If, like me, you are a devotee of Billy Childish's music, his poetry, his painting, or his mustaches, then I needn't bother to tell you how mandatory this book is. But to the Childish agnostic or the Childish ignorant, know this book is for you too. If you are even remotely interested in the gritty anthropology of underground music or high art scenes, in learning how obstinance and revolt can prosper in the face of corporate culture, or how one man overcame a truly Dickensian upbringing to single-handedly master all forms of cultural production and wrestle them into his own stubborn shapes, then trust me, you are in the right place.

Ted Kessler's formally unique collage of prose, oral history, poetry, and correspondence is the perfect vehicle for telling the story of Childish, an absurdly fecund artist who produces more culture in a week than most artists produce in decades. It is also a fittingly unsparing portrait of a man seemingly allergic to falsehood or pretense. Within these pages you will learn how Childish forged himself into a creative legend but also how he inspired a community of fellow travelers and how those friendships blossomed (and sometimes curdled) within the spheres of that shared creativity. There are tales of love geometries of far greater complexity than the triangle, plus UFOs, a literal goblin, Sasquatches painted in majestic oils, and of course ample tales of punk rock mayhem and trashed garage-rock brilliance.

Compulsively readable and hugely inspiring, Kessler's book is an overdue tribute to a man who not only contains multitudes but projects them relentlessly into the world.

—Guy Picciotto (Fugazi)

To Ease My Troubled Mind

The Authorized Unauthorized History of Billy Childish

Ted Kessler

AKASHIC BOOKS
BROOKLYN, NEW YORK

Published by Akashic Books
©2025 Ted Kessler

ISBN: 978-1-63614-213-5
Library of Congress Control Number: 2024940689
First printing

Typeset by Input Data Services Ltd, Bridgwater, Somerset.

Originally published in Great Britain in 2024 by White Rabbit, an imprint of the Orion Publishing Group Ltd.

Akashic Books
Instagram, X, Facebook: AkashicBooks
info@akashicbooks.com
www.akashicbooks.com

Contents

Foreword
by Stewart Lee

I first came across Billy Childish when he was supporting some grunge band at the Astoria in the midnineties, with Thee Head-coats. I forget who it was. It might have been the Afghan Whigs or Mudhoney, all them lot used to like him, didn't they, those Seattle types.

I thought it was fun, but it didn't make that much of an impression on me. He was doing this thing of not playing through the house PA, which in the larger venues means it doesn't really penetrate. So I thought it looked interesting and they were having fun, but I didn't really know what it was.

I came to appreciate him late: I saw him next at Glastonbury about twenty-five years ago, with the Buff Medways. That was when I thought, *This is absolutely amazing.* That, to me, was like seeing the Who in 1966. They just seemed absolutely incredible. I started to buy everything, worked back through it all systematically, and I realized what an incredible artist he is.

I wish I'd got into him earlier. I wish I could say to you that I liked him when I was a teenager, but I didn't. Although, to be fair, it was pretty hard to find out about him, because, unlike most things that are any good, he wasn't played on John Peel much, weirdly, given that in those days you could broadly have regarded the Milkshakes* or Thee Mighty Caesars as operating in the same

---

* Released music as both the Milkshakes and Thee Milkshakes. The former is used throughout the book.

field as some psychobilly groups, and Peel played Guana Batz and stuff, but he didn't play Billy Childish, so I might blame getting into him late on Peel.

After getting into the music I got into the writing, and I thought it was brilliant. I read the autobiographical stuff and the poems and everything I could get my hands on.

Then a few years back, after I met him, he took me to his studio in the Dockyard where he's now working on these massive landscape canvases that are almost illustrative, but have a slightly weird edge to them. And that was the point at which I thought he was a great artist. I thought he had real style before, and I thought he was good at knocking out a manifesto, and I thought he was good at concepts and ideas, but I think that no one would be able to deny the obvious skill and talent in what he's doing now. He probably does so well out of it that he has to keep quiet about how well it's going.

I've met him socially about four times in the last decade. Basically, whenever I'm in Kent, in the Medway towns, I'll tend to see him. The first time was in Rochester. I was keen to meet him because all of his family were going to see me perform, but he wasn't. I'm very surprised and flattered that he tolerates me, or when he actively seeks me out, because he knows that I'm a fan, and I think he has an admirably difficult relationship with people that are his fans, particularly if they're perceived as successful in some way. I think his independence is very important to him. He doesn't like to be in the orbit of anyone else, and I understand that. But I often end up getting on quite well with people who are described as difficult, certainly in music and comedy. I get on all right with the people who other people say can be hard to get to know—except for Jerry Sadowitz, who has always been difficult: he was supposed to be difficult and he is difficult. But most people I'm always all right with.

I'm very honored that Billy Childish would give me the time of day. His body of work is so vast and impressive; to be able to pursue those ideas, he's had to separate himself from the wider world of the music industry.

It's quite interesting what he's doing now, this sort of folk-rock type thing, the 1967 Dylan sound. It seems like each incarnation of his work drives a particular year of the 1960s into the ground, starting with the Hamburg Beatles in the Milkshakes, for example; Thee Headcoats were that beat sound with a bit of garage; and then the Buff Medways's stuff was like the Who. There's a parallel thing going on with things like the Musicians of the British Empire that's 1976/77 punk rock, as well, but he has an almost Cubist-like approach: he seems to make twenty albums or thirty albums in the style of 1965, and 1965 has been thoroughly exploded from every possible angle that the human eye can view it, and next he's moved on to 1966 and he'll do thirty or forty albums that sound like 1966. Even when he covers a Hendrix song, "Fire," it's perfect for that time: it's just as beat music starts to move into psychedelia, perfectly judged.

In fact, just now I thought, *I wonder what he's up to at the moment?* He's done about a dozen 1967 Dylan–style albums since I last looked, which must be about four months ago. It is overwhelming. His closest equivalent, I suppose, is Robert Pollard, the guy who did Guided by Voices, but Billy Childish makes Robert Pollard look like Taylor Swift in terms of his engagement with the media.

When I went to his studio, I had a really nice day there. He was getting on with painting and I just hung around and asked him the odd thing. He's very knowledgeable about all sorts of music-hall type comedy and old-fashioned comedy, stuff like that, which is quite interesting. The studio was breathtaking: every wall, these incredible landscape canvases. It felt like it was a real privilege to have seen that.

He kind of reminds me of my cat. Cats get on with what they're doing, don't they, and sometimes they overlap with you, but they're not seeking you out. They've got their things that they get on with. I think that he's a driven man, and he would do all this work whatever: I suspect that there's been a degree of quantitative easing caused by the success of the artwork that enables him not to have to worry at all about how the music lands commercially, but with all great artists you feel that the work would have to be done anyway. William Blake—who I guess is a not dissimilar character in some ways, one of the great English artists—talked about printing in the "infernal method," and that stuff was sort of hacked out of the printing plates, gouged out. It had to be, and that's what it feels like with Billy Childish. It's driven work that has to be made.

I also admire the fact that there's always an assumption that if you work in genre, you should move on. I know Alan Moore, who, again, is not a dissimilar character in some ways, feels that he wants to write comics, and yet he's always being told, "That comic would make a good film," or whatever. He'll respond by saying, "I didn't write it to be a film, I wrote it to be a good comic. I don't want it to be a film." What I like about Billy's work is you do hear the same two or three chords coming up a lot, and yet the little variations in rhythm and the emphasis of the song mean that their possibilities are infinite. A great artist can approach things in millions of different ways, or they can take a process and run with it forever to see what happens. It seems to me he's done that. He's done with rock 'n' roll what Henry Moore did with big lumps of stone: he's thought, *How many different things can you get out of this?*

Stewart Lee is a comedian and writer.

Ten Minutes on the Phone with Billy Childish, March 2021

"I'm really intense. I like truth, and things like that."

Billy, it's Ted.
Wotcha, Ted.

How are you doing?
I'm okay. I've had better times. But I'm all right.

What's the matter?
Oh, I had a nervous breakdown about three years ago and I get real repercussions from it.

Ah, sorry to hear that. Are you on the road to recovery?
I'm sometimes all right, but I don't take medication. I take natural stuff. Sometimes it feels . . . a bit excessive. It felt very difficult this morning in particular. I also have to have some tests for a pain in my side. But, you know, nothing is terribly wrong.

Just your mind and body.
Exactly. Just the bits holding me together. Nothing important.

What have you been working on today?
Painting. I always paint on a Monday. I just made an eight-by–five

foot painting. Then, this week we'll be working on music. We've recorded two more William Loveday Intention albums and I'm recording two more now. We have one coming out on Hangman in a couple of months called *They Wanted the Devil but I Sang of God*. That's all originals. Then we have one coming out on an American label, can't remember which, called *Cowboys Are Square*, and it's a really long extended version of "Cowboys Are Square" and "Girl from '62," which we did with Thee Headcoats, plus some originals. And we're doing *The New and Improved Bob Dylan, Volume Two*.

How come you've been making so much music?
I'm not entirely sure. I think maybe because I get bored painting all the time. I had this silly idea where I thought it would be good to do a career in a year. Ten albums in a year. It's the same with the painting stuff. We did a big book collecting four years of painting and it was essentially a lifetime's work collected in just four years. Then we did it again over the next four years. Obviously, this causes problems commercially, being so prolific, but nevertheless I thought I'd try a career in a year in music too.

The records you've been releasing have been very direct, lyrically. What emotional place do they come from?
It's not hard for me to tap in to that sort of thing because I had a very disturbed upbringing. I'm really intense. I like truth, and things like that. I'm not very political. I'm probably a little bit like that lad [Bob Dylan] when he was a bit more acid-tongued. I always have an axe to grind. For me, it's trying to get some clarity in my mind, so I'm not messed with. I'm always interested in people's motives. The spiritual development, the lack of spiritual development in people. I'm interested in God and death, I can always write about that. Often it's just we've booked the studio, so I better write a song.

Are all your secrets in your work?

Most of me is available for inspection, yes. Often I don't know what I'm going to say. I don't feel overly identified with what I do once I've put it out there. I was saying to [my son] Huddie today about my painting, I bet people think I like what I do. It's not necessarily the case. I do what I do. I don't do what I want to do, I do what I do. Very rarely does something go the way I want it to, but I just follow it, obey it. It's the same with the sound. It couldn't sound more differently to how we imagine it. We just try to make it come across with energy and humanity, some semblance of meaning. The idea is to keep it sounding like a group in a nice old wooden studio with soft reverb and some genuine energy.

In an interview you mentioned that "Hanging by a Tenuous Thread" was about your breakdown, but because there was no follow-up question I assumed it was a historic breakdown, perhaps around you quitting alcohol many years ago. I didn't realize it was recent.

I presume it was that. I didn't choose the subject, I just write the words down—"I'm hanging from a tenuous thread"—and think, *Oh, it must be about that.*

And you're still up and down?

Oh, I just had a bit of bad time recently, but generally . . . it was very bad this morning.

It's not harmed your work ethic at least.

It's strange, isn't it? I don't know why I'm made to do these things, but I have to do them so I do. In many ways, I'm very lucky because I am allowed to do it and people like it—that includes the painting. I must be doing the work that I am allowed to do. I don't like the way other people do stuff, so I do it the way I think it ought to be done. It helps me and it may help some other people, so it's probably worth doing.

Well, it's been very good talking to you and I hope you're on the upward swing soon.
I've got great family. I'll talk to you again, I hope. Stay in touch.

From: william claudius
Date: 16 August, 2021
Subject: billy calling—hello ted

---

hello ted

i hope your well

i unfortuntly had a 2nd break down - on meds and hope to be free soon

love billy

1.
Chatham Town Welcomes Desperate Men

In the beginning, before there was a book, there was an email. I wrote it in January 2022 to Billy Childish, who I first interviewed for a fanzine in 1990 and whose work, style, humor, and philosophical outlook I have loved for much longer. I also interviewed him in the mid-1990s, for *NME*, shortly after his band Thee Headcoats had released their "(We Hate the Fuckin') NME" single—a chorus I had as my phone greeting for a time while editing *NME*'s review section. I then interviewed him in 2002 for the *Observer* magazine, and in 2016 for *Q* magazine, while in 2015 he contributed a brutal chapter to a book about paternal relationships I edited called *My Old Man*. Sometimes it feels like I've spent my entire adult life trying to convince reluctant editors that they should allow me to write about Billy Childish.

My email to him explained that I was shortly to have a memoir published. I wondered if I could send Billy a proof so that he might consider giving me a quote for the jacket. He replied that of course he would be happy to do that. Then he asked—in his idiosyncratic and profoundly dyslexic manner—"whos ritting it? are they good?" reprising an old Tony Hancock joke about self-portraits.

Not particularly, I replied.

Soon after, Billy emailed back: "fancey doing one on my crap one day" he wondered.

I paused.

Billy Childish has released well over 150 albums with numerous different groups since his first with the Pop Rivets in 1979. He has published a dozen autobiographical novels and at least fifty collections of poetry, a couple of memoirs, along with several printed collections of his photography and art. He has produced thousands of paintings, and his work is exhibited around the world. And he's not slowed down since crossing the border into his sixties in 2019. In 2022, he decided that he would attempt a musical "career in a year" and release an album a month with his William Loveday Intention. He nearly succeeded as well, defeated not by a lack of recordings but by the availability of vinyl.

Every month brings a new Billy Childish release, publication, performance, or exhibition, stretching back decades. He is the UK's most prolific creative force—a painter, poet, photographer, musician, memoirist, and novelist who is in constant production of the goods.

How would I be able to describe both his life and artistic endeavors tidily? A vast task made much harder to untangle, as almost all of his work is unflinchingly autobiographical in nature. Most music journalists lazily prefer to tell a linear story of a singer-songwriter in a band who delivers three or four successful albums, takes a creative stumble, endures both commercial disappointment and personal toil—drugs, divorce, ideally prison—before some valedictory final release saves the day and they sweep in to tell the tale. I am no different. How could I keep up with and contain this enormous and evolving story?

I filed the Billy Childish biography in the back of my mind, to be revisited once my own book was published in July. Before then, however, Billy emailed again. In March 2022, he wrote: "can we talk about poss book."

I wondered what kind of book he wanted me to work on.

He replied: "it would cover my very strange up bringing—which sounds like a mad fiction all sorts of nonsence + painting writing music being part of that. family background. young skool. sexual abuse. art school punk, poetry, novels, (small) chapter on each main group)—christ—it goes on. but bite sized chunks with plenty of the funny strnge things that have lead to here . . ."

We agreed to meet for a coffee one Thursday when Childish regularly comes to London from his home in Rochester, Kent, to have breathwork therapy.

On Thursday, May 12, I joined Billy in the queue to enter Monmouth Coffee Company in Covent Garden, central London. Disappointingly, he wasn't carrying the fold-up scooter on which he once used to zip around from London appointment to appointment. A decade earlier, when I worked in a magazine office on Shaftesbury Avenue, I'd regularly see Childish being whisked upright at 10 mph along Seven Dials, flamboyant mustache leaning into the breeze, immaculate vintage suit or military camouflage hanging from his lean frame, a wide-brimmed hat on top of his well-maintained (very) short back and sides, weaving in and out of traffic and bemused tourists.

Inside the coffee shop, we each drank two strong Americanos and Billy ate three large chocolate truffles in swift succession, wiping his mustache in between mouthfuls, as we discussed what kind of book I might write about him.

Here's how it would go down, he explained. Billy would tell me everything that I might want to know about him. He'd put me in touch with anybody close to him who was willing to speak. I'd be able to reproduce any of his writing, painting, or photography—photos both by him or taken of him by the friendly network of photographers he has known over the decades. If he had research material on hand, it would be mine. He wouldn't want anything in return other than an attempt at even-handed historical accuracy. He probably wouldn't even read the book.

It sounded like an unusually inviting opportunity for a biographer. I asked him what was in it for him.

"We might enjoy ourselves," he replied with the soft, mischievous grin that punctuates even his most intense conversation—which is to say, all conversation.

And so we agreed to start work together on it after the summer.

In September 2022, I traveled to the North Kent coast to visit Childish at his painting studio in the Historic Dockyard Chatham. The dockyards themselves closed in 1984. For centuries, they built warships there, on the banks of the River Medway. At its height, 10,000 men were employed on the docks and the site stretched for over a mile, expanding into nearby Gillingham and including a large naval barracks. The Dutch even came to attack the British fleet in Chatham's dock in 1667, with the idea of sailing up to London afterward, but the plan came to naught and the Dutch sailed sheepishly home with just the flagship HMS *Royal Charles* in tow as their bounty, rather than the entire fleet of the British Empire.

Many famous British Navy ships were subsequently built in Chatham, over 500 in total. These included HMS *Victory*, which at 245 years old is the world's oldest naval vessel and, to Kent's dismay, is today docked in Portsmouth, and HMS *Temeraire*, which was so renowned for its action during the Battle of Trafalgar that J.M.W. Turner painted the *Temeraire*'s final journey before the ship was broken up in 1838. In 2011 Billy Childish honored it with a delicious folk-beat single, "The Fighting Temeraire," released by his Spartan Dreggs combo.

In the postwar twentieth century, after the navy phased out the dockyards as a provider of warships, nuclear submarines were maintained at Chatham instead. That's what was going on when Billy Childish was employed in the dockyards as an apprentice stonemason in 1976, from age sixteen to seventeen, in his first and last-ever full-time job.

While Childish was working as a teenager in Chatham's dockyards, there was an incident nearby in the North Sea, where a minesweeper got dragged underwater during a NATO exercise. Lives were lost. When they recovered the dead, they brought the bodies back to the dockyards in coffins aboard one of the nuclear submarines. The admiral was there, along with the local press, and all stopped work for the "Last Post."

Billy wasn't hugely interested in that, so he continued to carve his block of stone in the sunny breeze outside. As the press filed back from the ceremony, they paused to take a photo of this lad happily at work during his dinner hour. It ran in the local paper alongside a story about the joy Billy found as an apprentice at Chatham's dockyards, appearing beneath the headline "Chips with Everything."

Billy Childish was, in fact, not happy in his work. His six months as an apprentice stonemason were such personal torture that in between carving identical pieces of stone, he produced 600 drawings in what he describes as "the tea huts of hell," the best of which helped him eventually gain entry to St. Martin's School of Art. But not yet.

By the winter of 1976, Billy's older brother, Nichollas, was studying art in London at the Slade School of Fine Art. He lived in a squat in Chalk Farm that Billy would visit, sleeping on the floor. It was upon hearing the Sex Pistols for the first time on one of these trips, when "Anarchy in the U.K." was playing on the jukebox in the student union building at the University of London, that Billy's axis was shifted by the early tremors of British punk rock. Change was afoot—he could understand that loud and clear.

One day soon after, back at the day job in the dockyards, dressed in his overalls, carving away at his lump of stone, he decided he'd had enough. He'd seen what the working world had in store for him, an undiagnosed dyslexic who could neither read nor write. He believed that society needed stonemasons; that someone had to carve perfectly aligned pieces of rock. But it wouldn't be him. So he took a three-pound club hammer and smashed it down upon his hand, declaring that he'd never be employed again. In time, his injury would heal. His mind, however, was set.

He admits now that it was perhaps an overly dramatic resignation, but it delivered the intent of his message. He kept his word, too. He hasn't been employed since that day in February 1977, other than a stint as a ward porter at Oakwood Hospital, the local psychiatric hospital, and a day picking fruit.

The people Billy worked with at the dockyards told him he was mad to leave. At that time, in the 1970s, the vast majority of working-age people in the Medway towns of Chatham, Strood, and Rochester clocked in at the docks, if they weren't employed in one of the factories. Working there meant a job for life, they explained. He left anyway, as a job for life was the last thing he wanted. Then, seven years later, the dockyards closed, all those lifetime jobs disappeared down the plug, and the Medway towns were plunged into an economic despair they still haven't really fully recovered from. The only jobs going at the Historic Dockyard nowadays are as tour guides, security guards, in the gift shop, or when it's open as a film set.

Ironically, though, this is now where Billy Childish comes most regularly to work.

Every Monday, he returns to the Historic Dockyard Chatham from his home in nearby Rochester to paint. He became artist in residence at the Dockyard in 2011 and was awarded a big drafty studio above the Victorian Ropery the following year. He has since kept to a schedule of working here weekly, surrounded by his array of huge canvases, and painting latterly alongside his son Huddie, and his friend and occasional copainter Edgeworth Johnstone, while BBC Radio 3 plays in the background and his art collaborator ("no, not his agent, nor his representative") Steven Lowe sits glued to his phone and laptop, doing whatever he can to disrupt the art world's best-laid plans.

I stood next to Billy as he worked on a massive landscape canvas, dressed in his green overalls with a white hangman logo stenciled on the back, small-brimmed hat, and round spectacles. He was concentrating on a painting of a man in a checkered shirt, standing in a canoe beneath Mount Rainier—a large and active volcanic mountain in the Pacific Northwest of the USA, sixty miles south of Seattle. It's one of the most potentially dangerous volcanoes on earth, but the man in the canoe seemed unperturbed. The painting, Childish said, was called *Beneath Mt. Tahoma*, which is what the mountain is known as by the local indigenous people. When Childish married his wife Julie in 2000, in a park in Seattle, Mount Rainier could be seen in the distance behind them. It's always felt significant.

We had paint-splattered mugs of green tea and spoke about Billy's earliest memories for an hour or so while he painted. Then we embraced in farewell and arranged to continue interrogating his childhood by Zoom later in the week, perhaps when his son wasn't listening, as Billy hadn't actually discussed some of the family dynamics with him before. I said goodbye to Huddie, Edgeworth, and Steve, jogged down the stairs outside, following the road back through Chatham for the forty minutes it takes to reach Rochester station.

As I walked, I thought . . .

Over 150 albums.

Dozens of books. Dozens of groups.

Thousands of paintings, with a new one every week.

There have also been wives, children, several profound love affairs, a fractured, dysfunctional childhood home, and a thoroughly modern blended family.

I made a deal with myself to spend the next year gathering as much material as I could about Billy Childish, in the hopes that the conversations I had with him, about him, and my journey from one September to the next following these breadcrumbs, would become the book itself. I'd interview everyone who'd traveled in his orbit that I could and I'd spend as much time as possible with Childish in those twelve months, gradually building a mosaic of his life. The picture I gathered from these fragments across the year would be my portrait of him.

And that's how this particular Billy Childish story begins.

2.

For Whom Will We Inscribe the Grave?

He was born on December 1, 1959, in Chatham, on the Medway delta in the county of Kent, England, as the night wind howled in off the water and painted the gray-stoned town with salty rain. Soon after, his maternal grandmother, Ivy Loveday, officially registered the birth of her grandson, William Ivy Loveday.

Wait. William Ivy Loveday? That name doesn't sound right to John Hamper, the father of this boy. That's not what he'd instructed Ivy to do. So, in January 1960, he changed his son William Ivy Loveday's name to Steven John Hamper.

Since then, Steven John Hamper has answered to many names, mostly of his own invention. As a six-year-old child, he'd look up most reliably when hailed as Virgil. Other self-ascribed aliases followed.

In 1972, he became Horatio Hamper. In 1977, Gus Claudius.

Later, in that same year of 1977, the year that punk broke over the Medway, his friend Button Nose Steve decided he should be named Billy Childish. That one stuck. But others followed.

He opened his account with the Anglia Hastings & Thanet Building Society in 1980 under the name of the Dadaist painter, poet, and mentor Mr. Kurt Schwitters, reborn and domiciled at 181 Walderslade Road, Chatham, Kent. Around this time, he had a verse from a poem by Schwitters tattooed upon his left buttock—*I don't bother with the ideal / I eat the apple with the peel*—so he'd be able to note it down as a distinguishing mark in his passport, but the lettering has become so faded and blurred with time he's not sure it still passes muster in that respect.

He was called William Loveday for a while in 1981.

His passport is under the name of a William Charlie Hamper, the middle name a tribute to his grandfather's first, even though his grandfather returned from the First World War's Battle of Jutland and the Zeebrugge Raid, where he was thrown into the sea, apparently a changed and occasionally cruel man. Nevertheless, young Steven Hamper always got on well with him, so he added his name to his own.

For printmaking purposes he is Bill Hamper. Sometimes, his graphic work is attributed to Old 4 Legs.

The founders of Art Hate, 2009's mass rally against art, were called Dr. Albirt Umber and Karl Lampenshwarts. But that was him.

When working as a director for his Hangman Books imprint, he's Jack Ketch.

If you confused him with Charles Hangman he'd know who you meant.

Likewise, Sir Quentin Gaydish, a title chosen for him in the mid-1980s by his old colleague in Thee Mighty Caesars, Graham Day.

Rolling Slim, too, is the name he used sometimes when recording with the poet Sexton Ming (aka Gus Honeybum).

Danger Bill Henderson is credited with any photos he snaps and Odysseus takes the applause for a series of his novels. Should you admire his dexterity with Indian clubs, then Xerxes is the title he uses when handling those puppies.

If an email pings in from a certain William Claudius, then you know who's sent that message.

To many older admirers, he'll always be "Wild" Billy Childish, though, singer of raucous song and handsome, stylish, fearless wag, for that's who he was. And on occasion still is.

In some ways, the names he is known by are revealing. In

others, they mean nothing at all. We wipe away the titles, we scrub clean the nomenclature. We tumble down the barrel of time. Roll the film, please, from the very start . . .

Here he comes into view now. Focus the lens on a suburban Kentish house at the end of a long front lawn, an unhappy family home filled with recrimination, longing, stifled ambition, gnawing unease, and the sounds of traditional jazz whenever the brooding, distracted man of the house is here. Number 195 Walderslade Road, a newly built, end-of-terrace property, backing onto the woodland that lies directly beyond its rear garden in Chatham.

There he is, sitting in the front window's extended shelf. A very small boy, perhaps three years old, transfixed by a snail's slow but determined progress across the pavement toward the badlands of the estate on the other side of the road. But what's that? Oh, it's the postman, whose heavy tread announces his arrival to the serenading neighborhood dogs, and there goes our blameless snail, crushed beneath the postie's stride. Bye bye.

It's bath time now and Big Caroline next door is singing Beatles's songs through the wall. And with a love like that, you know you should be glad.

On the other side of the house on Walderslade Road, there is a large garden. Sometimes, in the sun, the girls who live in that house are naked in their little pool. You can peek over the fence and catch a glimpse. Or you can look over the fence when you hear an argument kicking off and . . . oh. There are two geese with their heads missing, oozing blood onto the grass, a fox jogging nonchalantly away.

Later, Big Caroline will explain that we all die and after we die there's nothing, forever.

That doesn't sound right.

When we die there's nothing, forever? He doesn't like the implication of that one bit. Those geese were alive, minding their own business one second, the next they were gone. Extinguished for all time. One day, the fox will be snuffed out too. As will you. Eternal nothingness for all.

Sometimes in the summer, Little Geoffrey from up the road will join him in the garden to catch bumble bees with their bare hands. The bees tickle them and make the boys very happy.

Tuning in the radio to listen to Cassius Clay beat the shit out of Henry Cooper. Good. We love Cassius Clay.

Big brother Nick has a pair of boxing gloves and uses them to reenact the bout, smacking his younger brother around the head until ears ring, knees wobble, brain throbs, tears flow, in an imitation of Clay decking Cooper.

He's out in the garden now, tidying up the leaves for his mother June. He senses movement and spies a large spider crawling speedily up his bright-blue jumper. He doesn't scream, he doesn't cry. He returns the spider to nature.

Big Caroline is off to see the Beatles play at Chatham's Invicta Ballroom, but five-year-old boys are not allowed in, so here's the next best thing: Mum will buy a handful of Jelly Babies so that Big Caroline can throw them at the band on your behalf.

There are some other groups our subject was too young to see play along the Medway, but that he might have liked to . . .

The Rolling Stones, at the Odeon Theatre in Rochester, on February 15, 1964, when they were still a good rhythm and blues band having fun, before it became serious business.

Also, more ardently, the Jimi Hendrix Experience, who performed at Chatham's Central Hall on December 1, 1967, alongside Pink Floyd, though Steven John Hamper would not have stuck around for them.

Jimi Hendrix, however. Jimi Hendrix! He fell absolutely in love with Jimi Hendrix from the age of eight, when his brother, who was a "wally" (i.e., an aspiring hippie), brought home the LP *Are You Experienced*. At first, and for a good while after, it just sounded like noise. It was impossible to understand what was happening. There was no context. In this house there were albums by the Beatles and lots of trad jazz, Louis Armstrong and the like, because his father was a "moldy fig." (Moldy figs in the context of the 1960s were purist fans of original jazz, who believed—ludicrously—that jazz took a wrong turn circa 1920 and everything that followed was frivolous and phony.)

Jimi Hendrix, who was welcomed—as he would reveal two years later in the song "Voodoo Child"—on the night he was born by a moon that turned a fire-red, and his mother cried out, "Lord, the gypsy was right," before she fell down dead . . . Jimi Hendrix sounded nothing like any of the records in the Hamper household. He wasn't like anything of this world to those young ears.

Nor was the Beatles's "Strawberry Fields Forever," for that matter, which the eight-year-old Steven John Hamper bought with his own money from Boots around this time. *Are You Experienced* and "Strawberry Fields Forever" were two experiments in colorful melody and dissonance that revealed themselves to him as eerie, outlandish noise. He had to check the needle for dust, to make sure there wasn't a manufacturing error. He felt like someone who'd never seen moving pictures, sitting in a cinema, afraid the train would emerge and crash into the room from the screen ahead.

The music was a distressing code he wanted to crack. After a few bewildering weeks, the notes started to settle and the noise began to make sense. The discordant crank of "Purple Haze" now made him strut. "Hey Joe" wasn't just a disturbing song about murder, it floated groovily through the air, and "Manic Depression," well, that rang a bell somewhere. This was no longer confusion, it was love. As it turned out, it was Steven's music. This was what he believed in.

It became apparent to our leading man that he was now a big fan of two creators. He was a devotee of Jimi Hendrix and he was in Vincent van Gogh's gang too. They were his heroes, his best friends. To demonstrate this ardor, he took his green hat, painted rainbows on the front with *Jimi* scrawled on one side,

Vincent on the other. Then he'd saunter out of the house, onto the suburban Medway streets, letting the world know which teams he supported.

Vincent van Gogh loomed large over the Hamper home, as a framed reproduction of his painting of sunflowers hung in their kitchen. Young Steven would gaze upon its majesty as he dipped doughy soldiers into soft yellow and white trenches, asking about the picture's provenance. Both of his parents hankered after art, a means to escape from their mutual misery, and the house was well furnished with books filled with famous paintings. His father, who worked for a time as an art director at the *Daily Mirror*, would paint at home in the short time he lived there, before splitting to pursue interests in fantasy and deception more seriously.

His mother—born June Lewis, previously married to Ken Frost, much later self-described as Looney June Childish on occasion—would read for Steven, because Steven could not read, nor could he write, even at the age of eight. He was a dyslexic, for whom all the letters remain jumbled to this day. So his mother would read to him, because he was very interested in stories, but he needed someone else to describe them to him.

After Steven had watched *Lust for Life*, the famous Kirk Douglas film about Vincent van Gogh, he asked his mother to read him the book by Irving Stone that it was based on. The book transported him. As with Hendrix, it made him aware of the power of creation.

He would've liked to have seen Jimi Hendrix perform. But he didn't. Instead, he saw the next best thing: a flying saucer. For, a few months before Jimi Hendrix hit Chatham, a UFO also visited the Medway region.

Steven was in the garden one warm summer's day, along with his brother Nick and Paul Ravenscroft from the house across the road. The trio heard a noise, looked up, and saw a silver disc revolving slowly above the house in the clear blue sky.

"Look," exclaimed Steven, "a flying saucer!"

"It's not a flying saucer," his brother Nick replied scornfully. "It's a jet."

The trio gazed at it a little longer. "Why is it round, then?" wondered Steven.

Nick became very angry. "It's a jet!" he shouted, and stomped off.

Steven and Paul watched it for a while longer without speaking, before it disappeared and Paul followed Nick inside. The incident was not mentioned again by the trio.

A decade later, Steven met Paul Ravenscroft at a gig during their punk rock awakening of 1977 and Paul finally broke his silence on the matter. "Do you remember that flying saucer?" he asked, by way of greeting.

You don't forget something like that. Nor do you forget seeing a panther, whose path Steven crossed one afternoon in 1974. He was on his way to his friend Dave Marsh's house through a field near his home, when a large black panther jogged out in front of him. Skeptical friends have suggested that he may have mistaken that panther for a large dog. Easily done. No. He saw the tail, the way it walked. It was a panther, twenty yards away from him.

It was an early, undocumented, entirely terrifying sighting of the Beast of Blue Bell Hill, which became the stuff of local legend over years to come. Blue Bell Hill, along which a stretch of road runs between Maidstone and Rochester, has long been associated with ghostly apparitions. Among them is a bride-to-be who died in a car crash on the eve of her wedding in the mid-1960s, and who has remained locked into the roadside ever since, seeking to be released by passing traffic from her purgatory. Steven has never seen her. But he did see a ghost at the end of an alley near his home once. And he had also witnessed weird shadows that moved through his house as a child. He and his friends would all see those, so he knows he wasn't imagining them. He saw his dead cat walking down the stairs once, and a man in full naval gear wandering through his home. Sometimes he was aware, too, of a dog-sized ant at the foot of his bed. That may have been a ghost. They don't self-identify.

But nothing was quite as supernaturally terrifying as what he witnessed by the fir tree at the end of the garden when he was fifteen. By then, he was living at 181 Walderslade Road, a cursed bungalow erected upon the site of an old shack where a German prisoner of war had lived with his English wife, who drank herself miserably to death . . . Steven was on his way to his kung fu class that day in 1975 and cut through the back of the garden. As he passed the fir tree, he noticed an unusual pile of sticks that he hadn't seen before. He moved in to inspect the bundle, pulling the top few back. There, lurking beneath the thatch, was a knee-high being staring back at him, radiating malice. Every hair on Steven's body stood up. The air left his lungs. And he ran as fast as he could from the goblin, screaming, "Don't you fucking ever come anywhere near me!"

Luckily, the goblin did not cross his path again. But that doesn't alter the fact that he was there—a goblin, in the garden, under a bundle of sticks.

Steven has come to believe, through his experiences, that the world is multidimensional. That there are different frequencies which we exist on and sometimes we can glimpse other frequencies, that we can have fleeting sight of parallel worlds. But he knows you may not believe that. He understands the skepticism. He feels no need to see flying saucers, giant ants, or goblins. But he has.

The American poet Robinson Jeffers wrote that he had seen a merman, sitting on a rock in the sea. Jeffers was a practical, outdoorsy man who described the human and natural condition in beautiful detail. He was not prone to fantasy. But he knew he'd seen a merman, sitting on a rock. Reading this, Steven felt kinship. For he has seen unexplained shadows, panthers in the Kentish countryside, ghosts, a giant ant, and a goblin.

Whether you believe him or not does not alter what he witnessed. Besides, the most evil and terrifying force that Steven John Hamper came across growing up was not a giant ant, nor a ghost, nor even that goblin under the sticks in the garden. It did not exist on another frequency in a distant realm.

It was a man named Norman who he met when he was nine years old.

i am billy childish

i am billy childish
ex drunk
and compulsive masturbator
late nite vomiter of good liquor
kisser of purple lipped women
riter of poems celebrating the
emptiness of my love
poems hungering for the moment
of my passion
wishing it could always be so
to never let my cock fall

i am billy childish
ex strongman
and 2-bit lover
late nite namer of names
corrupter of the literate
riter of poems that dare
to dream to pass down the centurys
and touch the harts of the
yet-to-be-born
wishing to hold them
to my arms
and kiss them all

i am billy childish
ex-poet
and failed suiside
late nite vomiter of truth and lies
kisser of the arses of girls
like the stars of god
ritter of poems to lick
the thighs of the dead
for ex-lovers to denounce
and teachers to hate
wishing to paint my life
and to never let my
voice quieten

Billy Childish (2010)

Childish Witness: Keith Gulvin

Childhood neighbor, teenage coconspirator, lifelong accomplice

"He's a highly principled person."

I call him Billy. He changed his name as a teenager and I understood the reason for that. He'd fallen out big-time with his father. His father actually said to him on one occasion, "You're so childish."

His family, they were strange. Let's be quite blunt about that. His father was absent most of the time. He was very aloof, I'd say he was stuck up his own backside. He ran a company, he was a partner, Hamper and Purcell, commercial artists. He did lots of design stuff. I remember his father did something for British Rail, the campaign they had in the seventies, "This is the age of the train": that was his father's work.

But his father lived way beyond his means. He kept mistresses in London, a London flat, and only came down to his house in Chatham occasionally, usually just to have a go at the family for wasting his money. He apparently disabled the central heating, Billy said, things like that. He was a complete arse, actually. He was awful, absolutely awful. His family were living on the breadline and he was driving around in a Rolls-Royce! You can get details of that if you read his books, which are written half as a work of fiction, but 80 percent of it is actually factual.

His brother was also a complete arse. Nick, he had a very inflated view of his own abilities. He was the one that went to grammar school and he was the star of the family, whereas Billy, because of his dyslexia, which wasn't recognized—it's something we shared—he ended up in Walderslade Secondary School for Boys, which was a really rough local school, so he was branded a failure for that.

His mother was very weak-willed. She did her best to look

after him. I thought they had a very close relationship, but in much later years Billy said she was a narcissist, and it wasn't what it seemed. So he had a very poor upbringing. He was trapped in a difficult family. On the outside, other people thought they were rich, had lots of money and all the rest of it, a good lifestyle, but I knew the truth.

We've known each other most of our lives. He lived across the road from me, hundred yards down or so. He's a couple of years younger. I lived next door to the Ravenscrofts: everyone in that row of houses feared them. Michael Ravenscroft was a real little weasel. Billy always said he was bullied by him and I suffered the same fate from his older brother, Terry.

Back in the fifties and sixties, because of the shortage of materials, if you had a private telephone, you had to share the line with another individual nearby. The dialing number was unique to your phone, but you could pick your phone up and you'd hear someone else having a conversation, and the polite thing was, you did put it down. Billy and I got into the habit of having conversations by agreeing to pick the phone up at a certain time, just for the hell of it. We shared a party line, as it was known.

We both had an interest in military things, particularly fortifications, so we hung around together. Where we grew up, Walderslade, on the outskirts of Chatham, there was lots of old military forts, and we were fascinated by these. We used to break into them from [the age of] about eleven, twelve with a group of other like-minded youngsters locally.

We formed our own miniterrorist group at one point: the Walderslade Liberation Army. The area we mainly used to play in was an abandoned orchard, behind what used to be quite a large house that was turned into a Catholic church many years ago, and the church sold off the land for housing. That was our play area, and we'd built a dugout in it. The bulldozers were steadily destroying it, so we decided we would react to that and we'd sabotage it. That led to us developing our own system of making weapons. I have to be careful, because it would now be regarded as terrorist activity. There is no statute of limitations in the United Kingdom. All I'll say is that in the local public library was a chemistry book that had a very good recipe for gunpowder. We constructed things pretty similar to very early matchlock muskets—and they worked, we could fire projectiles and things—and even minicannons. We were all young teenagers at that point. Billy's still got the pistol we made, I believe.

In the end, one of our number betrayed us to the developers and they totally destroyed our HQ, after which we'd lost our cause. So we morphed into a military research group. We said, *Okay, we'll carry on researching stuff.* Finding bits of old military equipment really fired our imagination. In Billy's dad's artist's studio, we formed the Medway Military Research Group. There was three of us originally. It started off as myself, Billy, and a guy called Steve Jennings, who was also at the same school as we were at—he was in the year below me, Billy was in the year below him—and he had an interest in military medals.

Strange as it might sound, it morphed into perhaps one of the most influential defense archaeology groups that was ever created. We were really ahead of our time, looking at mainly twentieth-century military structures. It wasn't recognized at that time, but this is mainstream archaeology now. I currently chair the Kent Archaeological Society's group called the Kent Defence Research Group, which looks at defense archaeology.

I carried on with it, but Billy dropped out when he went to art college. Before then, though, we produced a series of booklets and he illustrated those. I've got the originals of most of those drawings. They're some of my most treasured items, I'd never part with any. It was a unique part of his development as an artist. He copied the very nice copper etchings the nineteenth-century *Illustrated London News* used to do before photography moved into print. He used to draw in that style. For example, a picture of Fort Amherst with bricks in, he'd draw each brick individually, hundreds of them.

And the skill that took, I thought, was incredible, and the patience.

We published our first book, *The Medway Forts*, in 1975. We raised the money ourselves to pay for the production. It was miles ahead of the punk fanzine culture, but of course Billy really got into punk. I can still remember the very first gig he did, which was in a place called Detling, a little village tucked under the North Downs near Maidstone, in the village hall. His band the Pop Rivets were playing backup to a Maidstone group. They were a bit ropey, I suppose, but we thought it was great. We intimidated the supporters of the other band; I remember we had a large puddle of beer on the floor and we were dragging them by their feet through it, and then chucking the beer cans at the main group to get them to leave early so Billy could play longer.

I think Billy helped draw out the liberal in me. My parents were *Daily Mail* readers, typical working-class Tories. My brother was very right-wing—still is. Billy helped me see things from a different perspective. He would be questioning things, always from a very young age. He was very philosophical. And he also got me into another area which I'm still involved in, which is paganism—he got me on that path.

When we were still quite young, we spent one solstice night on top of a local megalith, Kit's Coty, near Blue Bell Hill, which is a 5,000-year-old Neolithic burial chamber, waiting for the sunrise, expecting to see some manifestation of the gods! We did a couple of camping trips to a farm nearby with other Neolithic remains; we were quite into it. We did early archaeological surveys on it.

As a youngster, he used to be like a hippie: he had the long hair, everything. He loved that sort of sixties, early seventies hippie lifestyle. He was a great fan of Jimi Hendrix. He always bucked convention with style, dress, everything, and that actually made him often a subject of ridicule and bullying. But he never changed because of it. He's a highly principled person. And I think that's one of the things that I greatly admire about him. He's always done his own thing, his own way. And as I say, I greatly admire him having the balls to do that, not bowing to convention. I used to think that way to an extent, but I ended up working and doing normal jobs and things, and doing my other stuff outside it, like most of us do. So I wasn't able to embrace that lifestyle. Like many people, you may aspire to it but you realize it's out of reach. But for Billy, it wasn't out of reach; he followed his own convictions. And then he was rewarded for it, by when his work became sort of popular, and he would never compromise.

He tried to live off his art, even at one point doing sketches for tourists in Rochester, signed as William Loveday. Gradually, his art took off, but all the time he was living in poverty. I don't think he liked being part of mainstream society, the slave to wages. That was not Billy. He would never compromise.

Many years ago, he was taking part in a poetry festival in Medway. I went along to listen in the auditorium. And immediately following Billy there was a children's reading session. So a lot of these proud mums and their little children had arrived early, and there was Billy, reading out a particular poem of his which was called "The Cunt." The word was used multiple times, I seem to remember. It was the look of horror on these lovely middle-class mums, trying to cover up their children's ears and then rushing them out of the room. But Billy didn't stop, he didn't pause: he carried straight on. It was his show, this is what he'd written, and if they didn't like it, they could clear off. There were complaints made, but, you know, Billy's poetry has always been full of expletives. I just thought, *No, good on you*: he stuck to his guns.

He's never compromised. Not once, in any respect. If you get an email from Billy, it is dyslexia and all. He won't use spell-check. I'm dyslexic, but I will spell-check; even the ones I do for Billy, I still spell-check them, because it's drilled into me. I had to conform because of the jobs I did, even though I was told at school—the same school that Billy went to—that if you couldn't spell, you were regarded as some sort of idiot.

And so I do know what Billy went through at school, because

I went through exactly the same thing. But the difference was, whereas I attempted to hide my problems or overcome them, Billy just said, "The hell with it, it's warts and all, you like it or you don't. It's your problem, not mine." I just love that attitude of his. And that hasn't changed: he will still do things his way. That goes for his music, his poetry, his other creative writing, and his art. His style is his style.

He is a very powerful character, very influential, and very uncompromising, but what he doesn't want is people saying, "Oh, you're a wonderful artist, aren't you the best": he doesn't need that. He never has. He's happy with being confident in his own abilities. To him, it doesn't matter if nobody else likes it, or wants to buy it or anything, it's just that, ironically now, yes, they *do* want to buy the stuff that he's got and will pay big money for it. I've got probably about thirty pieces of his work, I suppose, altogether. I would never part with a piece of it for anything. There's no price you could put on that for me. And because most of it is his early work, with *Steve Hamper* on it, no one would know what it was anyway.

**what
has
caused
my
brother
a
life
with
hart
frozen**

i
sing
of it
laughing

it
is
that
song
of
our
drunken
mother
being
pulled
backwards up
the stairs
the moonlight bouncing off her white arse
and our
father
bollock naked
screaming
– get back to bed!
and
so
we
lay
in
trembling fear
beneath cold sheets
and
her
scream
rising
in the grey dawn

Billy Childish, from *self portrate in a broken glass* (2023)

3.
At Home with the Hampers

In the 2010s, the Irish comedian and writer Sean Hughes worked on a documentary about Billy Childish. He filmed conversations with Childish and his family, as well as his artistic and musical collaborators, and, from the thirty-two minutes of edited footage that has been located by Hughes's friend Claire Gildersleve, it appears that his goal was similar to the aims of this book: to create a mosaic profile of Britain's most prolific creative force. Sadly, however, Sean Hughes died in 2017 before finishing his film, so it is with profound thanks to both Gildersleve and the Hughes family that we can reproduce these important historical excerpts . . .

NICHOLLAS HAMPER, ELDER BROTHER: Billy used to cry a lot as a kid. I can still remember his endless wailing. He did a lot of crying. And he wouldn't shut up. He was complaining from day one, about the injustices that were to be done to him. We tended to gang up on Billy when he was young, because he was so difficult. My dad didn't like him. I don't think he's ever liked him.

BILLY CHILDISH: I think they saw a threat from me because I would say what I saw—the way I still do. And they don't like that much either.

JUNE HAMPER, MOTHER: You couldn't tell him anything.

BILLY CHILDISH: When I was two or three, I knew my father worked in London. He worked for the *Daily Mirror*. I didn't see him very often. I saw him smash up some furniture and stuff. He was passably pleasant to me sometimes.

NICHOLLAS HAMPER: My father was drunk and violent.

JOHN HAMPER, FATHER: Well, there are regrets, yes. But I don't dwell on them. I push them into the recesses of my mind.

BILLY CHILDISH: He used to bang our heads together, me and my brother. He'd come up behind, grab your hair, and bash your heads together. It was always a shock. I used to get locked in the bedroom, too.

SEAN HUGHES: Did your brother take you under his wing?

BILLY CHILDISH: No, my brother bullied me incessantly.

SEAN HUGHES: Did your brother ask you for help?

NICHOLLAS HAMPER: We were just there, two little kids witnessing this horror. It was awful. And it's really fucked me up for years. It still fucking hurts.

JOHN HAMPER: I don't think I was particularly viewed as a terribly nice bloke. But I was so involved in what I was doing. It was a really very difficult time. We separated gradually.

BILLY CHILDISH: My father used to come home on average once a fortnight to collect the shirts that had been starched for him. My mother was in constant fear of these visits, because he rang every day and said he was coming home. He'd say he was on the train or he was at Chatham station. Complete baloney. He was in London, pissed. Also, we didn't get any money from my father. He kept my mother on a very tight, short leash. He would always be on the point of shutdown.

SEAN HUGHES: When I spoke to Nick, that period of his life has affected him quite a lot.

JOHN HAMPER: I'm sure it did affect them. It affected me as well. But I don't talk about it. I don't need to.

SEAN HUGHES: You don't speak to your dad now much at all, do you?

NICHOLLAS HAMPER: No, he's a seriously damaged person.

SEAN HUGHES: So you don't intend to have a relationship with Nick or Billy, you don't see your grandchildren?

JOHN HAMPER: I've seen two of them. I haven't seen the little girl [Billy's daughter Scout, born in 2010, who has yet to meet John]. Obviously I think about it, but I haven't got any plans to pursue anything in that direction at the moment.

SEAN HUGHES: There was an assumption that Billy exaggerated his upbringing, but he hasn't.

NICHOLLAS HAMPER: No. It was horrible. Mine was horrible in a different kind of way, but his was fucking grim.

SEAN HUGHES: Do you find the songs that Billy writes about those days hard to listen to?

NICHOLLAS HAMPER: Yeah. He writes some pretty evil things about me as well.

SEAN HUGHES: Are they true, though?

NICHOLLAS HAMPER: Probably.

JOHN HAMPER: He's written quite a lot about how horrible I was. He's had an opportunity to make something interesting from it. That's okay, I don't care.

SEAN HUGHES: Of course you care.

JOHN HAMPER: I don't care. I don't care.

Today, Nichollas Hamper is an artist working in France. John Hamper lives in Wittering, West Sussex. June Hamper died in 2021.

From: william claudius
Date: 6 July, 2023
Subject: billy—sean's film

ive watched a bit - Nick is drunk isnt he. John is so strange with that put on voice

i like both of them - nick has joined in with john now in not wanting to deal with any of it - neither will talk to me - or the kids - funny fellows

4.

From Across the Kitchen Table

When people from Rochester talk about their town, they describe its imposing Norman castle, which looms over the River Medway and sits beside its other main attraction, Rochester Cathedral. Then, perhaps, they'll mention that Charles Dickens grew up here and in nearby Chatham, returning in his later years to live and write. Many of his stories and characters were based on local people and places; the quaint cobbled high street of Rochester is littered with Dickens-related blue plaques. His Swiss chalet now sits behind Eastgate House on Rochester High Street—it used to be in the garden of Dickens's home in Gad's Hill and was where he was writing *The Mystery of Edwin Drood* on the day he died, in 1870. Today, on a wall just behind Eastgate House, there's a twenty foot–by–eight foot mural of Billy Childish's face painted by a local artist, Sam Collins. Childish doesn't know how he feels about it: "It's odd some people imagine I had something to do with it. I'm not that much of a maniac!"

Locals also point proudly to how quickly one can get away from Rochester, now that the high-speed train between the Kent coast and London runs through their town. You can be in Stratford in thirty minutes and in St. Pancras in under forty. Despite this, Billy Childish is disappointed there hasn't been a greater influx of "East London ponces, who have friends who are lawyers." That is what his hometown needs, he feels. For while there are plenty of pretty tree-lined residential areas filled with imposing and varied Victorian housing stock, commanding dramatic views of the Medway's grand sweep from the streets that rise above the cathedral, the castle, the High Street, the theater, and myriad Dickens-related attractions . . . there aren't enough poncey places to eat. There's a Pizza Express. A Costa Coffee opened and vies for customers with a couple of other local cafés. And you can always grab some pub grub, or a kebab, a curry. There's a tapas place, too.

But there aren't enough places for us ponces, bemoans Billy. So let's go and have a coffee at his house instead.

Out of the station, across Corporation Street and then over the High Street, up by the Jaggers cocktail bar (named in honor of Mr. Jaggers from *Great Expectations*), in between the cathedral and the castle, beyond the sprawling independent King's School, and on to the steep climb of St. Margaret's Street. You're on the right track now. When the mansions start to thin out at the top of St. Margaret's, you'll pass the barracks for 579 Field Squadron and the Prince of Wales's Royal Command on your left, as the street morphs into Borstal Road, which leads eventually to the parish of Borstal, whose youth prison lent its name to the nation's detention system for under-eighteens in 1902.

But we're not going that far down Borstal Road. Long before then, you'll spot a large detached house with a blue plaque above the door. The plaque commemorates Oswald Short of the Short brothers, who owned this place after the Shorts moved their pioneering aeronautical company from the Isle of Sheppey to the banks of the River Medway in Borstal in 1915. At its peak, Shorts employed 12,000 locals here and at Rochester Airport, developing the Second World War Shorts Stirling bomber in Borstal and testing its famous Empire and Sunderland flying boats on the Medway. Billy Childish exhibited a large-scale painting of their Canopus flying boat in 2023 to mark the seventy-fifth anniversary of the Shorts closing their Rochester factory and moving to Northern Ireland instead.

Before then, Billy designed the impressive four-engine, airplane-shaped knocker that hangs from his green front door beneath that blue plaque. It's modeled on the Short Sunderland flying boat, because he is an admirer of Oswald Short, who, he says, "was a great employer, a free-thinker, an aeronautical engineer and pioneer of flight who treated his workforce out-standingly." For example, during the recession between the wars, Short turned his factories over to the building of buses to keep his people employed.

Give that knocker a big swing and stand back. Maybe ring the bell, too, because this is a roomy and solid four-story pile, with a long, wide garden at its rear that Billy has just learned how to mow, so he could be anywhere within its grounds. Eventually, the door will open to reveal him in a long-sleeved white vest and a pair of navy vintage sort of jogging pants held up by suspenders. He smooths down his mustache. Big grin.

"Wotcha."

Let's step inside. Down the hallway and, groin first, straight into the nose of the family's extremely waggy dog, Captain Frank Worsley, named after the fabled New Zealand explorer who served as captain of the *Endurance* on Ernest Shackleton's epic Trans-Antarctic Expedition of 1914 to 1916—Captain for short.

There are stairs heading upward ahead and a long sitting room filled with furniture, a sewing machine, instruments, and paint-ings to the right, but we're going down, past the many Childish paintings, into the basement: a light-filled sitting room with large windows facing onto the lovingly maintained garden that leads down into woods and eventually to the Medway on your left. There is a bathroom in front of you, and ahead, through a door to the right, lurks a kitchen. But we're going to stop before reaching there and pull out a seat at the hardworking old wooden dining table, laden with neat piles of pending administration, small boxes of protein powders, a laptop, bottled carbonated water, and a teapot. Now we're ready to discuss some of the many cross-contaminated contours of Billy Childish's life and work.

Over the coming months, we'll pull out this seat to interview his old friends, as well as his wife Julie, who this morning is out practicing ballet. Most usually, though, we'll be with Billy alone, discussing his love life, his paintings, his journey through various therapies, his thoughts on creativity, the knotted weeds of family, his many musical groups, his personal escapades, his poetry, the childhood abuse he endured, and his long search for a place of comfort in this sometimes bewildering world, among other subjects; all while his ancient and befuddled cat Shackleton occasionally stands in the hallway and honks in distress, having become disorientated by accidentally wandering from beneath Billy's feet into a room its aged memory momentarily doesn't recognize.

And after we have locked eyes with Billy for hours of intense, largely one-way conversation, by turns upsetting, confusing, and quite often wryly hilarious, we too will make like Shackleton, hugging farewell to our host and emerging onto Borstal Road honking in distress, disorientated, and ecstatically befuddled.

From: William Claudius
Date: 13 October 2023
Re: god and reincarnation update

morning ted

i believe in god - which makes me the same as someone who dosent believe in god. 'believe' being the key word. and what do i mean by god?

i could say i believe in the creation. a creation is created. the maker and the substance being one and the same. i belive in the holographic creation that is always becoming and unbecoming. There is intelligence so it is intelligent.

reencarnation - i belive in reencarnation- which makes me the same as someone who dosnt believe in reencarnation. i have no requirement for my beliths to be correct. im going on guess werk surgested by the energys i encounter.

To Ease My Troubled Mind

i cant prove god anymore than someone can disprove god.
people are very upset with god, or at least the word. people
enjoy being upset. the wold is full
of idealogs. whats best? a good christen or a bad atheist? whats
best a good atheist or a bad christian? the answer is simple -
who cares what you believe? lets see how you act.

billy.

5.
Pedophile

A single called "Pedophile" was released in 1992 by Thee Head-coats, a band with which Billy Childish played guitar and sang throughout the nineties. There was no chorus to this song, no verse. No lyric sheet either, because there are no words. Just a riff and a rhythm, carved from a fifty-foot wave of menace that rolls over the listener, drowning you with dread.

In the dead center of the cover for the "Pedophile" single is a photo of a little man in white pants, a black V-neck sweater, and round-rimmed spectacles. He is seated on a banquette, smoking a cigarette and plucking a guitar. That's Norman.

A little while later, in 1993, Thee Headcoats released a song called "Every Bit of Me." The original was furiously noisy, Child-ish smearing the words over a blurred punk motif. Many years later, he redid the song with his Singing Loins group as a jaunty English sea shanty, but the message remained the same:

He was forty years old inside my jeans
I was nine years old and feeling unclean
He told me it was a secret to keep to myself
I wanted to hate him
But I hated myself
With every bit of me, with every bit of me . . .

There had been several active pedophiles at Walderslade Sec-ondary School for Boys. At least two were arrested while Billy was a student there in the 1960s. One of these, a science teacher, was infamous for closing the blackout curtains in the lab and taking boys' temperatures anally. He ran an after-school club for students that he invited Billy to join, and Billy agreed to give it a go. The teacher had long hair and played a guitar. Billy thought they'd maybe sing some songs together, go on a nature trek. Instead, the teacher told all the boys to lie down with him in the back field, before declaring, "If anyone wants to leave now before we start, they can." Billy ran.

There was also a curator at the Royal West Kent Museum who maneuvered Billy into one of the back rooms when Billy asked him about the Royal West Kent Regiment. He tried to molest Billy, but wasn't strong enough to pin him down, so Billy was able to escape. He never forgot his face, though.

But before all this, there was a convenience store on Walderslade Road called Crook's, run by Bert and Joan Crook. The Crooks also owned a canary-yellow chalet called "Nelly" in Seasalter, on the Kent coast near Whitstable, one of a row of chalets on sticks by the sea, with a septic tank you emptied into the tide when full.

John and June Hamper were friendly with the Crooks, so they would sometimes holiday in "Nelly" as a family. Next door to canary-yellow "Nelly" was a blue and white chalet called "Como," where Norman, a widower, and his daughter Susan would also spend their school holidays. They were from Blackheath, in southeast London, where Norman worked as a school woodwork teacher.

The two families became friendly. John Hamper got on well with Norman: John played trumpet, Norman guitar, and they both liked booze. Bert Crook, meanwhile, was handy with a ukulele. They'd all go to the Old Sportsman pub, where the adults would get drunk and play music together while the kids stayed in the parking lot making their own entertainment. After John Hamper left the family home when Billy was seven, he encouraged June to continue taking the children to stay in the chalet in Seasalter—possibly so he could have the house to himself in

Walderslade. Upon learning of this, Norman suggested that the two families save money and share a chalet . . .

How would that work, Norman? Where would everyone sleep?

Well, Susan and June in one bed. Nick can have the sofa bed. And Norman and Steven can bunk up together in the other bed . . .

Can you keep a secret? Can you?

Of course he can.

Steven Hamper kept the secret each night they were forced to share a bed together, but after the third night with Norman he refused to share the bed again. He said he'd take the sofa bed.

God, why are you so difficult, Smell!

Billy Childish kept the secret for many years, bottled up, eating away at him, until he could keep it no longer as an adult, and the humiliation, anguish, and disgust came spilling out in song, verse, prose, and painting for all to see and hear again and again.

But while it was still just a secret between Norman and Steven, Norman pursued him. He tried to take him on walks in the woods—Steven refused. He tried to pick him up from school and take him to his blue and white estate, even though Steven's home was only 300 yards away—Steven refused. He tried to fill the vacuum left by John's absence, fixing Steven's broken torpedo boat—but Steven refused to let him groom him, even though there was a fatherly vacancy.

Eventually, Norman faded from the Hampers' lives. But when he was old enough, Billy sought him out. He tried to track him down. He asked around. He put out feelers. No dice. He even stuck his face on the cover of a single titled "Pedophile." But he never heard from Norman again.

6.
Bates Motel

The old man blew us out, he packed us off down to Seasalter, then absconded. We couldn't afford the rent on
a shack by ourselves so we chipped in with a friend of
the family, Norman and his daughter Sue. Nick kipped
on the couch, Sue slept with my mum, and I have to
sleep in the big bed with Norman. And that's when he
got it out. All nite he keeps asking if I can keep a
secret, he tickles my leg and repeats it.

'Fred, can you keep a secret?'

Of course I can keep secrets, I tell him loads of
times. Then he groans and gets his willy out, he slaps
it in my palm, like a sausage, brown and hot, and all
these crinkly grey hairs. That's odd, all those hairs,
I haven't got any of those. Then he tugs my knickers
down and plays with my little pecker, he makes it go
hard and then he sucks on it, he does it for ages,
then he starts grunting, and kneels over me and wags
his thick one in my face. I can feel the heat coming
off it, he slaps my arse with it, hot, denuded, growing . . . It went up and out like a stick. I look at
it, that makes me go cross-eyed, he plunks it into
my hand and I remember something my brother told me
about, 'wanking' . . . about rubbing your willy until
this stuff comes out of it. So I do it, I kind of move
it a bit and he starts dribbling. This must be what
they call 'Wanking'. This must be 'The Facts of Life'

my mother keeps talking about . . . 'It's about time you learnt some Facts of Life!' Must be that my father can't tell me because he's too busy at the office. My mother must have asked Norman to tell me. I wondered if that's what it was, if me mum hadn't asked old Norm to show me 'The Facts of Life'.

He slaps it into my palm, then starts having some kind of fit, he jiggles about all over the shop, his eyes popping. That's something I couldn't get used to, his eyes without his specks, like some kind of hideous dwarf, snorting through his nose. And that thing sticking out of all those grey hairs, that sausage between his legs, hot and steaming. I let it go, I drop it double quick, just as soon as he starts moaning and dribbling. I thought that I'd hurt him. That maybe I'd done 'the wanking' wrong, it seemed that way . . .

And he was a school teacher, you go messing with them and they're just as likely to put you on a detention, or hit you or something. And that's when he did it, he flips me over on to my belly and puts his thing between my legs, he noses it in there, he sweats on me, he gurgles, he trembles at the knees. And the sound of the shingle, that's the waves . . .

I used to have to go to the bedroom in the afternoons, I didn't breathe a word to no one, I was guilty as sin, I kept schtum . . . I was implicated just by virtue of being born. That's sad.

So now I talk, I dare him to come back, old Norman, I dare him to come back here and try to shut me up! I'll give him juice! We can talk about his dick and the crummier aspects of his intricate personality. I know his address, I have contacts. Well, I remember and I won't forget. The sun slanting in through the drawn curtains, pale blue sea horses and cockle shells. Afternoons, you could hear the kids playing outside, the beach, the seagulls . . .

Excerpt from *My Fault*, Billy Childish's autobiographical novel (1996)

7.

An Afternoon in Walderslade, 1973

Steven Hamper walked into his mother's bedroom, opened the doors of her wardrobe, and placed a finger to his lips. *Ah, there it is.*

He reached up and lifted June's smart, two-piece tweed suit off the rail. The tailored suit had a rich, green weave to it, a tidy postwar cut with detailed pockets on the jacket, and an above-the-knee skirt.

Steven laid the suit down on her bed. Then he opened her drawer and removed stockings and suspenders, placing them next to the dress on the bedspread. June was a petite woman, about five foot three inches in her bare feet, but eleven-year-old Steven was a similar build and size. He knew his mother's suit jacket and skirt fit him perfectly, because he'd worn them occasionally already. So he slipped them back on again, smoothing the skirt out just above the suspenders he'd attached to the stockings.

Sitting at June's mirror, Steven applied lipstick. When finished, he wrapped one of his mother's headscarves around his shoulder-length blond hair, before standing to take a final look in the mirror. All in place. Carefully minding his step in his mother's shoes, he made his way downstairs. On the way to the front door, he picked up a copy of the family's Holy Bible, tucked it under his elbow, and crossed the road to let the inhabitants of the Wild Weeds Estate opposite his home in Walderslade know all about the good work of the Lord.

He knocked on a few doors. Some people on the estate opened

up, took one look at the little-old-lady Bible-basher, and swiftly closed the door. A few politely told him they weren't interested, thanks. Steven thought that Keith Gulvin's mother lingered a moment or two longer at her front door, taking in his attire and registering, perhaps, that the Hamper boy was beneath the lipstick and headscarf. She smiled faintly, shook her head, and closed the door wordlessly.

Eventually, Steven grew bored of the enterprise and headed back across the road, pausing only to lift his skirt at a passing bus. As he reached his home, he remembered that his key was not in his mother's suit. Luckily, it was Wednesday, the day that his grandmother Ivy, Nana Lewis, came to visit. He knocked.

Ivy opened the door, sporting a quizzical expression. "Yes?" she asked.

"Oh, hello. I'm letting people in the area hear the good news," began Steven. "Would you like to buy a Bible?"

"Oh, I don't know, dear," replied Ivy, closing the door slightly.

"Nana!" shouted Steven, laughing. "Nana, it's me!"

Nana Lewis took a long, confused second look. Was this little old lady really her grandson?

"Nana," he repeated more quietly, stepping past her into his home. "It's me."

8.

I, Gus Claudius

Steve Simmons was two years above Steven Hamper at Walder-slade Secondary School for Boys, but he knew who Steven was. His younger brother was in Steven's year, as were some of his cousins, but that wasn't primarily why he was aware of him. There was just something about Steven when you crossed paths in the school, something in his eyes behind their curtain of long, wispy blond hair; a melancholia. From a distance, Steven reminded Steve of Pip from David Lean's film adaptation of *Great Expectations*. That face . . . it's too strong to say it haunted him. But it stayed with him.

At that time, in the early seventies, Walderslade Secondary School for Boys was a rotten institution. It was a place for boys from Chatham who couldn't get into the grammar schools, for lads being molded to work locally in the dockyards and the factories, somewhere to help keep the supply of that workforce flowing. It was where Medway poured away its dregs. That went for the teachers, too, many of whom were war veterans, wounded and damaged, with axes to grind, or otherwise student teachers in their first positions, overwhelmed and unable to maintain control of their charges. The cane was used with grim regularity. "It was awful," says Steve Simmons now. "It was just like the school in that film *Kes*. There was terrible bullying going on. It was a horrible, horrible place."

Steve and Steven were well versed in the school's regime of corporal punishment. Both were profoundly dyslexic, but then, in 1972 or thereabouts, you may as well have said that you were from Jupiter or another dimension. Teachers just thought the boys were thick and lazy. Steven Hamper was sent to the bottom stream, where there were no real exams to tax him, but Steve Simmons was relegated even further below that into a remedial class. They were cannon fodder for the teachers.

Among the cruelest was Mr. Marrs, nicknamed Goebbels by the students on account of both his looks and demeanor. He was a teacher who viewed illiterate boys like Steve and Steven as a particular affront and dealt with them accordingly. Rather than a cane, Marrs favored a slipper, which he named "Whispering Willy," and he took great relish in threatening boys with it before pulling them into a private back room for its administration. "He used to really wallop you with it," recalls Steve. "And it actually hurt much more than a cane." Decades later, Billy Childish used Marrs's remarks in his school report for music as the title for a compilation album of his called *17%—Hendrix Was Not the Only Musician!*

Steven and Steve lived on opposite sides of Walderslade Road, oblivious to each other: Steve in the Weeds Wood Estate, Steven in a semidetached house. Steven had fish fingers or Birds Eye beef burgers for tea; Steve had bread and jam, "like the British Army." Steven had a Rolls-Royce parked in the garage; Steve didn't even have a fridge in a kitchen. Neither family had any money, though. Steven's just had the appearance of it, carefully manufactured by the absent father of the house, who spent what he had on himself.

The boys left school a couple of years apart, but they both ended up in the dockyards. While Steven took an apprenticeship as a stonemason for six months, Steve worked on the nuclear submarines, maintaining the reactors. His uniform included a Geiger-counting badge that filled up throughout the day, and when it reached a certain level he had to clear out. He says, "I was down in the bilges, cleaning them. I worked on the *Conqueror* and the *Poseidon*. Most of the people I worked with in the nuclear subs are dead now and I don't think that's a coincidence, you know."

Steve Simmons spent a year in the dockyards. Then he became a laborer for a while, before working at the oil refinery on the Isle of Grain. He flitted from job to job, trying to make enough money to fund his real passion: Marc Bolan and T. Rex. He grew his hair long and curly, got glammed up, and joined the other die-hard fans in the front wherever Bolan's T. Rex played across the country. There are photos of Steve standing next to Bolan at a gig in Paris in 1977 and they look so similar they could be related. But simply dressing up in glam gear and letting your hair grow into long curly locks made traveling by bus back to Weeds Wood Estate from a night out a highly risky endeavor in 1970s Chatham. "You had to really watch it, looking like that," he says. "But I come from quite a tough family, my cousins were boxers. I could run with the pack if needs be. I was never a bully, even though a lot of them were. I could just act tough if I needed to."

The pair of ex-Walderslade boys had a mutual friend named Kev Harding, who lived opposite Steve in the Weeds Wood Estate. One day in May 1977, Steve convinced Kev to come with him to Hastings to watch the Damned play at the pier. He'd seen them support Bolan the previous month and was by now a big fan of not just the Damned, but some of the other punk bands Bolan enthusiastically endorsed. Bolan had recently anointed himself "the godfather of punk," and that was good enough for Steve. He was on board—even if he didn't look at all like a punk.

With his short, dyed-red hair, Oxfam-sourced tweed jacket, and vintage sixties jeans, Steven Hamper, on the other hand, did look somewhat like a first-generation punk. Kev Harding spied him in the Poacher's Pocket in Rochester that May afternoon on their way to Hastings, where he was sitting near the pool table as the sun streamed in through the pub window. "There's someone you should meet in here," said Kev to Steve, as he made for the door. "He's the only other punk I know in the whole of Chatham."

Steve, twenty, and Steven, seventeen, hit it off immediately. They shared a silly sense of humor shaped by *The Goon Show*, Spike Milligan, comic books, and the comedy duos Laurel and Hardy and Abbott and Costello, but they were both at that moment enthused by punk above all. As they stood in the pub swapping names of new bands they wanted to see, Steven suggested a plan. They should bunk the train to London together next week and head to the Vortex on Wardour Street in Soho; there's a punk club opening there on Monday and Tuesday nights where all these bands play, £1 to get in, it might be a laugh . . .

Forty-six years later, the pair are once more laughing together in Rochester, chuckling at the memories of those few short golden weeks when punk was breaking, spreading its DIY message to dead-end kids like themselves, who were marooned beyond the capital in the suburbs and satellite towns, and desperate for some relatable youth culture, in that brief moment before the tabloids and TV fully cottoned on . . .

Soon after they first met, Steven Hamper told Steve that he would now be known exclusively as Gus Claudius. This alias was in tribute to *I, Claudius*, the BBC drama series about the Roman Empire that had captivated him the previous year. The "Gus" part came from learning that his mother had intended to call one of her boys Gus, but John Hamper vetoed it.

Yet as he stood watching Gus Claudius goon about on the escalators at Victoria station, miming climbing a rope upward while traveling down, before collapsing at the foot of the staircase and pretending to have a fit, with tutting commuters stepping over and around him, Steve Simmons considered that nickname was perhaps off the mark.

As a dyslexic, Simmons was a big fan of comics. He loved Billy Whizz, the "fastest boy in the world" from the *Beano*, and *Billy's Boots*, a weekly about a football-crazed kid with magical boots.

Seeing Hamper roll around on the train station floor, it suddenly struck him.

"You're not Gus Claudius!" he shouted, laughing. Rather, Steven was a character in his own comic fantasy, about a lad trying to create entertainment in a sternly gray, friendless world. "You're Childish! Billy Childish!"

And, lo and behold, he was.

Indirectly, Billy Childish is also responsible for Steve Simmons's nickname. Another day, later in 1977 or maybe even 1978, when Childish's band the Pop Rivets were setting up for a gig, drummer Bruce Brand turned from his kit and called over to Billy, "When's your mate coming down?"

"Which mate?" wondered Childish.

"You know . . . button nose?" replied Brand.

"Steve?"

"Yeah, Button Nose Steve." That also stuck.

Today, August 3, 2023, Billy Childish and Button Nose Steve are sitting at Billy's kitchen table. Both their wives are down the hill in Rochester together, shopping for fresh fruit—particularly raspberries—so we have the house and the boys' rusty old memories to ourselves.

These are two glorious sixtysomething physical specimens, rosy of cheek, heads topped with thick hatches of hair, in loose-fitting cotton work shirts, suspenders, and baggy canvas trousers. They are in great health (apart from the mystery pain in Billy's side. And that unexplained lump in his throat. And his persistent summer flu bug . . .)

Steve Simmons has a small farm down toward Canterbury, where he lives with his wife Denny. They have a few animals on-site, and they also volunteer their time and home to half a dozen regulars with learning disabilities.

"He and Denny give them a life," explains Billy. "Most of them have never been out of an institution, so he brings them over, lets them pet his animals. Takes them on jaunts. He nearly killed some up a mountain. You go round there, open a cupboard, and there's one just sitting in there! They're a weird bunch, aren't they?"

Button Nose smiles. "Oh yeah, but you get used to it. I've had two live with me for twenty-seven years. The others come for five hours on Tuesdays and Thursdays."

Button Nose and Billy have been friends for five decades, but they don't live in each other's pockets. They get together a couple of times a year, and Button Nose always tries to catch Billy playing live when he can: "I'm not just saying this, but Billy's my favorite group."

Let's fade their conversation in as they remember those first carefree days together in the early summer of 1977 . . .

STEVE: The Vortex used to be on a Monday and a Tuesday night: five bands for a pound and it wouldn't start till about nine or ten, finished about two.

BILLY: Siouxsie and the Banshees would always play.

STEVE: I remember Eater [early punk band from Finchley, north London, fronted by Andy Blade] always being there.

BILLY: They played a lot. Because he was only fifteen, his mum and her friends were there too. We were scared of them; we didn't realize they were just posh birds. They were all standing at the back being scary girls. We didn't know anything about girls, did we, going to Walderslade, a boys' school.

STEVE: X-Ray Spex played.

BILLY: Yeah, and we used to talk to Siouxsie. And we used to talk to that guy who turned out to be in Sham 69, we were friends with him.

STEVE: Jimmy Pursey.

BILLY: We used to chat to Shane McGowan on the Victoria platform. I became friendly with him a lot later, he liked us.

STEVE: It was a very short period of time, but it was a very important period of time.

BILLY: You know what my problem with punk is? It's like in that CTMF song, where I said, "I did everything Uncle Joe said, never took drugs to get out of my head, then we had to give up hope, the second LP was *Give Us Enough Rope*." Because, being a provincial punk, I believed all the bullshit.

STEVE: Me too.

BILLY: So I believed that this was a code of honor.

STEVE: What I noticed about Billy straightaway was an antagonistic thing. That's carried on, of course. Like meeting Joe Strummer—Joe Strummer wasn't a star but the Clash were known, they were big in the punk world, but Billy weren't going to cut him any slack. Me, I'd have been, "Hello, Joe, all right mate, can I have my picture taken with you?" Billy was giving him stick. I mean, we actually got in a barney with him and told him to fuck off!

BILLY: They were telling off our friend Gabriel. Gabriel was a Black guy wearing a Nazi armband. They told him he had to take it off, we told them to leave him alone.

STEVE: He had a swastika on his arm. I mean, the Sex Pistols had done it, and Siouxsie Sioux. He was just a kid, he'd gone along with the look like punks do. He had a gold band dyed in his hair, he had the safety pin, and he had the swastika.

BILLY: He was one of the only Black kids there.

STEVE: We're just standing in the Vortex chatting, and Joe Strummer comes up, spitting thunder, "What are you fucking wearing that for, my fucking grandad was persecuted by the Nazis!"

We're saying nothing, he's going on and on at him, but he went on about ten seconds too long. So we went, "Fuck off, leave him alone!"

BILLY: "He's doing no harm," we said. Strummer and Mick Jones. I asked Mick if I could have his badge and he wouldn't give it to me after we told them off.

STEVE: Mick and Joe, we used to chat with them.

BILLY: I was a massive fan. You didn't like them, but I really liked the Clash a lot.

STEVE: And you liked the Jam, didn't you?

BILLY: We went to the Battersea Jubilee in [June] '77 to see them.

STEVE: Yeah, Battersea Town Hall, with the Boys supporting.

BILLY: You've got photos of us there. I nabbed Paul Weller's plectrum—you've got a photo of me with it in my mouth on the train on the way back. We're sitting in first class in Victoria.

STEVE: And you've got the fanzine *48 Thrills!*. Billy said that day, "I like the Jam, but they're just going to be big stars." And I thought, *Fucking hell, they're not going to be big stars! Who's going to get them? They're good, but they're not stars!* He was so right.

BILLY: You sort of came round to the Clash, but . . .

STEVE: I hated them at the time.

BILLY: You thought they were too political.

STEVE: Yeah.

BILLY: A lot of people thought that. The Damned were pure rock 'n' roll and Steve's a big Damned fan.

STEVE: What I really liked about punk—and this is why me and Billy hit it off—what I loved was the fun. A lot of people missed the humor in punk. As soon as you knew the punks, knew the people at the core of it, you realized those were all art students. They were all very gentle, but they scared the shits out of everyone else by how they acted, they really did. People were scared of them. It was this big act. But with Captain Sensible and the Damned, it was just fun.

BILLY: We used to have jaw ache, watching them, from laughing.

STEVE: Yeah, they were so funny.

BILLY: Do you remember sitting there at the Vortex and there was that bird sitting next to us who pushed a safety pin through her lip? Most people who wore them used fake ones. This girl sitting next to us did it for real, stuffing a safety pin in her lip. We nearly threw up!

STEVE: She pushed it right through! It was like, *Argh*.

BILLY: Remember at that one night those people berating us, because they wanted us to go on the Right to Work march? They said, "There's a Right to Work march, you need to come on it!" I said to them, "Is there a Right Not to Work march?" Then, next week, we found out the Clash played at it, and we were pissed off. Felt like the end of fun. I wasn't into it to try and get a job. I was working too hard at *not* getting a job.

STEVE: They were saying, "Right to Work!" and we was like, "No, we want to be on the dole so we can come up here!"

BILLY: But it was already the beginning of that thing that lives to this day, the thought police of the liberal left. You can't get much more liberal and free than me and Steve. That's why I wrote [the Pop Rivets's] "Fun in the UK." I mean, "Anarchy in the U.K." was brilliant. I had the 45. But I wanted the same energy about having some fun for a change. That was the direction I wanted punk to go in. Everything was already serious and po-faced enough.

STEVE: It's hard to think of it now, but we had absolutely no money. We'd go to London with nothing in our pockets. It wasn't an easy thing in them days.

BILLY: We'd jump the train.

STEVE: Maybe had enough for one drink between us. Nothing else. You used to be able to buy a platform ticket in those days, if you wanted to meet someone on the platform or see them off. We might get those and then we'd get on the train.

BILLY: You had to do the Charing Cross line because they didn't have guards. Second World War carriages with no corridor, no guards, so you could do that. Onto the Victoria line, they might check your ticket, then you'd have to jump the barriers.

STEVE: There was a guard in Victoria—he always reminded me of Chuck Berry—I remember thinking, *Cor, that Chuck Berry's a bit of a nasty one,* because he got really angry. He spent his time searching for us. And he'd know we were coming up there on a Monday and Tuesday. We'd get there and you'd see him looking like he was after us. And if he saw us, we had to go back down to the train, hang around, and then try and make a bolt for it. We called him "Under the Rock."

BILLY: When we got to Victoria, we then had to walk to Wardour Street. Not that close, really. Then after the show, we'd walk from Wardour Street back to Victoria station, get the milk train if we could. Then walk three miles from Chatham station up to Walderslade, and we'd split at King George Road. You'd go up the estate and I'd go up the Walderslade Road. Then we'd wake up and I'd come up your house about two o'clock and say, "Are you coming tonight?" And Steve would be, "I'm not coming again!" I'd say, "Come on!"

STEVE: Billy used to drive me on to go up again. I'd be knackered. We weren't getting indoors till about six in the morning. But we'd go the next night all the same, do it all again. It wasn't very easy to find out about, either, that punk scene. You had to seek it out. When we went to the Vortex there were probably two hundred people in there. Punk was a tiny scene in reality.

BILLY: Oh, yeah. History shows punk as sweeping the nation or whatever. Not true. It was really hard to find out about this stuff.

STEVE: So, the Vortex, there's two hundred people in there. No other punk gigs on a Monday in London and certainly not outside Greater London or in the Medway towns, or wherever. There's just two hundred people in the whole of fucking London who were into punk enough to go and watch some punk bands play! We always joke that we were the only two punks in Medway in the summer of 1977—but we probably were. Because if you took two from Chatham, two from Gravesend, two from Gillingham, up through each town in Kent . . . eventually you'd have still made up more than two hundred before even reaching London. But as soon as we had a taste of it, it was, "What's the next thing? We want more of this." It was addictive, wasn't it?

BILLY: When we went to see the Jam at Jubilee Week, it took us forever to walk from Victoria to Battersea Town Hall, trying to find the place. We knew nothing about London. We ain't got an *A to Z* or a clue. Then we queue up to buy a ticket and just go in. Not once did we ever go to anything you couldn't get into. It was very small-scale.

STEVE: But you heard people talk about that gig for years: how many people would have been there if they were all telling the truth! It's not to brag. It was by chance that we started going to them gigs. As soon as we each found someone we could go with, we're gold.

BILLY: We were scared to go on our own. I was terrified of punk rockers.

STEVE: Go across town, get to this gig at that time of night, risk getting beat up walking back through London to get on a train at four in the morning that took the newspapers down, get off, walk three miles back home . . .

BILLY: With no food or drink. All good fun. But then it went a bit wonky.

STEVE: As soon as the masses get on to it, they ruin it.

BILLY: Those skinheads really turned me off it, the Sham 69 audience.

STEVE: Idiots. Worse than Teds. Remember Spider Wrassell?

BILLY: He was the only Ted at the school. He had an earring, a cross, and no one wore an earring. People were scared of him. Spider lived up on the estate near Steve.

STEVE: He said to me, "You tell that Hamper, if he comes past my house dressed as a fucking punk again I'll break his fucking legs."

BILLY: Do you remember the Fonzie Bar? It was a coffeehouse on Military Road. All the Teds went there. As I was going off the punk thing, I started wearing more fifties gear, leather jackets, old Levi's. I went to the Fonzie Bar with Bruce, feeling pretty brave because they were terrifying. Bought our coffees, turned around, and literally bumped into this lump. Look up . . . it's Spider Wrassell. He just nodded a "watch it" and walked by. My disguise worked! He didn't know I was the punk he wanted to torture.

STEVE: Spider Wrassell.

BILLY: What a brilliant name.

STEVE: We never got round to starting a punk band together, did we?

BILLY: You had a Woolworth's guitar. I said to you, "Why don't we do a group and you play guitar?" That was before I met Bruce.

STEVE: I could only play about three or four chords.

BILLY: I said one day, "I'm trying to get that Dave Marsh," a friend of mine, to play drums. We thought, *Oh, we could do the Chatham Forts,* because I was into the military thing. That was a good name for a band.

STEVE: I remember one little get-together playing, trying to do a song I thought I'd written, but I still thought you had to be able to sing or do something, you know?

BILLY: You didn't realize you didn't! And that you didn't have to have any talent at all. I wasn't allowed to be in the school choir. They said I couldn't sing. I had nothing musical in me but I really took to heart that [punk fanzine mantra] thing of, "Here's three chords, now form a band." It still took me four years to be able to distinguish what the bass or the guitar was doing when I was in a group, mind. I had no idea what the fuck was going on! Plenty say I still haven't.

STEVE: I think you know what you're doing now. You've got the hang of it.

Punk Rock Enough for Me

Louis Armstrong's Hot Five are punk rock enough for me
I said, Louis on a Dansette is punk rock enough for me
Leadbelly in a field is punk rock enough for me
I said, Leadbelly and the Grey Goose is punk rock enough
    for me!

Oh yeah
Yeah, yeah . . .

John Lee Hooker without Santana is punk rock enough for me
I said, John Lee on a half-track is punk rock enough for me
Hendrix in Beatle boots is punk rock enough for me
Freddie and the Dreamers are punk rock enough for me

Oh yeah
Yeah, yeah . . .

P.R.E.F.M! P.R.E.F.M!

The Beatles at the Star-Club are punk rock enough for me
I said, The Beatles without George Martin are punk rock
    enough for me
Joe Strummer and the 101ers are punk rock enough for me
I said, "Keys to Your Heart" is punk rock enough for me

Oh yeah
Yeah, yeah . . .

Billie Holiday and a piano is punk rock enough for me
A cup of tea is punk rock enough for me
Dostoevsky and Gogol are punk rock enough for me
Knut Hamsun and John Fante are punk rock enough for me!

Oh yeah
Yeah, yeah . . .

P.R.E.F.M! P.R.E.F.M!

Bo Diddley humming "Mona" is punk rock enough for me
Son House crying blood is punk rock for me
Robert Johnson at the crossroads is punk rock enough for me
The Downliners Sect are punk rock enough for me
Punk rock enough for me!

Jimmy Reed's wonky wheel is punk rock enough for me
I said, "I Told You I Love You" is punk rock enough for me
The Who before rock is punk rock enough for me
The sun pinned on God's sky is punk rock enough for me!

Yeah, yeah!
Oh yeah

P.R.E.F.M! P.R.E.F.M!

Buddy Holly and Bill Haley are punk rock enough for me
Wire at the Roxy are punk rock enough for me
Posing in a photo booth is punk rock enough for me
Miming in the mirror is punk rock enough for me!

Oh yeah!

    Wild Billy Childish and CTMF (2014)

From: Ted Kessler
To: William Claudius
Date: 5 April, 2023
Subject: Music/Art/Books

It would be good if you were to pick out some of the records/
groups art/artists writers/books, even comedians or films that
have had the most impact on you.

To Ease My Troubled Mind

From: William Claudius
Date: 5 April, 2023
Subject: Re: Music/Art/Books

---

sure ted

Vincent Van Gogh - and painting
Jimi Hendrix - and a record
Fyodor Dostoevsky and book
Kurt Schwitters and poem
Edvard Munch and painting
John Fante and book
Hans Fallada and book
Robert Walser and book
Knut Hamsun and book
The Beatles and record
Billie Holiday and record
Huddie Ledbetter—and record
Charles Bukowski and poem
Peter Cook

9.
The Tea Huts of Hell

Working as an apprentice stonemason at Her Majesty's Dockyard in Chatham, Steven stepped outside, into the icy wind of the winter of 1977, into the snow, with his bag of inadequate tools and his snatch of tobacco. He went shivering out there alone to carve a huge chunk of frozen granite.

His governor Bill couldn't go out, not with his chest, not with his health being as it was, not in this weather. Not possible. He had to stay in the tea hut with his brew, while Steven Hamper took his push-bike and his bag of rusty tools out into the bleakest of midwinters, a storm rolling in off the Medway, biting into bones, freezing his tears as he repeatedly chipped the granite, unable to carve it properly . . .

Stop for a moment. Think about the future.

He placed his left hand onto the granite.

He raised a three-pound club hammer high into the gray, godless sky, then he smashed it down upon his hand. Again and again and again and again. Once more, to make sure.

And that was the end of that. Off to the infirmary with his battered, bloodied paw, his final day as a member of the nation's salaried workforce in the rearview. From this day on, Steven Hamper would become an artist, a musician, a writer and poet. To that end, he signed onto the dole as soon as possible, remaining on unemployment benefits for more than a decade.

But before then, in the tea hut over the previous months, to blank out the bullying, the teasing, he'd taken to drawing. In those six months, he drew 600 sketches in his pad between tasks.

Now, Steven decided to take those drawings to Mr. Holborn, one of his old teachers at Walderslade Secondary School for Boys.

Holborn wasn't a benevolent teacher who'd encouraged Steven, someone who'd put a fatherly arm around Steven's shoulder when he could see the student overwhelmed by his dyslexia, when his home life drama threatened to drown him. No, that wasn't Mr. Holborn. He was a disciplinarian. Steven had told him he wanted to be an artist, but Holborn couldn't see it himself.

Yet now Steven brought those drawings back to Holborn, because Steven wanted to apply to art school, and he didn't know how to do so, as he had absolutely no qualifications. Qualifications were apparently necessary. Why do you need qualifications in science and English if you want to learn how to draw? wondered Steven. Anyway, Steven took those drawings from the tea hut to Holborn and asked for his advice.

"Finally, you've listened to me and learned how to draw," said Holborn with evident satisfaction that his code of "teach them mean, keep them keen" had born fruit.

So Mr. Holborn wrote a glowing recommendation for Steven Hamper and, lo and behold, Steven was accepted onto a foundation course at St. Martin's School of Art on the strength of his tea-hut drawings, as "a student who lacks qualifications but shows outstanding promise."

Unfortunately, he was refused a grant. So—as a student lacking in qualifications but showing outstanding promise—he was instead accepted locally by the Medway College of Design.

That didn't go well. Steven's argumentative, questioning, occasionally querulous and anarchic attitude was not widely appreciated and soon he was put on probation. At the end of the college year, Steven was not granted a certificate.

So what? What is he going to do with a certificate anyway?

This is 1977. A landmark year for Steven Hamper, soon to be Gus Claudius, before a final metamorphosis into Billy Childish. 1977: the year punk breaks into the suburbs; the year Billy

Childish sees the Jam, consequently buying a pair of black and white Jam shoes, which in turn facilitates a momentous meeting with Russ Wilkins in a Chatham boozer, on account of nobody else daring to spike their hair and wear a pair of black and white Jam shoes in a Medway pub . . .

In 1978, he will once again apply to St. Martin's School of Art, to study painting, and is accepted this time as a student who lacks qualifications but shows outstanding promise—but he'll only last a term before dropping out, disillusioned. And in 1980 he will again be accepted as a student who lacks qualifications but shows outstanding promise (and he'll be banished early on for producing "obscene" materials).

But for now we are in 1977. The year of his first intense romantic entanglements, of new creative alliances in poetry and music, of his first public performances and publications. So long, dockyards, farewell to the working week. Sayonara, Steven Hamper.

This is the dawning of Billy Childish . . .

10.

Top Ten Hits in Another Universe

Date: 28 July, 2023
From: Ted Kessler
To: William Claudius
Subject: Songs

Billy, I just wanted to say that I've been compiling a Billy Childish playlist to listen to as I write and I'm finding loads of songs that I missed over the years. I can't get over how much music you've released.

Ted

Date: 28 July, 2023
From: William Claudius
To: Ted Kessler
Re: Songs

---

a-okay

i have a few i like.

we really have made a few top 10 hits - but in another universe.

billy

When you've recorded well over 150 albums, not every song is going to be good.

Let's say conservatively that Billy Childish has made 160 albums (nobody can definitively confirm a number) and that there are ten or twelve songs on each one: that's around 1,900 songs, plus B-sides, etc. Considering how many lineups of different bands he's been in, it's unlikely that anyone other than Billy Childish has even heard them all.

Ian Ballard runs the Damaged Goods label that has released at least half of Billy's records over the last thirty or so years, but Childish's back catalog remains opaque even to him. The last words Ballard shouts to me across an east London roundabout after being interviewed for this book are, "Let me know if you manage to get a discography of all his stuff together—we'd love to know everything he's recorded!"

There are consequently some issues with quality control. Childish is not like many artists of his generation who took five years to record an album at a host of different studios, perfecting their craft and smoothing out perceived glitches. He records an album over Monday and Tuesday, does the artwork on Wednesday, sends the package out to his label on Thursday, and then forgets about it until it's time to flog it a few weeks later. When, for example, he'd finished recording the final single with his band Thee Headcoats at Toe Rag Studios in London in 2000, he used the remaining studio time that afternoon to record the first single with his new band, the Buff Medways; as one drummer and bassist filed out of the room for the last time, a new pair trooped in for the first.

Turnover of material is high. But Childish is right: he really has made a few top ten hits in another universe. It's a dimension where good lyrics are really important, and where the best records sound like they've been recorded by, as he says, "a group in a nice old wooden studio with soft reverb and some genuine energy." Here, the guitars crunch. The choruses make you gasp, and laugh—if they get it right, you'll do both at the same time—and they're very easy to sing along to, even if occasionally the words make you wonder if you should. There's rhythm, there's blues; there's fury, there's pain. There's an at times uncomfortable level of personal honesty, as well some hard-to-bear universal truths masquerading as jokes. Sometimes the songs are silly fun, often they're madly funny. They usually make you bop, or pogo, or punch the wall.

There's a reason Jack White was once such a fan he appeared on *Top of the Pops* with *B Childish* written on his arm, why Beck asked to work with him, why Kurt Cobain regularly cited his influence in interviews and why Graham Coxon of Blur started a label to put out Billy's Buff Medways records. There's no one really like him—he's a singular, instantly recognizable songwriter, performer, and vocalist in the lineage of so many postpunk stylists who've proven influential, from Paul Weller to Edwyn Collins . . . but without any of their commercial success.

He's made rock 'n' roll records. He's made punk records. He's made blues records, he's made rhythm and blues records. He's made folk records. He's made spoken-word records. He's made records that sound quite a bit like a Kentish John Lee Hooker, Link Wray, Star-Club Beatles, or, most recently, and perhaps surprisingly, Bob Dylan. He's made lots and lots of raw garage rock records. But he hasn't as yet made any UK or US hit records.

They all sound like Billy Childish records, though. You'll recognize the riffs, and the melodies, and the rhythms. Did he rip it off directly from the source, or did he rip off himself ripping something off from many years back in his catalog, or is he ripping off someone else ripping off someone else ripping off him riffing off someone else? It doesn't matter. It only sounds like a Billy Childish record when he's on it. Even if he didn't actually write it, or even sing it.

And he made the first of those records in 1979, a year after forming the Pop Rivets.

11.

Blimey, You Need Your Bleedin' Head Felt, Mate!

An Oral History of the Pop Rivets, the Milkshakes, and the Delmonas

"Most bands are fighting to get out of pubs. We were fighting to get *in* them."

Featuring:

BRUCE BRAND: Pop Rivets guitarist; drummer in the Milkshakes and many other Childish groups, including the Delmonas and Thee Headcoats; now (and then) a commercial artist (and musician)

RUSSELL WILKINS: Pop Rivets and Milkshakes bassist, Delmonas musician/producer, as well as for several other Medway-related bands; now in the Gruffmen and also Lord Rochester; runs Rochester Cutting Rooms, an Edinburgh record service specializing in limited-run lathe cuts

SARAH CROUCH: aka Ludella Black, member of the Delmonas and Thee Headcoatees; now a ceramics artist, living in Chatham with her long-term partner, Mick Hampshire, once of the Milkshakes

MIKI BERENYI: teenage Milkshakes and Delmonas devotee; the ex-Lush singer is now a musician and writer

BILLY CHILDISH: Billy Childish

"I'm Gonna Kill Myself"

BRUCE BRAND: Before I met Billy Childish—B.C.—I was in a band with Russ Wilkins, on guitar.

RUSS WILKINS: Chatham Technical High School for Boys: that's where I formed a band which we eventually got Bruce into, playing rock covers. When I left school, I wanted to work in a recording studio, and at that time, when you went to the careers man, you were destined for either Chatham Dockyard or the army or one of the factories. I said, "I want to work in a recording studio." He just looked at me blank, as though I'd said I wanted to be an astronaut or something. I managed to get myself a job in a TV rental place and they sent me on what's called a City and Guilds to get a qualification in TV and radio repair, which served me very well over the years with band equipment. In all the bands, I've been the technical bloke, and fortunately, I'm quite interested in it.

BRUCE BRAND: It was Russ's idea: "Let's form a punk rock group." I said, "Okay, that's you and me and who else?" He said, "I bumped into a punk rocker the other week, he's called Steven, Steve the punk, and I don't know if he can sing but he looks like he could be a good front man."

RUSS WILKINS: I first saw Billy Childish around town in '75, '76. This very shy boy with long, wispy hair like Johnny Winter. That was the caterpillar and then the next year I met the butterfly in the Bull Hotel in Rochester. It was the night after the Jam played at Hammersmith—he'd been to that too. You kind of stare at each other across the pub before you eventually go up and start talking to each other. We got on fine and pretty quickly decided we should form Medway's only punk band. We started off as TV21 and then became the Pop Rivets.

BILLY CHILDISH: I had a pair of these black and white Jam shoes on, my straight trousers, and my dyed barnet. I went into the back of the Bull Hotel, to the old Victorian bar, to have a pint. I was on my own and this guy came over and spoke to me, because he clocked me, talked to me about music. Hardly anyone was interested in that music, but he saw somebody that was. His name was Russ Wilkins, and he said he was a TV repairman. He asked me what I was doing. I said, "Well, I've got to go to this art college in September." He said, "I've got some pals at art college, we play in a group." I said, "Oh, right, I want to do something with a group." And he said, "Would you like to see me and the group?" and I said, "Yeah."

BRUCE BRAND: 1976-ish, I met Russ in a queue for a Damned gig at the Astoria. He said, "Oh, yeah, Steve the punk's coming, so you'll meet him." This bloke came bounding up, spiky orange hair, he talked a load of rubbish for about ten minutes. I think I was at art college, Russ was an electrician or something, Billy said he was going to go to art college. I said: "What are you going to do after that, then?" "Kill myself." That hasn't happened yet!

BILLY CHILDISH: I thought I wasn't going to live beyond twenty-one. I had this presumption in my head, like, *How can this carry on like this?* The world didn't seem real or concrete. I thought I was going to be born into a world of fairness, where adults were adults—I still struggle with that. Anyway, Bruce came up to me: "Oh, you met my friend Russ and he said you want to sing in a group," and that we should do a rehearsal. So we did a rehearsal with an acoustic guitar and a cardboard box.

BRUCE BRAND: Russ and myself practiced on a field outside the art college a couple of times, in the open air, with prospective drummers, and we ended up using our old drummer from the band we used to be in beforehand called Night Shift—every town at the time had a band called Night Shift, playing all the rock hits of the day. And then we got Billy to front it, to sort of sing. I mean, he couldn't sing for toffee, but he was great at *not* being able to sing for toffee.

RUSS WILKINS: Myself and Bruce, we'd been in bands and we'd done the lugging Hammond organs up and down stairs and all that shit. Billy hadn't done anything, so there was an element of swanning around with his notebook, not doing very much. There wasn't a great work ethic, but it was all new to him.

BILLY CHILDISH: We called Russ Wilkins "Big Russ" because the drummer was also called Russ, Little Russ. He really was a small man. The other Russ is normal. He was mean to me in those days, very mean.

RUSS WILKINS: We had this defense mechanism, you'll find it in quite a lot of people from that Medway music scene. It's not something I'm overly proud of, but we would mercilessly take the piss out of people. If there was any opportunity to take the piss, we would. It's a bit laddish, but also insecure. It was pretty relentless. I became exhausted with it by the time I left the area.

BRUCE BRAND: I seem to remember the local punk band was called Gash, and it was the one single solitary punk rock group for the whole of the Medway area; we saw them a couple of times and decided that we could do a lot better. They were probably fine; that's just the way you are when you're eighteen. Anyway, they booked a gig at this place called Detling Village Hall, and somehow or other we got to open for them.

BILLY CHILDISH: So we started rehearsing up at my parents' house, and we strung together a set over two or three rehearsals, then went along and did the show. That was my first.

BRUCE BRAND: I kept forgetting it was their gig. It was a sea of spiky hair and leather jackets and whatnot, all bobbing up and down. We always did lots of sixties songs. I think the start of the set was "Whatcha Gonna Do About It?," "Hippy Hippy Shake," "Love Comes in Spurts" by Richard Hell and the Voidoids, "You Really Got Me," a truncated version of the *Stingray* theme—and we also did the *Fireball XL5* theme, hence the name TV21, which was a very popular comic that had all that stuff in it. I remember doing "Born to Lose," oh, and "Wild Thing," but more like Jimi Hendrix's version than the Troggs's, which was completely against the grain, but that's the way we rolled. When I say it was like Jimi Hendrix, obviously it was nothing like Jimi Hendrix, but it had that sort of meandering arrangement.

BILLY CHILDISH: After we played, we went straight to the pub next door, because we weren't interested in seeing Gash.

BRUCE BRAND: After about ten minutes, a sea of spiky hair and leather jackets came barging in the pub and said, "If you don't get back onstage, we're going to trash the gig." "Oh, okay then, better do that, I suppose," because it was probably our gear. So, we played another set, or at least half a set. That was the start, and the rest is history. Anything else you want to ask?

BILLY CHILDISH: Big Russ said he wanted to move to London and go for the big time. He didn't express it that way. Me and Bruce were left there in Chatham. I was with my first true love, Rachel Waller, but she was a problematic girlfriend—in that she caused me problems and I caused them too probably. Bruce also had a problematic girlfriend. So me and him hung out and I said, "Why don't we write songs?" Bruce said, "Well, I don't write songs, I've not done that before." I said, "We should do one, I've written some lyrics."

BRUCE BRAND: The first song we tried to write was at his mum's house in Walderslade. It was called "Blimey, You Need Your

Bleedin' Head Felt, Mate," which was kind of an Ian Dury, Blockheady type thing. I think we practiced it, went through it a couple of times, then completely forgot about it, for obvious reasons.

BILLY CHILDISH: I wrote some lyrics when I had this idea for a group called the Chatham Forts before with Button Nose Steve, but I had no idea about music at all, couldn't play anything, had no musical background, wasn't allowed to be in the school choir because I'm tone-deaf, etc. So anyway, Bruce came round my mum's. I was really into the Kray twins and I'd written this lyric, "Kray Twins." I was also fed up with "Anarchy in the U.K.," so I'd written a thing called "Fun in the UK" as an answer to that. We needed a bass player, so we put an advert up and there's a guy called Romas Foord who could play a bit of bass and became our bass player.

BRUCE BRAND: We played a few gigs locally, at pubs.

BILLY CHILDISH: Big Russ saw us and wanted to come back in, so we booted the other fella out.

BRUCE BRAND: That's show business, unfortunately. Then Russ started writing stuff as well.

BILLY CHILDISH: Big Russ was the powerhouse behind the Pop Rivets making the first album, which we released ourselves with a backdated benefits check. We did the album ourselves and that was mainly Russ's instigation. I still couldn't tell the difference between a bass note and a guitar note or anything. I didn't know what was going on!

BRUCE BRAND: We recorded it at a place called Oakwood, which was somebody's bungalow in Whitstable, their front room. The bloke who recorded it was called Grahame—Grahame spelt the posh way with an "e" on the end. He had a Noel Edmonds haircut and teardrop aviation shades, but he was quite forgiving. We were recording away and then at six o'clock his old man came through the door and went, "Right, news is on, shut up!" Bang! So we had to sit there in silence for half an hour while he watched the news on the telly. Then we started up again. I think we did it in two or three days. We thought, "Well, it's the first album, obviously we should call it *The Pop Rivets's Greatest Hits* and then quit while we're on top."

Hopp Schwiiz!

RUSS WILKINS: Little Russ, the drummer, he had a Swiss girlfriend he'd met.

BILLY CHILDISH: She had to go back to Switzerland for tax reasons; they drove through France and Germany, all the way to Switzerland, and they took the album to clubs they passed and asked if they could play them. All of these clubs said yes! So when they came back, we had to try and get a secondhand Transit van. We then headed out and played this string of gigs through Switzerland when no one else was playing, and Hamburg, and we met all those connections that the Milkshakes exploited a bit later on.

BRUCE BRAND: We put this tour together in Switzerland and Germany. We were off for six weeks or something ludicrous, in some knackered old Transit van. We got gigs while we were over there, on the way round. "Oh, there's a likely looking place, they do gigs," and we would go in and say, "Hello, can we play here next week?" and they said, "Yes, you can come here and play next Saturday." "Okay!" So we'd drive halfway across the country to play this little dive that we'd booked the week before. That was proper. I'm not saying we brought punk to Switzerland, but there were no other punk bands playing there, that's for sure.

RUSS WILKINS: If you want clichéd stories of people climbing out of windows in a moving van on the motorway and so forth, they all exist. Young boys drunk abroad for the first time. We did all that.

BRUCE BRAND: We had a friend called Mickey. He had an Everest double-glazing van that he used to drive us around in. He was like our roadie, and he had a friend called Bertie who helped us, so we had a driver and a roadie. They formed this band called Mickey and the Milkshakes, who used to support us sometimes. They played rock 'n' roll and punk hits and "Tiger Feet" by Mud. It was a college band. We were still at college. I think Billy had got thrown out of about three colleges by then. Mick was in the graphics department I was in at Medway. Mickey and Bertie would come on tour. We did a couple of tours of Germany and Switzerland, made two albums, then . . .

BILLY CHILDISH: Then we began to fall apart, of course. The drummer left and they tried to throw me out. I was told in Germany I should be more like Jimmy Pursey, by the Swiss girlfriend who thought she was the manager, which didn't go down well with me. Then Little Russ left and there was an uprising. I was going to be expelled.

RUSS WILKINS: We could have possibly gone over to Europe again and earned a bit more money, paid off our debts, but Russ left, without any warning. We'd borrowed money to buy a PA and stuff, and Russ said, "I don't want to do this anymore." I think he walked away from the debt. We actually owed his girlfriend's sister money, which was a bit messy, as those things are. We were committed. I'd given up work. It was going reasonably well, so we wanted to carry on.

BRUCE BRAND: I can't actually remember why Little Russ left, he probably got fed up with it, because he did it as a favor to us in the first place. He was a top-notch drummer, though.

RUSS WILKINS: We had a John Peel Session, and Russ just walked out, which was really frustrating. So we had to rehearse up somebody pretty bloody quickly. He was a big fan of Rush and he had long hair. There was a real paucity of people you could use at the time.

BRUCE BRAND: Called himself Cecil Bass and he was a Phil Collins fan. An okay drummer, but a bit fancy.

BILLY CHILDISH: He hated me, but we did the Peel Session. Then it all fell apart.

BRUCE BRAND: We accidentally fell out with Little Russ quite badly in the end. We had a friend on the local paper, the *Chatham Standard*, called Steve Rayner, and he'd write glowing reviews of us no matter how awful we were. We would run down there, Billy and I, tell him we'd bought a new pair of socks, and he'd print it on the music page. But when Little Russ decided to leave, we ran down there to tell him and we made up this cock-and-bull story. We said, "Yeah, he was always a bit odd, the way he wore women's clothes," and this, that, and the other, just made up a pack of lies to make it sound funny. Unfortunately, Steve Rayner wasn't there and there was a bloke standing in for him and he wrote everything down that we said and published it as we'd said it, as if it was true, because, ah, well, being young and foolish, it didn't occur to us that that's what the press did; we thought if it was our mate, Steve Rayner, he'd know, he'd go with the flow. It didn't work out like that. So a couple of days later, it was there in glaring black-and-white: it said, "Yes, we kicked Little Russ out because he was a bit weird and wore women's clothes," which was . . . in the late seventies, that kind of thing was not quite as accepted as it is these days. We'd arranged a meeting with Little Russ to divvy up the proceeds from the PA we bought and it was all done in a stony silence. Very uncomfortable.

RUSS WILKINS: We got the airplay on John Peel, which was good, but by then it'd lost momentum. When you're in a band, it's you versus the rest of the world, and that's important. Not having Little Russ play the drums in the Pop Rivets anymore, it's not four of you against the world, it's three of you against some other bloke.

Eight Legs, One Brain Cell

BRUCE BRAND: By that time, we were getting heavily into more R&B and sixties music. In fact, the reason I got into punk in the first place was because it reminded me of listening to the Kinks and the Who when I was a nipper. We all started listening to more of that stuff. I remember hearing a John Peel Session of the Rezillos—or the Revillos—and they did "Hippy Hippy Shake" and a couple of other things that we did, and it was like a carbon copy of our arrangements. We thought, *Let's face it, any contemporary punk rock or new wave band, given those songs, they'd probably do them too fast, too loud, and too wacky.* You'd compare them to the originals and think, *They've got something else going on. It's not a gimmick. It's got more joy to it, and it's got a quality that transcends just playing things loud and fast.* You think, *Wouldn't it be great to capture that?*

BILLY CHILDISH: Mick Hampshire and Bertie were in my favorite group, Mickey and the Milkshakes. Mick playing guitar, singing; Bertie on bass.

BRUCE BRAND: The Pop Rivets fizzled out in the end. We used to play the art college a bit. We did one, they had a sixties party and they booked us to do it, or we demanded to play it, under the name of the Dead Beats, with another drummer called

Yan, who made his own drum kit. We did this one gig and he wanted to play guitar on a couple of songs. Previous to that, I'd just been playing guitar.

RUSS WILKINS: Bruce is one of these strange people who can just pick an instrument up and apparently start playing it.

BRUCE BRAND: I took no notice of drums whatsoever. But since I'd been listening to these rock 'n' roll and sixties and R&B records, I'd started noticing the drums, mainly because they weren't overbearingly loud and just going *dush-dush-dush* to everything, clattering away in the background. *Wow, no one plays like that anymore*, I thought, *I'd love to do that*. It was either heavy rock or disco drums at the time. I don't know how I found out I could do it, but doing this gig, on two songs I was on the drums. I really enjoyed it.

SARAH CROUCH: I was at Medway College of Design. I was twenty, twenty-one, doing a vocational course in ceramics. Billy had left college but he used to pop in to the pottery department and I met him there. I took on a room at 107 Rochester Street, but because he'd left college, Billy wasn't entitled to rent a room; I managed to get him one. We just said that he was still a student. Mickey and the Milkshakes then reformed with Billy and they used to rehearse in the cellar next to the kitchen. That's when I met Mick. We lived in a student house together for two years, from around 1980. I've been with Mick ever since.

BRUCE BRAND: Everyone left college and Billy and Mickey started to get tight. They locked themselves in Mickey's room. We'd shown Billy how to play two chords on the guitar during the Pop Rivets: he could play A minor and G over the solo in one of our songs. I don't know if that was the biggest mistake we ever made or our gift to humanity. He and Mickey learned how to write songs together and after about six months, they came out with beards dangling along the ground.

BILLY CHILDISH: I wanted to do more rock 'n' roll songs. I really liked Gene Vincent and wanted to go more in that direction. Mick was interested in the Beatles and we both loved the Star-Club album. We hated New Romanticism. There was common ground there.

SARAH CROUCH: The new version of the Milkshakes was Bertie, Mickey, Billy, and a chap called Tramp on the drums.

BRUCE BRAND: He was kind of a biker bloke, I think he was a Hells Angel.

BILLY CHILDISH: Tramp was a lovely guy but he wasn't very reliable.

BRUCE BRAND: They played a pub in Rochester and I went to see them. It was the funniest thing I'd ever seen. They were playing this rock 'n' roll stuff and their own songs. Every time one of them took a solo, they'd go up on tiptoes and their tongue would come out, like a cartoon! I wish I could show you, but you know, someone sticks their tongue out and it leaks out of the side of their mouth—every time one of them took a solo, that would happen. It was kind of useless but brilliant. And I thought the only thing that let them down, apart from being useless and brilliant at the same time, was the drummer was just playing standard rock drums, which didn't really suit the music.

BILLY CHILDISH: Bruce was a really great guitarist in the Pop Rivets, so we made him learn to play drums in the Milkshakes.

BRUCE BRAND: The dynamic of the group was that Billy and Mickey shared the same brain cell. They lived in the same student house in Rochester and they were joined at the hip. You'd go round the house for a rehearsal, nine times out of ten they'd be tumbling around on the floor with their hands round each other's throat and threatening to batter each other's brains in, while giggling like schoolkids! They were always writing songs together and they'd always be credited to both of them, even if one of them had written it. And it wasn't necessarily whoever sung it wrote the song: they'd both write the songs, either together or independently, and then whoever got to sing it, sung it. So it wasn't all Mickey's songs sung by Mickey or the other way round. Let's not call them the Medway McCartney and Lennon, please.

BILLY CHILDISH: We really liked the energy of the earliest Beatles stuff and rock 'n' roll. There wasn't much of that around in 1981, so we thought it would be good to get some of it back.

RUSS WILKINS: If you asked me about Billy's musical philosophy, the most obvious thing is latent plagiarism. It's about delivery of a good song, or performance. So, we may have done a cover in the Milkshakes, and done it well—but it always sounded like us and nobody else. And Billy's done that with all his stuff. I mean, all this Bob Dylan stuff he's been doing recently, it's Bob Dylan! But it's also obviously Billy Childish so I think it's too simple to call it plagiarism.

MIKI BERENYI: Of course, the music was derivative—some would say pointlessly so. Might as well be a covers band. But for me, punk and the sixties were both legendary eras that I missed out on, and the Milkshakes encapsulated both. And it really did have an explosive energy, raw and exciting. Mickey and Billy would dance while playing their guitars, really move; if you were down the front, it felt like they were dancing *with* you; and they were funny and raucous, confident, without a shred of self-consciousness or pompous artifice. They looked like they were having a blast, and that was infectious. You wanted to lose yourself in the energy and dance along. Everyone—including the band—would be dripping with sweat, properly dancing, like when you see footage from the sixties of kids in dance halls letting loose. You came out of their gigs feeling exhilarated.

BRUCE BRAND: We had a residency at the Hope and Anchor in London, but the gigs, I can't remember much about the gigs, because there was a lot of alcohol involved. It's all a bit of a blur, to the point that everyone else would remember what had happened, and they were coming out with all these stories, "Remember when we did this and we did that and we played there and we played here and we met this bloke and that bloke and they said that?" and I thought, *What are you talking about? I've never heard of any of these people or places.*

RUSS WILKINS: My dad was a pub singer. I think if I have to have anything on my gravestone, that's probably what I am. Most bands are fighting to get out of pubs, but we were fighting to get *in* them. Not because you want to get pissed but because those small venues are the best places to play. All of the best gigs I've ever been to have been in small places. I've been to gigs in massive places, I saw Led Zeppelin and stuff like this: it was horrible, really horrible. Yet seeing the Damned at the Hope and Anchor was just earth-shattering.

MIKI BERENYI: I think what really did appeal was that you could dance down the front. I was seventeen and there were a lot of girls; it didn't feel like girls were sneered at for joining in. They had a kind of flirtatiousness: they did a lot of guitars being aimed at the girls at the front; that way they engaged with their audience, knowing that there were loads of girls there, used to drive Tracey [Emin] absolutely fucking bonkers. I think that was partly why I didn't even realize Billy was going out with Tracey—I didn't really realize until I'd already got off with him, and I was like, "Oh, fuck, you're actually with her?" The big thing, I think, was it was music you could dance to, and not fight to, which made it so much better than all those psychobilly bands then.

BRUCE BRAND: We recorded the first album, *Talking 'Bout*, at the same studio, Oakwood, with the same engineer, but at a different location. He'd moved up to above the El Ranchero tearooms in Herne Bay, which was a bit more like it. It was a proper down-home recording studio, rather than his dad's front room. That's where we recorded the first album, the second album, the third, and a couple of singles.

The Sex Pope

BILLY CHILDISH: We did these little tours in Germany through our old connections, but Bertie was disillusioned. Bertie was into funk and Led Zeppelin. We also made him cut off—well, we didn't make him—but I cut off all his dreadlocks when he was round my house. My mum came in and said, "Oh, there's all caterpillars in the bin." I said, "That's Bert's dreadlocks, Mum."

BRUCE BRAND: Bertie eventually decided to leave. He went and joined a local funk band, I don't blame him for that. The name of his group escapes me now.

BILLY CHILDISH: Big Russ came back in on bass after Bert. He met Hilary then, and that's when we formed the Delmonas.

MIKI BERENYI: God, I loved the Delmonas. They were such an important group for me. The Delmonas, at that time, consisted of Sarah, Louise, and Hilary, who were the wives/girlfriends of three of the Milkshakes. The girls did the singing, the Milkshakes played the backing music. Interestingly, the only girlfriend of a Milkshake not in the Delmonas was Billy's girlfriend, Tracey Emin. I often get asked to name women in music who inspired me to form a band, but it is usually the attitude and the enthusiasm that are as galvanizing as the music itself. Seeing ordinary girls with no professional training sing and play gigs made me realize that this could be something achievable—and fun!

BILLY CHILDISH: The original Delmonas lineup was Tracey and Sarah, which never performed because we soon realized Tracey couldn't ever do it. Then Bruce started going out with what's-her-face, Louise, who I had a big falling-out with when he got married to her. That's the reason we didn't do [BBC Music TV show *The Old Grey*] *Whistle Test*, because of my refusing to play with her.

SARAH CROUCH: It was Bruce and Louise, his first wife, so they were a unit, and there was Russell and Hilary, they were a unit. Russell and Bruce were very keen to push their wives. I was Mickey's girlfriend, but Mick never used to get involved in pushing me in any way at all. And Billy didn't care. For Billy and Mick it was more just to have fun. Me too. I just wanted to sing some songs.

BRUCE BRAND: We started getting lots of tours in Germany. In Hamburg, the bloke who was booking the tour said he knew a photographer from the old Star-Club, the guy who photographed all the old beat groups there. I thought, *Hmm, interesting.* Somehow he managed to wangle us a gig at what used to be the Star-Club, which was now called the Salambo Erotic Sex Theatre, run by a bloke called the Sex Pope—his name was René Durand but he called himself the Sex Pope, which was a bit exotic—what's going on there, then? We were traveling around Germany and the man at the Salambo Erotic Sex Theatre on the Reeperbahn said, "Yeah, you can play next Sunday on their night off." Again, it meant driving across the entire width of the country to get there, but we did it. Apparently the original Star-Club stage was underneath the stage we were playing on; they were raffling off bits of wood from it. I found some old curtains, some old black drapes backstage. "Yes, this is original Star-Club curtain." "Ooh, I'll make a lucky Star-Club tie out of those!" So I ripped a bit off and it crumbled to dust in my hands . . .

SARAH CROUCH: There was this jokey thing that whenever you asked them what they got up to on tour in Germany or wherever, they'd say, "Keep your nose out of band business!"

BRUCE BRAND: We played this place, the Salambo Erotic Sex Theatre; the sex club people said, "Oh, yeah, Eric Burden's going to come and Tony Sheridan's going to come, and two of the Liver Birds live in Hamburg, they'll be there . . ." No one bloody came, of course. It was just full of these old geezers. But anyway, we did that, we played the Star-Club; we were the first group to play there for, I don't know, eleven years or something, however long it hadn't been the Star-Club. The next time we went back there, it had burned down, nothing left, so we were presumably the last group to play the Star-Club as well.

Self-Inflicted Wound

BILLY CHILDISH: Big Russ was married, he'd had children, so Big Russ left the group, and John Gawen, who was a young fan of the group, we brought him in on bass. And then there was a gradual decay of it.

RUSS WILKINS: I upset the apple cart when I left, but I don't think it was quite as much fun for Billy and Bruce. When somebody leaves it kind of takes the wind out of your sails. I'm not saying that the albums after that weren't any good; I mean, *They Came They Saw They Conquered* was okay, *Thee Knights of Trashe* was really good. But it wasn't really any surprise when maybe a year or so after I left, Mick just said, "I don't want to do this anymore." Maybe I saw the writing on the wall.

SARAH CROUCH: Mick and Billy were really, really good friends in the early days. The four of us, me and Tracey and Billy and Mick, we used to hang out and do everything together. But they were all drinking so much in those days, and the Milkshakes was like a working group. That's all they did, they were on the dole and they went to Germany and all around Europe, they'd play pretty much every week. So the drinking got a bit heavy with all of them, really. Mick just decided that he didn't want to do it anymore.

RUSS WILKINS: One interesting thing is that nobody took drugs, ever. It wasn't like a creed or something, it just never really came up. It was just booze. Much too much booze, but just booze.

BILLY CHILDISH: Mick suddenly left. Sarah and Gawen were in the van with us, we'd just played at the Hope and Anchor.

SARAH CROUCH: Mick just announced, "By the way, I'm not going to do this anymore," and it was quite emotional. I remember Bruce saying, "I was going to do that first!" I think Billy respected that Mick was going to leave, but I don't think he ever really forgave him for leaving. It was at the time when they'd just played on telly on *The Tube*, and they were really taking off. But when they'd say, "Who's the band's spokesman?" Billy would reply, "I am!" It got a bit like that, and all these things were storing up. That's just my opinion, may not be entirely true but seemed that way.

MIKI BERENYI: I was a little heartbroken when Mickey left. Mickey had a cheekiness, but it was less wild than Billy. There's more gravitas. There was nothing childish about Mickey. When he sang those slower songs, like "Jezebel" (I remember Tracey once telling me it was "her" song—which was a reason I never twigged early on that she was with Billy, because it was Mickey and not Billy singing it), his voice sounded amazing and he completely held the stage, like some star crooner from a bygone era. I don't want to take away from Billy's achievements—the Caesars, Headcoats, etc., were great—but I really missed Mickey. He seemed to keep Billy in check, like an older brother.

BRUCE BRAND: I could not believe Mick had got his resignation in before me.

SARAH CROUCH: I think now Billy probably does think that he had far more ambition than Mick did. But Mickey just wanted it to be like a rock 'n' roll band. It was quite nice that they got offered tours, *The Tube*, and they got BBC sessions, but that wasn't what he wanted to do. I mean, that's him, he doesn't want to sell his paintings: he's just a very unassuming chap.

BILLY CHILDISH: Gawen was crying and Sarah was crying. I said to Bruce, "Do you want to form another group?" And one of the main reasons I wanted to do it was because John was so upset because he hadn't been in the group long, so I thought, *I'd better form something.* That's why I did Thee Mighty Caesars.

BRUCE BRAND: Thee Mighty Caesars was basically the Milkshakes without Mick. We had a couple of rehearsals round the back of the Nag's Head and Billy recorded it on his Revox, which became the first album. My thought was, *Ah, this is all right, but . . .* I didn't see the point of doing it without Mick, really. I didn't like it without Mick.

BILLY CHILDISH: I think Bruce had some big problems with me. A lot of people feel that I need taking under control, have my wings clipped; a lot of people see that as their main job. A thankless task! I can't be sure of that, but I do occasionally get told what type of an arsehole I am. My character flaws have been pointed out in the past, on numerous occasions. Actually, from the get-go, from the cradle! So I'm resilient, I'm obstinate.

BRUCE BRAND: I was particularly good at picking arguments with his lordship. I'd open my mouth and everyone else would take a step back. I eventually learned many years later in Thee Headcoats that it's better just to keep my mouth shut, take a step back, and let Billy get on with it. I didn't necessarily have to agree with it, but saying anything or complaining about something or stating a point of view had no bearing whatsoever. It just led to me feeling like I was hanging off the bottom of the food chain.

RUSS WILKINS: There are a couple of things that made the Pop Rivets and Milkshakes different from other groups. The Revox E36 is the key to the Milkshakes's sound, a load of Billy's stuff, Mighty Caesars, a lot of the early Prisoners stuff. The Revox was a valve tape recorder and what was really good about it was, because it was horrible, if you pushed it into the red it gave this really amazing sound. All of the Milkshakes's backing tracks were recorded on that, all of the good stuff anyway.

BILLY CHILDISH: We never play through a soundman on a mixing desk.

RUSS WILKINS: The other thing was live always playing quietly through amps. It came from seeing Jonathan Richman at Hammersmith Odeon in '77, right in the middle of punk, when everything was loud and in your face. I loved Jonathan Richman, the first three albums, great. But I went to see him at Hammersmith, big old place, and he had a band that all had tiny little amplifiers and you couldn't see the PA. The speaker cabinets were on either side of the stage, but they were tiny. It was very much like, *Shut up and listen.* And it wasn't, *Shut up and listen, I'm preaching, you've got to listen to the words;* it was, *This is what we do and this is how we do it, and if you shut up, then you'll hear it, and if you talk or make a racket, then you won't.* It sounded so good! It's actually much easier carrying a couple of PA columns around and a 100-watt amp or whatever, than carting bins and mixers and all that shit. I mean, you go to venues these days and they've got it all there for you and they're all fucking awful and run by idiots. If there was a Medway sound, that's it.

BRUCE BRAND: People now call it the Medway scene, but it was after the fact. A bit like doo-wop: it wasn't called doo-wop at the time. I don't remember it being called the Medway scene. There were a few bands knocking about, and they were all kind of more or less sixties-influenced: we all had that in common, us and the Prisoners. The mod revival of '79 probably had something to do with it.

BILLY CHILDISH: I used to play mods-and-rockers when I was a kid, when I was five or six; we used to pretend to be mods and rockers—I wrote "Lambrettavespascoota" in the Pop Rivets because I was really into sixties crap, which I used to wear. This was before the mod revival.

BRUCE BRAND: When Billy and I started writing songs in '77 to '78, we thought, "Oh no, let's not be punks, let's be mods. Do you remember mods?" "Oh, yeah, blokes in the sixties, they wore fancy suits, and that, yeah, that would be good, wouldn't it?" We got suits from charity shops and put black velvet half collars on them, stuff like that, tried to look smart. We bought Beatle boots and whatnot. Then the next thing we knew, the headline in the *NME* was about the mod revival, because *Quadrophenia* had come out—"Oh, bloody hell, *we* wanted to be mods!" We wanted to be a clique.

RUSS WILKINS: I get on pretty well with Billy nowadays. The last time we spent any time together was in Spain last summer after the CTMF played with the Wildebeests and we sat there till stupid hours in the morning, just talking with him and Julie and me and [partner] Saskia, and John and Lenny from the Wildebeests, just smoking fags and drinking, which I haven't seen him do for many, many years. Nobody was trying to impress anyone, just chatting about family and so forth. It was just normal stuff. Nobody wanted anything from him, so he could relax.

BRUCE BRAND: I've been in a lot of groups with Billy Childish. I did count them up once. There were the Pop Rivets, Milkshakes, between the Pop Rivets and the Milkshakes we did one gig with the Dead Beats, and . . . Thee Mighty Caesars briefly, then Thee Headcoats, and . . . that's it. Oh, and the Blackhands! I last played with him a couple of weeks ago, at a CTMF gig, did a couple of songs. I was summoned. We ended up doing the first song the Pop Rivets ever played live, which was "Whatcha Gonna Do About It?" I have spent a lot of time with him. When we were hanging out together and best buddies, I'd get every book and everything ever, every record that he did. But it did feel like after Thee Headcoats that I was kind of like the rusty tool in the toolbox. I don't miss it probably as much as I should.

RUSS WILKINS: There is an intensity in what Billy does now, which wasn't there before. I think the pressure is pretty hard work, from two sides: one, he's trying to maintain the credibility of what he's doing, but there's also the pressure that he puts on himself. He seems to be work-work-work-work-work. I've got amps on the bench that I'm repairing, I've got my cutting equipment, I'm working on my computer, you know, all this stuff. I'm quite happy doing that, but I do enjoy getting the fuck away from it as well, and I don't know that Billy gets that opportunity very often. But I think that's self-inflicted. There's a song in there: "Self-Inflicted Wound." One of his own.

From: william claudius
Date: 2 November 2023
Subject: billy ted - poem ritten today (ive written about 50 over the last weeks)

**the
mystry
of
unbecoming**

from
a
kid
i
loved
the
mystry
of
unbecoming
the
flickering
lite
of
black
and
wite
soldiers
who
remained forever thin . . .
rusting ralings
discontinued

lines . . .
stepping
the
cracked pavement
a
lover
of moss
its miniture world . . .
the
lost
the redundent
the
gaunt
the
broken
and
the
looser . . .
the decay
of
my
grandfathers world
dissapering
into
the
smoke haze

From: Ted Kessler
To: william claudius
Date: 2 November 2023
Re: billy ted - poem ritten today (ive written about 50 over the
last weeks)

Thanks for sharing. When you're so prolific with one discipline,
do you find you spend less time on music or painting?

From: william claudius
To: Ted Kessler
Date: 2 November 2023
Re: billy ted - poem ritten today (ive written about 50 over the
last weeks)

---

i wish

we've been playing/rehusing 4 groups
+ novel
and painting normal output

i sent this one as it tells something of my feeling
about what people call the past

12.
Sanchia

Over time, Billy Childish has come to understand that charisma is an extremely dangerous weapon. He knows this now, as a man in his sixties, because he is dangerously charismatic. "If you have charisma or charm, your job is to not exploit that gift," he says, "or at least make your victories very small and polite." He has grown both weary and wary of its power to enable selfish gratification and to dominate others. He deploys it in moderation. But that was not always the case.

Steven Hamper did not grow up as someone whose good looks and easy charm melted barriers and made friendships easier. He was always an outsider, bullied, easy prey as an awkward yet forthright boy, treated as the runt of his family's litter, and then as a teenager who did not run with the crowd.

Sometime in the late 1970s, however, once recast as Billy Childish, he found that punk had unlocked a new freedom of expression for him (and that his hormones had settled). He discovered that he was a tall, handsome lad, actually, with an elegance all of his own, armed with a mercilessly sharp wit that became turbocharged by alcohol. He was funny, cheeky, and good-looking. Brash, unforgiving. Threads of timeless design hung stylishly from his skinny frame, no matter how worn they might be. His eye contact could be devastating.

Women naturally also became aware of his many charismatic attributes. The absence of love and affection that he experienced when he was growing up meant that Childish was extremely susceptible to their attention and charms, though his childhood abuse meant he found it very difficult to make sexual advances himself. He says he found it hard to read signals and often missed them. This didn't prevent him from being sexually active as a young man. Indeed, he went through a fairly lengthy period before the turn of the century when he experimented, he says, with having an ill-advised "harem." This might seem far-fetched—his description of a "harem"—but here we are, once more in his basement kitchen, discussing his love life, and the "harem" is one of the knottiest detours we embark upon.

There are tent-pole women in his life, relationships that have changed him, molded him, and tested him, providing huge reserves of material for him to write, paint, sing about. If you want to understand anything about Childish's work, then the romantic relationships of his life are absolutely key. They all shape his music and art, his writing. It's all there on the page, time and time again. After a few minutes of nodding along to his memories of these lovers, I make a mental pledge to seek out as many of these women as possible for their sides of the stories too, as Childish is unsparing in his summaries of the rise and fall of each affair.

Not all are available or willing to talk about Billy, either by virtue of not being alive, or if they are still among us then perhaps they'd rather not revisit such overwhelming emotional turbulence. Most are happy to speak, though. Their stories circle above us, awaiting clearance to land, like that of Sanchia Lewis . . .

"Christmas 1979: everything was looking fine
Sanchia said she'd still be mine
by the end of the year, I was crying . . ."
From "Christmas 1979" by Billy Childish (2007)
for Wild Billy Childish and the Musicians of the British Empire

Before Sanchia, there was Rachel Waller. "A very strange relationship," says Childish now. The affair ran hot and cold for a few intense months during the blooming of punk in 1977, just before he started writing songs with Bruce Brand for the Pop Rivets.

"Rachel treated me quite badly," he remembers, "and I was a very sensitive young man. She'd draw me in, being full-on, and then she'd be super cold. It was cruel, I thought."

It drove Childish crazy in the way that only an overwhelming young crush can. When she stopped talking to him, he went around to her parents' house and sat on the wall outside, disconsolately refusing to leave. "It was tragic teenage stuff."

Childish used to call her Barbara Wire. He wrote the following poem for her, which opens his 2021 novella *the student*, published in thirteen parts by Vipers Tongue Press, an imprint of Hangman Books. Attributed to "Odysseus," it is about a young man at art school in the 1970s, with a miserable love affair at the story's heart. The novella's subtitle is *barbara wire*, and accompanying the publication of *the student* was a set of three posters of Childish and Waller larking around in a photo booth, as is his lifelong wont. The nostalgic longing oozes from the pages.

barbara wire

her his thou then mine
is it her soft flesh
or is it her long limb?
Or is it her soft firm flesh or her long limb

oh desire
oh i desire
limbs intwined in barbara wire
design desire oh barbara wire

    gus claudius (1977)

"She absolutely broke my heart," Childish recalls, but they are nevertheless occasionally still in contact. "Because I wrote the novel about her I thought I'd email," he explains. "She was very engaging, she'd email me back and then completely stop, cut me off. I thought, *Wow, this is incredible. This is just how she operates with me.*"

Today, Waller lives in New South Wales, Australia. After Childish, she started a relationship with the middle-distance runner Steve Ovett, who won gold in the 800 meters at the Moscow Olympics in 1980. The famous *I love you* hand signal he made upon crossing the finishing line in Moscow was for her. They married, had kids, moved first to Scotland and then to Australia, but are now divorced. "I feel with all the significant people in my life I have this deep love and longing that remains," Billy tells me, "not sexually, but on another level they are imprinted on me."

Few have left quite as deep an imprint as Sanchia Lewis. She is one of the figures in Billy Childish's personal Mount Rushmore of romances.

Nowadays, Sanchia Lewis lives on a street of typical terraced houses in a south London suburb—except it's something of a disguise. The area behind the house used to be a builder's yard, while the small two-story building at the foot of the garden was once a stable. It's where she now has her studio, working as a painter alongside her fellow multiformat artist—and husband—Jeremy Youngs. On a bright midsummer's morning, hers seems like an idyllic life, setting off on artistic quests in her bright upstairs studio, which overlooks the neighboring playing fields, aware that her partner is elsewhere on the premises, engaged in similar pursuits but available for the occasional chat. Today, she ushers me into her garden with the promise of tea and the generous offer of lunch—if there's time, perhaps?

Childish thought it unlikely that Lewis would want to talk about their past, as she's moved on from their relationship, which, as it ended in 1980 when she was twenty years old, is perhaps a reasonable assumption. Yet she replies to the interview request within forty-five minutes and suggests I head over.

On YouTube there's footage of an event in London that Childish read at in May 1997, sitting alongside Tracey Emin, who swigs from a can of lager and listens with resignation to poems he's written about her. During the event, Childish says (to the obvious pain of Emin): "Sanchia was the first love of my life, which I never quite recovered from. And probably the girlfriends that came after her were suffering from my anger. I was making them pay for her."

"Oh that's a load of rubbish, probably," says Sanchia Lewis today, batting away the thought, embarrassed. She is soft-spoken, self-effacing, and unwilling to accept responsibility for someone else's behavior.

Some of the evidence of Childish's work contradicts this, however. Sanchia is the subject of a number of his poems, songs, and paintings, while the striking cover to his 1994 collection *Poems to Break the Harts of Impossible Princesses* is a reproduction of their photo-booth shot from fifteen years earlier: Lewis sitting upon his lap, both subjects radiating youthful, beautiful, mutual misery. She also has three full pages devoted to her in Childish's 2020 photography book: the photo-booth shot, as well as her in her bra posing in the King's Cross squat he briefly lived in while at St. Martin's in 1978.

One thing the pair do agree upon is the intensity of their relationship. At age eighteen, Lewis arrived at Medway College of Design in 1978 from her family home in Blackheath, London, after a period in a hospital where she had been treated for "some sort of breakdown; I had a terrible family background and my one way out seemed to be to go to art college." She'd been offered a place provisionally if she got the right O levels, but was unable to take her exams as she was in the hospital. "I was so doolally," she says, "I just went to Medway anyway." Nobody checked her credentials and so she started her foundation course regardless.

Childish had left Medway the year before and was now at St. Martin's, where he'd remain for barely a term before being booted out for publishing obscene work; but that didn't stop him from making regular appearances back at Medway—much to Lewis's delight.

"I didn't like it at all there, it was very boring, but Billy was always bursting into people's classes," she recalls. "The first time I saw him he was pretending to be our tutor, chatting away to the class, giving his opinions on philosophy, which was what we were meant to be studying: 'Hello, everyone, I've come to take the class.' We were so young we just believed him, until the real tutor arrived and chased him out. He had incredible bare-faced confidence."

Even though he was no longer a student at Medway, the stories of his behavior in Lewis's foundation course the previous year were still scandalous. "After he left the class, we all spoke about him with the tutor, a hippie type," she recalls. "He had been a thorn in the side of the academic staff, doing things such as running along an internal concrete balcony ledge and jumping down onto the next floor, luckily not breaking any limbs. He then returned the next year with two parallel scratched marks under each eye and wearing bright-blue shoes he'd painted himself."

She went to see the Pop Rivets play in the Chatham town hall one evening. Afterward, Childish approached her in the crowd. He told her he liked the way she looked, that she was "stunning," even though they'd not spoken previously. A shy and quiet young woman, whose confidence had been shattered by her recent hospitalization, Sanchia was deeply flattered. She invited him to a party in her shared house nearby on Ordnance Street: "And from then on, we were going out, I suppose."

"She's was an attractive lady," Childish says today. "I like intimacy—and by that I mean one-to-one truthful honesty. But at the same time I'm highly superficial, in that I like the aesthetic of everything I look at. It doesn't have to have perfection, it has to have balance, which is what I look for in my paintings, and my music."

He fancied her. "She had quite a good sense of humor, she was intelligent, she was interested in art, history, books." She introduced him to classical music. "She played me Bartók, things like that. She was a nice middle-class girl with a fucked-up family, but she had a funny way of looking at things, a good way generally. Most people I know are worse when they're drunk; she was actually better. She was good with a drink. Generally, she was fun."

At the time, Childish was learning the guitar and this would infuriate Lewis. She was trained in the viola and had played in the Kent Youth Orchestra. "She had perfect pitch apparently, and I drove her mad," he says.

"I remember trying to get him to sing in tune," she agrees, laughing at the memory. "I tried to tutor him because, yes, it did annoy me. I did think it would help him to be able to sing in tune and play properly, because—well, he always says he doesn't want to be famous but I thought he wanted to be the center of attention. He's an outsider, I suppose, but I always thought, *Oh, he's going to be well-known.*" In the end, this was one of the tensions that condemned the relationship. "I didn't want to be the person behind him all the time. I thought that would mean that I would have to disappear . . ." She trails off, and touches her face, worried. "I don't want to put him down—it was such a long time ago. I was so young. It doesn't matter really."

Yet when they were together, they were extremely tight, bound in all endeavors. They'd hang out with Billy's new poetry pals from the Medway Poets, Bill Lewis and Sexton Ming, of whom Sanchia was particularly fond: "Sexton Ming is fantastic, so talented, so funny. He loved Virginia Woolf and had a shrine built to her in his bedroom. We were always mucking around together. We'd go and stay at Billy's parents' house when they were away, the three of us. Billy's dad was quite horrible. He had a Rolls-Royce parked in the garage and had made a special window into the garage so everyone could see it! Sexton got in the front seat, pretending to drive it, and when he got out he smashed the door against the wall, denting it. That was a drama."

Childish remembers Lewis being an avid reader, reading *Lolita* by Nabokov nightly to him. "She was also really interested in killers, in Nazis—not as a fascist, she wasn't like that. She was just fascinated by evil people. I remember her spending hours in a biography of Hitler, reading out her favorite bits. She also really liked Bonnie and Clyde: she used to dress up like Bonnie around town. Generally, she was just really interested in murderers."

While Childish was away on tour in Germany with the Pop Rivets, Lewis decided upon a whim to catch a train to Hamburg to see him. "It was very stupid of me," she admits, "because the van only had enough room for the exact number of people already in it."

Childish gallantly offered to hitchhike with her, as neither had enough money to catch trains to the next gigs. "I remember spending a lot of time on the motorway with Billy, thumbing lifts. He could've missed his shows doing that, but he looked after me. It was very heroic of him."

Back in Chatham, however, there were tensions. "In our own ways, both of us were quite controlling people," says Sanchia. "Billy loved being the center of attention and hated being ignored. One evening, a few of us were sitting around the kitchen table. A full moon was shining through the window as we were talking, but it must have been a conversation that Billy felt left out of or wasn't interested in. All of a sudden, with no apparent reason, he screamed and yelled and smashed the kitchen chair that he had been sitting on. I remember the full moon, as it made me think of the lunacy of the incident."

Childish was by now writing songs with Mick Hampshire, designing the Milkshakes in their shared house. He explains, "Sanchia said to me that I needed to concentrate on the relationship. It was the group or her, sort of. I ended up doing the group, but I thought I could get away with that and still see her. I couldn't! It's one of the massive, great heartaches in my life."

Lewis remembers it differently. "I don't think I said that," she insists. "I might have, but it wasn't why. I do remember walking out. They were all rehearsing in the living room and I just thought, *Oh, I can't stand this anymore.*"

The impetus to leave had been bubbling for a while. Lewis felt she was being dominated by him. She found his rigidity hard to cope with as well: "He's really adamant in what he thinks, what he likes, and everybody around him just has to agree—but then he'll change his mind about something and everyone else has to agree with that, too. I couldn't. If I didn't like what he liked, then I was wrong. We had lots of arguments because I wouldn't back down either." A few times, she says, she tried to leave him but he'd persuade her that she was making a mistake, that there were too many good reasons to stay together. "He really has the gift of the gab."

In the end, a friend told her that there needn't be a reason to leave someone if she was unhappy: that was reason enough. So she gathered her things from his room and bathroom, packed her suitcase, and walked back to her student digs around the corner. She says, "The reason I left when they were rehearsing was because I knew he wouldn't be able to chase after me to persuade me to stay."

Childish did not accept this breakup easily, but in the end he had to. It's reasonable to deduce that people withdrawing from him cuts particularly deeply. "Due to my upbringing, I can fall in love very easily," he says. "Very deeply—I presume from emotional damage I've suffered. After Sanchia, I was devastated, really crushed. My mind went. Perhaps because she left so suddenly, I don't know." In the depths of despair over Sanchia, he vowed not to allow himself to become so submerged in relationships again. "That wasn't very successful," he notes.

Lewis is surprised to have been such a profound source of artistic inspiration for Childish over the subsequent years. "It's strange, isn't it? I know it was the same with Tracey and Kyra, though; they were all over his work, some others too—but we were so young and though it was two years, it's sort of fleeting, isn't it?"

They're not in touch now, though there was a brief alliance when she joined the Stuckist art movement that Childish was part of at the turn of the century. Lewis went to the first Stuckist show, *Stuck! Stuck! Stuck!*, in Shoreditch, east London, in 1999. Like the Stuckists, she was in favor of figurative painting rather than conceptual art, and Childish suggested she might want to be a part of Stuckism's steering group, founded by Charles Thomson and Childish. In the end she agreed to become one of the eleven founding members. Like Childish, she soon came to regret this decision. "I'm a loner," she says. "I shouldn't be involved in groups. I'm not a team player; they had all these strict manifestos and I didn't agree with it all."

One of the main sticking points with Stuckism for Lewis was that it seemed to be born from jealousy at the financial success of the Young British Artists. More acutely, however, she hated that it was a weapon to bully Tracey Emin: "I like Tracey, even though she's not straightforward. But this whole thing was based on Tracey saying to Billy that his art and he was stuck, stuck, stuck—that insult. It was then heavily focused on being horrible to Tracey, which I couldn't be part of. She was always nice to me, as well as being direct and sometimes honest. I remember Tracey sitting in the kitchen in Ordnance Street one time saying that if she became rich she would buy all her friends a packet of cigarettes."

Childish left the Stuckists during the first exhibition. He recalls, "I went to that and told Charles [Thomson] then and there, 'Oh, this is absolutely diabolical—I want to leave.' He said, 'Would you consider pretending to stay in the group for a year or so?' I said, 'Doesn't bother me,' but I never attended another single thing they did."

Lewis wasn't far behind, quietly fading into the background rather than making a big showy exit. The pair haven't really spoken since, but there's no reason for that. It's just life. "It's like a room in a house I lived in for a while growing up, somewhere I spent a lot of time for a short period: the door's closed now, but I still remember its interior," she says.

Standing in her hallway, saying our farewells, she suddenly remembers something very important she wants to tell me about Billy Childish. "You mustn't call him a genius," she says, locking eyes with me for perhaps the first time that day. "Billy's not a genius. But he is incredibly influential. Everybody who came into close contact with him became extremely productive, and that is down to him. He influenced all of us, his attitude, how prolific he is. That's his gift."

Sanchia Lewis and Billy Childish, lovers between 1978 and 1980, and an unresolved ache forever after in Childish's heart, from which we'll catch a final throb or two . . .

Her name was Sanchia, and it meant everything to me, and her name is still Sanchia . . . All the little intimacies that we held together, they belonged to nobody but us two. And now they've gone for good.

I should've seen that kidney punch coming. Sanchia was only biding her time. The signs, the hints, building up over the months, I knew it, but I didn't want to know it. In fact to know doesn't even help in the end. I went down and I didn't come back up. That was some punch, it lasted for years, revolving, repeating on me, I can still feel it now, if I sit quietly for a moment.

I swear to die, if only I can . . . of a ruptured heart . . .

The door went, her things disappeared and my heart

beat, and the clock ticked. No more her hair in the plug hole, blonde and matted. I lift it out and fling it to the floor. No more her eyes and lips . . . she is as dead to me as a lost hand or an eye . . .

I walk the streets like a dead man, I look for her on passing busses, in the nite rain. I gripe and I complain . . . I indulge myself, boring my friends, licking back salt tears and staring into my whisky. The faces drift away, the place is closing up . . .

So I drink and I storm, my fragile ego so ready to burst anybody else's. I live on a memory, trying to recreate those same heart-felt feelings with the next woman, and then the next. I even use the same shameful chat-up lines. The same tired conversations, until in the end I can't remember if I ever meant any of those sweet sentiments of youth.

All mine and Sanchia's young love talk was flushed down the crapper like a used Durex on the 19th December 1980.

Excerpt from *My Fault* by Billy Childish

hurt me

your face is smooth and cold
it glistens like the rain
your mouth is bright and soiled
there is a rusty stain

come on and hurt me
im naked without you
come on and hold me
im hated with out love

your face is lovely to behold
you smile through the pain
your eyes are bright and extold
they are so nice and plain

lying in the sun
you begin to unfold
the day has just begun
and you are so bright and bold

come on and hurt me
im naked without you
come on and hold me
im hated with out love

i see shining just like gold
and nobody to blame
i see hands that enfold
and your lips they speak my name

come on and hurt me
im naked without you
come on and hold me
im hated with out love

Billy Childish for Thee Headcoatees (1998)

We move now into the next room, where Billy Childish is standing with fist and teeth clenched above John Hamper, who lies bloodied and whimpering at the foot of the stairs . . .

13.
Our Father, Who Art in Prison, Hallowed Be Thy Name

JOHN HAMPER was a graphic designer and a figurative painter. If you google him, some of his paintings can be seen on a dead Facebook page: landscapes, figures walking through woods, and a spooky pencil self-portrait.

NICHOLLAS HAMPER is an artist, trained in fine art at Slade and the Royal College, who employs some unconventional tools in his work such as car spray and Hammerite, but he also paints.

BILLY CHILDISH is an internationally renowned painter, with exhibitions in the UK, Germany, throughout Europe, the US, South Korea, and, in the future, China. (He is also, of course, a distinctive and skilled graphic designer, woodcutter, photographer, etc.)

HUGO HAMPER-POTTS—son of John, younger half brother of Nichollas and Billy—is an exhibited artist and a gifted painter of portraits and landscapes.

HUDDIE HAMPER, son of Billy, is an artist who studied fine art at Slade, specializes in figurative and landscape painting, and has also been exhibited.

JUNE LEWIS (ex-Hamper) painted as a child; in her fifties she started making earthenware pottery, some of which was exhibited in New York when she was in her eighties.

Additionally, Billy, Hugo, and Huddie all record and perform music. John, Nick, and Billy have all, by Billy's estimation, been drunks at times, though not all three have perhaps officially recognized and corrected this pattern of behavior. John, Nick, Billy, Hugo, and Huddie are all unusually snappy dressers, each with their own distinct style.

It's fair to summarize that—either through nature or nurture—there are strong characteristics and callings that are shared through the generations by the Hampers. However . . . only John Hamper has been arrested and imprisoned for drug smuggling. That's the one thing that he alone has accomplished in the Hamper family.

When Billy Childish talks about family dynamics with his teenage daughter Scout, with whom he hopes lines of communication are always open and clear, he tells her that his job as a loving parent is to show her what a man can be, while his wife Julie's job is to show her what a woman can be. He believes that a parent's role is to instill values in a child, and to explore how to solve problems and resolve issues that living among other humans may offer up.

This presents challenges. "Let's face it, we know men are dicks," Childish explains. "Not saying women can't be dicks, but men usually are because we are so weak. I don't mean we're not manly enough, but strong men need to be able to access love and the feminine side in equal measure. Many can't do this."

In his own relationship with Julie, he thinks he's managed to achieve a kind of gender-free state, as there are no sex differentials between them; there is no male or female. "Apart from the actual sex, the intimacy, that's the only time I'm a man and she's a woman." This is perhaps the only thing he can thank his own father for. He had to witness the worst a man could be in a family dynamic to help him choose his own diametrically opposed parenting path (though the route he took initially was unconventional and winding).

There are so many gruesomely snappy anecdotes about John Hamper—but which to choose? We've heard the one about knocking his infant sons' heads together, the one about calling his second son "the Smell" or "Stinky Steve"; we've already discussed his having a Rolls-Royce parked in the garage with a special viewing panel for the neighbors in the door, while simultaneously disabling the family electricity in order to save money. We all know about how he left home, only to return sporadically to cause domestic terror and violent mayhem (and to collect his starched shirts).

But what about the time June looked in one of those shirt pockets and found a note from the woman who ran the shop up the road, offering John some more sex whenever he wanted? That's a good one.

"Oh, I think I'm going to have a nervous breakdown," said June upon reading that.

I think I'm going to have a nervous breakdown: her catchphrase for over a decade, says Childish, who reluctantly took on the role of her confidant throughout, even though he was only a child with plenty of his own problems.

How about all the times John's mistresses called up the house to speak with June, particularly one named Ann who was always keen to let June know how happy he was with her, about their plans for the future, how one day that house would be theirs? *Well, I think I'm going to have a nervous breakdown this time for sure.*

Or that time in the summer of 1968 when he packed June and the boys off to West Beach in Whitstable for a two-week holiday; when the trio returned there was a brand-new Hoover in the house and all the pots and pans had been rearranged: John and Ann had been living there, marking their territory, while his wife and children were away . . .

So many stories.

How about the one where John and his new girlfriend get caught smuggling a large quantity of hashish into the country in 1980? That's a good one, no doubt.

But the snappiest tale, the one that most tidily casts John as the tragicomic antihero in the story of his own life, is when Billy managed to get ahold of him on the phone in Reading Prison, while John was on remand awaiting trial.

Billy wondered how John was getting on.

"They're treating me like a bloody criminal!" blustered John Hamper down the line, aghast and scandalized to have fallen victim to the consequences of his own actions for once.

"My father is a complex, sociopathic narcissist," says Childish today. "Not a bad guy, it's just the way God made him."

In the end, John was sentenced to eighteen months. Upon his release after a year inside, Billy took his girlfriend Tracey Emin to the Bull Hotel on Rochester High Street to talk to his father. This may have been a little antagonistic, as his father hated Tracey, having referred to her as "that Turkish whore" in the past. Perhaps now that he'd spent time in jail he'd treat her with a little more humility.

John Hamper was in the bar of the Bull, where he was staying under an assumed name: Lord Hamper. He was drunk on brandy and upon seeing his son and Emin, he asked them to order another bottle. "Tell them to put it on Lord Hamper's tab—nobody knows who I am here. I'm a mystery figure."

Childish went to the bar and ordered the brandy, requesting the barmaid add it to Lord Hamper's bill.

"Oh, that fellow over there, is he your dad?" she whispered. "I thought I recognized him as soon as he walked in here. Drugs he was inside for, wasn't it? I read it in the paper: 'The Downfall of Debonair Director' . . . What a shame. I don't mean to be rude."

That afternoon, Billy laid out some new rules for his father.

He was to stay away from the family home: on no account was he to visit them. John Hamper was being pursued by creditors for over £100,000; he'd misdirected company funds—"on whores and alcohol, and the smuggling," says Childish—and was being catapulted out of his design company by his partner on account of this. He had his eye on the family home as one way to satisfy his debts, but Billy was wise to this and had finally convinced his mother to divorce John after years of begging her to. Otherwise they'd lose their home and John would swallow her equity.

John absorbed this information, along with another slug of his drink. Then Billy outlined some ways he felt John could get himself back on track and reconstruct his life without June. After a couple of drinks, he and Tracey left John Hamper to his new existence back in the community.

Sometime soon after, John Hamper turned up at the family home, drunk. He said he was collecting things, but it looked a bit more like he was *taking* things. During a disagreement with June, he made to hit her and Billy pinned him against the wall, told him to clear off. Billy was twenty-one going on twenty-two; his dad was around fifty and reasonably fit. But he was pissed and Billy was fairly handy, so he vamoosed.

A week later, Billy came to see his mum and, while she offered him tea, she let it slip that John had smashed some of Billy's paintings he'd found in his studio, as Billy had been using it in John's absence. And now he was upstairs in her bedroom, refusing to leave.

Right.

Billy Childish ran upstairs and told his father he could sleep in Nick's room or on the sofa downstairs that night, but he had to leave June's bedroom. John Hamper told him to go away and pulled the cover over his head, which Billy yanked from him.

The disagreement continued to the landing. And that's when Billy Childish punched his father down the stairs.

He Can't Figure Out Where My Hatred's Sprung

I speak to him, I summon my courage and open my trap.

'Dad, can you sleep downstairs please, Mum wants to go to bed.'

He looks at me, a moment's recognition, then he pulls the covers back over his head . . .

'Look, she can't sleep up here with you in the room.'

'Go away!'

I stand there, stammering, I feel my knees going. I lean in again and re-tap his shoulder. *Bang!* He sits bolt upright, his dressing gown falls open, a naked chest, golden hairs, expanding, un-aged.

'Go to bed Steven, it is time all little boys were in their beds!' I feel my hackles rising. I suck my teeth, there's no spit, but I suck, that makes me curl my lip. And I grab him. I claw at his sleeping bag. 'Listen you, you're sleeping downstairs!' I feel myself going to say it, the words jam up like a great wad of blood in my throat, I have to spit them out. I force myself to jump, an impossible leap, my knees knock, then I push off . . . I feel myself flying . . . a surge of beautiful hate, nursed at my bosom, matured and now full grown. It bursts out of me like a dam, rushing out through the top of my head. I spit cataracts, I snort them out through my nostrils. My ears go *pop!* and I pull him wriggling from his sleeping bag . . .

I feel my strength, the strength of the weakling, of the underdog. I lift him and throw him sprawling out across the landing. He scrabbles to his hands and knees, he slips in his own shit, whimpering . . . I grab hold of his dressing gown and launch him across

108

the floor, the blood pounding in my ears. I've got to get him up, to get him off the floor and out of this room, because I never ever want to hear my mother talk of this man, this house, this marriage ever again!

I breathe in great gulps of cold air. He crashes down on his back and I stare at my clawed fists, his dressing gown in tatters . . . He pulls himself up and adjusts his dick . . . I don't move in, I stand off, still his son.

'Now you sleep downstairs, alright?' I look at him in desperation .. . . that this situation shouldn't turn to murder. 'Please!'

Now I think back to it, I should never of said that 'please'. Please isn't the language of the conqueror, it's the language of the underdog . . . Straight away he's on to me. He re-finds his balance and comes strutting back in, pulls himself up, re-adjusts his G-string and pats his pecker into place. He looks me up and down, finds his bluster, then starts laying down the law the way he sees it.

'You stupid little child! . . . You think you're a man with your pathetic tattoos, don't you? But you're not a man at all, Steven, no you're just a silly little boy! . . . I think it's past your bed time, now run along like a good little boy, mummy and daddy have some very important matters to discuss, Out! . . . Do you hear me? Chop-chop! Out of my house!'

He bristles his whiskers and jams his face right into mine. I've got his gander up, that much is obvious. I let him sound off, let him have his say, but one more push, so much as one more piece of his crummy advice! . . . I fix him with one of my stares, I hold him with it. His hands flapping at my chest. My ears go back, I can feel them burning . . . the heat rushes through to the tips . . . tingly.

'You think you're a man with your tough man tattoos, but in fact you're just a silly little boy! . . . You think you're a man, but you're just thick! Thicko!'

He liked that word 'thick', he repeated it, 'thicko!' . . . I like it too, I lunge and groan . . . I go for his beard . . . I let him have it, twenty-two years' worth in one go! He's finally got my goat.

I grab his fancy suits off the peg and ram them into his chest. I scream it out. 'It's you who's leaving, you fucking cunt!' I open my eyes so wide that they ache. His face registers panic, he can't figure out where my hatred's sprung from. He backs off, cringing . . .

'Steven, I wouldn't hurt mummy . . . mummy . . . I wouldn't hurt mummy!'

He's playing ga-ga now, five years old . . . And I give it to him, I put my fist in his face, five knuckles, a whole bunch . . . A perfect hatred, finely honed over years of silence and compliance. It bursts out of me like a disease, crawling and malignant . . . I grab up a pile of his fancy togs and jam them into his bread basket. I shake my head and fill my veins . . . He falls back, his eyes questioning. His little world isn't functioning properly anymore. He grasps at the air, he staggers, hands flapping under my nose. I cover my balls.

'Mummy, mummy . . . I wouldn't hurt mummy!'

And *sock!* I stick one on his bracket. I sight along my thumb and lay one on him. I coil up and spit it out. It lands, an explosion between his eyes . . . He topples, he hangs there for a moment, caught in time . . .

He teeters on the brink, then his knees give way . . . I watch him go, he lifts off and flips back, bouncing down the stairwell . . . He revolves taking three pictures with him, he cartwheels and bounces down on his bonce, one step at a time. Then a crack as he hits the bottom step, his piece of masonry, hand-built in green slate. He examines his handy-work at close range. The special type of grouting, the general effect, *crack!* On his final bounce.

I run down after him, leap over him, holding up my fists, bunched, ready . . . my chest tightened into a ball of fear. He's knocked for a loop, he whinnies . . . his tongue hanging out . . . his hair-do fucked, his little china blues . . . dribbling . . .

'If you want more, you can have it!' I'm shouting, I'm dying, I show him my stupid fists. I feel foolish, but I say it anyway. I mean it . . . He sags, propping himself on the bottom step. His left eye, it swells, a purple slug, one end of it opens and it splits its guts and starts pouring . . . He shakes his dumb stupid head and tries to pull himself to his feet.

'You can have more of it if you want it!'

The truth is, I should have killed him the instant he went down, throttled him on the spot. But the moment passed, my hatred spent, souring to my stomach.

'Blood' he says 'Blood . . . What have you done to me? . . . Juny, what have you done me? . . .'

The morning comes and I hear him moving around downstairs collecting his personal effects. He wanders about in the garden, his head bandaged, hiding behind his dark glasses. He dithers about, tinkering with the lawn-mower. He packs and double fiddles with everything. He tells the old girl to call him a cab and stares forlornly up the garden path. This sad old ritual, never to be played again . . . He paces around in the driveway till the taxi sounds its horn out on the road. Then his face relaxes, he comes back in, sits down on the step, unbuckles his shoes and starts repolishing them. First the uppers, then he turns them over and concentrates on the soles. He takes his time about it, spitting and licking, as fastidious as a pussy cat. He buffs them till they burn like coals, then admires his whiskers in them. The meter still clicking away. That's his style, nonchalant, thirty-five minutes. He likes to keep people waiting, one of his little pleasures.

I help him carry his cases to the taxi, a suitcase in each hand. It's a tough thing to do, carrying your old man's cases, to load him up on his way to the nut house . . . He's ready to leave.

Excerpt from *My Fault* by Billy Childish

It would be another ten years before Childish spoke to his father again. Billy phoned him and John told his son that he'd had another child, Hugo, in the interim. John also came as close to an apology as he could muster, saying to him, "I've not been a very good father, but what can I do about it now? Nothing." Self-reflection and empathy, says Billy, are beyond John.

We now step out of the tableau where Billy stands above his bloodied father at the bottom of his mother's stairs, fist in John's face, asking if he wants some more while John whinnies about "not hurting Mummy." There are more desperate, surprising twists in Billy Childish's story, as well as plenty of revelatory and poetic beauty, but Reginald John Hamper will not be a main character again. He's down there in West Wittering, busy with his own memories.

the day I beat my father up

the day was breathing without a sound
the dog was dead buried in the ground
the sun shone like 16 golden fingers
it shone like diamonds in my mother's windows

the day I beat my father up
it was sunny and raining and i
was fucked up

i punched him clean down the stairs
the blood was oozing from his golden hair
a bruise grew on his cheek like a purple slug
then it split its guts—i was standing like a thug

the day I beat my father up
it was snowing and nite
and i was fucked up

the nite was shining black as my mother's pint
the cat kept his nose buttoned on tight
i was holding everything I ever had
he was bloodied and naked and looking quite sad

the day i beat my father up
it was cold and damp and i was fucked up

Billy Childish for Thee Headcoats (1993)

To Ease My Troubled Mind

From: william claudius
Date: 6 August, 2023
Subject: important tings of note

---

my mother was an assistant in a dept store when she left school

I was my mother's confident from age 7 - messes kids up badly

I got my mother to divorce my father when he went inside as
she would have lost the house and anywhere to live (I tried to
help my father after he left prison - as he was suicidal)

I only beat him up after he was attacking my mother

my mum then served at the fish and chip shop on the estate and
did washing up at a local hotel

later I had to go against my mother's wishes to try to have a
relationship with my father

when my father's 2nd wife temporarily left him I again talked him
thru his suicidal intent

he stopped talking to me again after I reported him and he was
arrested for beating his wife up (he was 70) and his wife - my
age - was going insane and they had a 7 year old kid in the
house.

John Hamper with Steven,
Walderslade, 1960

June Hamper with Steven,
"in normal loving pose"

June, Nick, Steven, Seasalter, 1965

Left Steven Hamper at work
in Chatham Dockyard, 1976

Below Billy Childish on the
train, returning from watching
the Jam, June 27, 1977

Bottom Billy, Gabriel, and Button
Nose Steve at the Vortex, 1977

Billy in a hand-painted punk outfit, 1977

Billy Childish and Tracey Emin, 1982

Left Childish and Julie Hamper, 2020

Below Childish and Kyra De Coninck, early 1980s

Opposite page top Billy Childish and Huddie Hamper in Childish's studio at Historic Dockyard Chatham

Opposite page below Childish and Edgeworth Johnstone

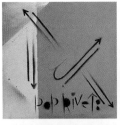

Grid of album sleeves

14.

Groningen and Brussels

The Milkshakes regularly played and toured with another Chatham-based band, the Prisoners, a quartet who were heavily indebted to garage-band psychedelia and the muscular sixties mod-preening of the Small Faces. They were several years younger than the Milkshakes—they recorded their first album in 1982 when some members were still nominally at school—but they had two secret weapons that elevated them above most groups of the postpunk era playing in dingy basements: they had a couple of talented musicians in their ranks.

Singer Graham Day had a soulful vocal range and played guitar with the occasionally showy flair of another era; while Jamie Taylor was a period rarity in that he had total command of his keyboards. By the time he upgraded his kit to a Hammond organ in 1984, he could be classed as one of the great rock organ players in circulation, an influence on subsequent groups such as the Charlatans. Later, he found lasting commercial solo success with his jazzy James Taylor Quartet (and more recently, in 2022, he recorded some lovely parts with Billy Childish's William Loveday Intention and Guy Hamper Trio).

The Prisoners were inspired to form by the Pop Rivets and were fans of the Milkshakes; they shared a 1960s aesthetic that cast both bands at odds with other groups they met on the moldy pub and club circuit—often macho psychobilly bands with whom they were sometimes disastrously billed. Because of this and by virtue of coming from the same town, the Prisoners and the Milkshakes regularly played together, alongside other Medway-based, mod-like bands such as the Daggermen. None of which convinced the Milkshakes not to bully the Prisoners mercilessly.

"We called them the Pensioners," remembers Childish. "Which they didn't like, so we called them that even more."

Joint gigs would often descend into drunken chaos. They'd flip coins to see who went on first, with the band who were on second getting drunk and heckling throughout the first band's set; the headliners would then be plagued by regular stage invasions from the openers.

European tours together were particular mayhem. In Groningen on one early tour, the Prisoners invaded the Milkshakes's set naked, which inspired the Milkshakes to strip too; soon both bands were onstage, playing in the buff. (Recollections vary about which band was naked first.)

"Bear in mind, this is in front of a sparse and quite confused audience," says Childish. "Nobody was encouraging us. I turned around and Johnny [the Prisoners's drummer] is standing on the house monitor laughing and pissing on someone at the front, which didn't go down very well." Johnny, the youngest band member, had form for this. "He was always trying to piss and shit on people," sighs Childish. "I remember outside one gig, I saw he was balanced really high up, very dangerously, in the well of a building. I said, 'What are you doing?' 'I'm trying to shit on Graham!' Graham was below chatting to someone."

Childish shrugs. "They all went to the maths school [Sir Joseph Williamson's Mathematical School, a boys' grammar school in Rochester]," he says by way of explanation. "Some weird born-again Christian crap went on there."

After the gig in Groningen, Childish put his clothes back on and went upstairs to see the promoter about payment. "Because even when I was drunk I never blacked out, I stayed compos mentis. I go in and ask for the fee. This guy is furious: 'It's the most disgusting spectacle I've ever seen!' Which, given this is Holland, was surprising." The promoter had already called the police during the set, he told him, so both bands made a swift exit.

Many years later, Billy Childish returned to the venue in Groningen for a sold-out show with Thee Headcoats. Incredibly, the same promoter was still there. After the Headcoats's gig, Childish made his way upstairs again to collect the fee. He found the office filled with well-wishers who were listening to the promoter regale them with a tale about the last time Billy Childish played there: "It was a legendary show. An incredible night. Chaos! Billy Childish was pissing on the audience."

Childish, standing unnoticed behind him, soberly corrected him. "I wasn't pissing on anyone."

"Ha, ha!" said the promoter, swiveling around. "You were! I saw you with my own eyes, Mr. Childish!"

"You don't know what you're talking about."

"You were all so drunk and wild, you wouldn't remember. I saw you!"

"Look," said Childish calmly, "I'd be more than happy to piss on your audience, but it wasn't me. And if it was such a legendary show, why did you keep back our money and call the police on us?"

The room fell silent. Billy Childish collected his band's fee, and headed back downstairs and out of the venue.

Back on the road in 1983, the Milkshakes and the Prisoners pulled into Brussels, for a packed show at Ancienne Belgique, attendance swollen by a contingent from Medway who danced throughout and infected the rest of the crowd.

Laying her eyes upon the swaggering Milkshakes for the first time was a fifteen-year-old local, Kyra De Coninck, who only found herself inside the hall by accident. Earlier, she and her friends had seen some local lads trying to rob a bequiffed Englishman down the road from Ancienne Belgique and had intervened, chasing the two thieves away. The man was so grateful that he invited the gang of girls with him to see his friends who were playing that night, the Milkshakes.

De Coninck was bowled over by what she found inside. She'd been listening to a lot of German and European punk up until that point, and had never seen or heard music like the Milkshakes's before: sixties pop music with a punky attitude and a sense of humor, a group that didn't take itself too seriously, but at the same time wasn't a joke. She found herself dancing along with the throng, in itself unusual as many in the front were girls only slightly older than herself, and she took careful note of the stylish vintage clothes everyone was wearing, too. She needed a new wardrobe.

Afterward, Billy Childish found himself alongside Kyra in the group massed by the stage door. They started to chat. Her English was reasonably good and Billy asked what she was into. Kyra explained that while she liked music, her main interests were writing and literature. She liked poetry, too, and was something of a history geek. Her grandfather had fought Franco in Spain and had been head of the West Flanders resistance during the Second World War, while her grandmother Rochelle was a Jewish communist who had also been high up in the Resistance.

"What are you reading?" asked Billy, his interest substantially piqued.

She replied that she was working her way through Louis-Ferdinand Céline's prewar novels. Childish's eyebrows were raised. So was he. "This was a great relief from Tracey, who was my girlfriend," he says now, "and who had no interest in anything interesting whatsoever. That may sound cruel, but you can't help the truth."

Kyra asked Billy how the gigs were going and Billy wondered if she wanted to see the band's van. Anyone earwigging this invitation may have grimaced: a twenty-two-year-old man inviting a fifteen-year-old girl to come and look at his vehicle? In truth, Childish was simply incredibly proud of the band's van. It was an old GPO mobile office, an ancient bus made from wood and painted green. He took her down the hallway, into the backyard, and showed her the vehicle. Then he led her back into venue.

"I said, 'There's the van,' because it really was an impressive old van. 'Right, let's go back in.' I don't think she really thought I was actually going to be showing her the van when I offered to show her the van."

As they returned to the venue and started walking toward the stage, they watched Johnny of the Prisoners come striding up behind the massive PA system that had been causing both bands issues all night. When he got to it, he pushed the PA right over with a grunt and it smashed to the floor with an almighty crash.

Suddenly, there were loud shouts from within the venue and Johnny came tearing past Childish and De Coninck at full pelt. Within moments, a gang came running up the corridor. They stopped by Billy. Where'd the drummer go? they demanded. Billy and Kyra pointed in the opposite direction. "He'd been an arsehole, but we didn't want him to be a dead arsehole," he explains. It was perhaps time, however, for both bands to make their excuses once again. Billy paused.

"Here," he said to Kyra, scribbling down his address. "Send me a letter sometime; tell me what you're up to, what you're reading."

And that's exactly what Kyra De Coninck did.

15.

The Ballad of Tracey Emin and Billy Childish

art or arse

damien hursts got his fish in the tank
some say its art others think its wank
dave stewart says hes doing quite well
you gotta make art and you gotta sell

theres a man named herr b
hes fucking whores and hes living at the (ahem)
he needed something new and this he found
if you aint got an idear hang it upside down

i was bored and had nothing better to do
so I went to see schwitters at the pompado
2 bus tickets and a pot of glue
oh poor boy—he didn't have a clue

there was a boy called pablo picasso
he was an art star—don't you know
his wife had a face like an african mask
in place of her nose he painted her arse

i've been slated cos i ain't very avante garde
but to copy deuchanp—that ain't very hard
or maybe i should be an abstract expressionist
or become a tutor go down the pub and get pissed

is it art or is it arse
what do you think
you be the judge

ompa-pa-ompa-pa-hey

Billy Childish for Thee Headcoats (1995)

Bill Lewis—Billy Childish's great friend and collaborator in the Medway Poets and other endeavors since 1978—says that Tracey Emin and Billy Childish are two people who should never have been together, romantically. You will not find anybody who knows either who disagrees with this assessment. And yet, Billy Childish and Tracey Emin were romantically together between 1982 and 1985.

"In that time," says Emin, "I think Billy kissed me maybe three times."

Childish offers this background information: "She was a fucking sex maniac."

What is indisputable is that Emin was a great muse for Childish and that he was the defining influence on her future art, for which she is internationally famous. He was her first love.

What's also true is that after Emin was nominated for the Turner Prize in 1999, Childish says she called his home and told his then-partner Kyra De Coninck that she should pass on the message that "Billy is no longer my friend and he is not allowed to speak to me ever again." They didn't speak to each other for ten years, until 2009.

We will now consider statements from the two primary eyewitnesses to this relationship.

Tracey Emin

"He married his ex-girlfriend while he was with me."

When I first met Billy, it was in 1982, and there was a train strike. Our friend Arthur had a party in Gillingham. I went to Medway College of Design, so I'd have to stay over because of the strike.

When Billy turned up, for some reason—I don't know why—I hid from him underneath a table. He comes in and sort of pulled me out by my leg, like a cat or something, and then he asked me what my name was. He thought I said Dolli—no, he didn't, Dolli comes from somewhere else.*

But anyway, Billy always called me Dolli, he never called me Tracey. That's the first time Billy met me.

We spent ages talking that night because Billy's really funny— ha ha—and I'm quite irreverent with my humor, and then we kept in touch. And then he came to see me in Margate at Easter and we just started seeing each other.

I write lots of letters, always have done, so I wrote him a lot. And he sent me lots of things. He sent me records and stuff, before we even had our first proper date. Billy didn't have a telephone, so he used to have to go to a telephone box in Chatham train station. It sounds so old-fashioned, but this is 1982. He used to have to queue at the telephone box to call me, quite sweet really. And Billy was only twenty-one, twenty-two, he wasn't old. People think Billy's always been old, but he was young. We were both really young; I was just eighteen.

---

* Billy explains: "Dolli is the other nickname, Dolli Bambi. She had this photograph of herself with a white leather handbag, a light dress, a big bow in her hair, and white patent leather shoes, from when she was about three. She told me this story, as did her mother, that they were at a hotel, and every day the man on reception said, 'Hello, little girl, you're very beautiful, what's your name?' and she would just turn away and walk off. On the last day at the hotel, the man said, 'Hello, little girl, you're very beautiful, what's your name?' and she said, 'My name is Dolli Bambi.' So we used to call her Dolli Bambi."

Billy was a really larger-than-life character, very forthright and formidable. He knew what he wanted. In that respect, Billy was a really good influence on me. Billy really, really pushed me to draw and to paint, but I actually really liked printmaking. He really pushed me to do the fine art side, because I always wanted to do fine art, but I didn't have the qualifications to do a degree or anything. Billy encouraged me. He really made a big impression.

I was also a big influence on him. One of his old friends said that at the beginning, he always thought it was me running off with Billy, but the more he got to know about it, it was the other way around. It was a bit like that with the influence. My influence on Billy would have been much more subtle and less obvious, because Billy was so forceful with everything no one would have really noticed that I actually was influencing Billy.

And it depends what you talk about with the influence. I mean, 100 percent not music, because I liked Bowie and Lou Reed and the Velvet Underground, but Billy was firmly punk, rock 'n' roll, garage. He wouldn't fucking move from it. But with art, Billy was focused on really quite traditional art. I liked a lot more expressionism and abstract art. Billy was very particular about what he liked: he was rigid, absolutely rigid in it.

His art that he liked was the same as his music: it was Lead Belly, blues, rock 'n' roll, two-beat, and it was the same with the art that he liked, you had to be able to see what it was. It had to be clear, it had to be obvious, it had to have a narrative, all of those things—figurative and clearly defined of what it was saying. Whereas I was a lot more messy than that, really.

Billy knew that I was really creative—he could see that in me, that's why he was attracted to me. And also, Billy used me as like a muse for years, even while we weren't together anymore, really quite stalkerish. Billy loved the way that I looked and the way that I was as a personality, so whether he was painting me and drawing me and stuff, it wasn't like he just thought I looked nice; he liked the energy as well.

Me and Billy were really fiery together, quite dramatic as well. We looked like caricatures. The way we used to dress: we looked like we'd just walked off a film set. My figure, as well: Billy used to be able to put his hands around my waist, I was so thin; I was about six and a half stone. I was always falling over. I was quite an unreal character at that time, but Billy was, too. We just looked like kids. Most people of our age would have been at school till they were eighteen, but me and Billy left school really early.

The photos of us were sort of iconic. We were something together. When we split up, Billy wouldn't let go of it, and that was a problem, because Billy was always unfaithful. Billy couldn't cope with just having one relationship. He wasn't unfaithful, actually, I've got to be fairer than that. He liked to have multiple relationships, and this was very hurtful. I wouldn't have it. Some people, especially if they're young, they'd just be fucking around, they wouldn't care. Billy wasn't fucking around; he was actually having other relationships.

This is a good story. Billy always kept his diary by his bed, and he always used to say to me, "Are you going to read it?" and I'd go, "No," and Billy knew I never lied about anything, so I said, "No, I'm not interested in reading your diary. It's your diary, I'm not interested." Never read it, never read it, never read it. I never read it in a whole year. And me and Billy used to read phenomenally. We were always reading. We'd fuck and we'd read, we'd fuck and we'd read: we never stopped reading.

Anyway, Billy's dad never used to like me. Billy's dad visited his mum at Walderslade and we were there. I had to hide in bed while Billy's dad was there. Billy's dad didn't like anybody at that time. Maybe later he softened, I don't know. So I was in bed and I finished my book, whatever book I was reading, Anaïs Nin or whatever, and I lay there for ages and ages *and* ages. And then, you know, I picked up his diary. I thought, *Nah, I don't want to read it*, but I turned the first page and the first thing it said was, "Me and Sheila got married . . ."

I thought, *Oh, what's this?* and I read it. He'd married his ex-girlfriend while he was with me. That was end of 1982. I was beyond devastated. Because it wasn't like he'd fucked someone; he'd gone and *married* someone! That was really painful, that was one of the worst things that anyone has ever done. And the weird thing was, in actual fact, Billy wasn't doing anything to me, he was doing something to someone else. He got married to some-one else. He got up in the morning on his birthday—I stayed at home with his mum and made him a cake—and he went and got married. Then he came home and spent the night with me, and he never told me. He never told me.

I don't think he slept with her. I know that they did it to get a council flat in Brixton, people did things like that then. But it wasn't a very good thing of Billy to do. At the time, I was suicidal. I was hysterical. I wouldn't talk to Billy, and Billy said to me, "You read it, didn't you?" Yeah, I had.

I came back down to Margate. I don't really know how I left Billy. I can't remember it. I can't believe I actually did it, because he had such a hold on people. You know, you're madly in love, you're nineteen, you think you've met the person you're going to be with forever—and you read they got married. Then you realize they spent their wedding night with you. I mean, how did Billy keep it to himself?! Well, he didn't keep it to himself because he wrote it in the fucking diary, and of course he wanted me to read it. He never had the guts to tell me.

Billy would say, "But I've told you the truth." He'd sleep with someone on tour. He'd come back, tell me, and go, "Well, I told you the truth." Like the truth made up for what he did wrong. If Billy didn't tell me something, then I didn't think it happened.

He's really complicated. I got asked in an interview once: what was it like being with Billy Childish? I said, "I wasn't with Billy; it was like being with the fucking Manson family." But it wasn't that bad. Billy was a very, very, very strong, powerful, wilfull person, but also Billy was very good. He is really good at encouraging, not just to me but to lots of people. He helped so many people creatively, with music, art, poetry, publishing, performing—lots and lots of things—so that energy that he had that seemed demonic and negative was also very, very positive.

He gave me gonorrhea, though, sleeping with a whore in Hamburg. And that kind of fucked up everything for me, in lots of ways. Well, not everything, but it meant that I never had children, it meant lots of things. I did get pregnant, though, thinking I couldn't get pregnant, which was another big fuck-up, but the gonorrhea was pretty horrific, and I was really ill with it.

I stayed with him during that period. I stopped seeing Billy when he was with Kyra. But Billy didn't want to stop seeing me; Billy wanted to carry on seeing me while he was with Kyra, but I wouldn't. He's living with someone else in his house, and thinks he could still be with me. Definitely a bridge too far.

But, can I say something about this? We were really still very young then. We were still early in our twenties. Kyra was like eighteen or something. It was all very rock 'n' roll, it was all very Charles Bukowski.

With Billy, whatever book he read, he became like a method actor around it. When he was reading Charles Bukowski: "Oh, fucking hell no!" Because he'd take on that whole persona of it. He'd read Hemingway and become really macho. When you're really young, of course, you're influenced by things. I was. But being with someone like that was quite hard. We never lived together, though. We always had our own places.

I really helped him with Hangman Books. I didn't just run it, I did it with him, for quite a long time, and got the books sold in bookshops. I used to go around to bookshops, saying, "Hello, would you like to buy some of these books?" That was good because I met really cool people. I met brilliant writers, I met Bernard Stone, a writer who had Turrets Bookshop. I met all these great characters from the eighties to do with literature, and that was all by knocking on people's doors, saying, "Do you want to buy some of these books?"

So what I'm saying is, even though I was working with Billy doing that, I got a hell of a lot out of that. Being with Billy wasn't all victim; it wasn't all, "Oh, you know, he was a sexist brute." It wasn't all like that, because I was really—I still am—pretty determined in my own way. I know what I like and know what I don't like, and there was a lot about Billy that I liked, and I got a hell of a lot out of our relationship. What is amazing is that over forty years later, we're still in touch and we still care about each other. We're still friendly. We're still friends.

Of course, there was over a decade when we didn't talk! There were fourteen years that we didn't see each other, actually. But that wasn't so much Billy's fault, that was the stupid Stuckist idiot people. Billy was cool, he was doing his stuff. Billy always had a sense of humor; Billy was always approachable. It was those other people that were latching onto him who weren't, who made it really difficult for me, and quite nasty. It made me keep away from Billy and anything to do with him. It was not on. They were really pretty vile toward me.

But Billy actually didn't really have anything to do with them—they used him because Billy's really talented. They really weren't. They used Billy as their front man.

When me and Billy saw each other after the fourteen years, I said to Billy, "Oh, your mustache is pretty big," and he said, "Not as big as yours," because I always had a mustache, hair on my top lip. It was so funny. We were really laughing. It was like I'd seen him the day before.

He has changed, of course, because he's such a better person than he was. He's kind, he's considerate, he's gentle, he's a Buddhist: he's really a pure person.

I don't think he's really got one greatest talent. He's much more of a Renaissance person. Billy really works hard, but I think he's lazy because he never pursued one thing really strongly. He always was insistent on spreading himself out on everything.

I think Billy now, looking back on everything he wrote about me, if he could rewrite it, he would. Because it's pretty misogynistic. There's some people who will dismiss Billy because of that. I know that was his truth then, but that's why you dismiss him, because what a bad truth that was! That's what I mean about Billy and about the truth: he will say that it was the truth, so that makes it all right. It doesn't make it all right. But Billy's apologized to me. I don't think Billy feels good about the things that he did with me. I think he'd like to take it back, some of it.

It was the beginning of the eighties, it was still the Dark Ages. It wasn't like now, where people have a lot more conviction about their moral compass and what's politically correct. There was none of that stuff then. Billy was so fucked up from his childhood.

His dad was really cruel to him: cruel, cruel, cruel. His dad had an experiment between him and his brother—one of them went to private school and had money and all that, and Billy didn't. Billy had to make his own way.

Nick, his brother, was always really nice to me, and part of that was because I got on so well with June, Billy's mum. I loved her, really loved her. She was one of the sweetest, loveliest women in the whole world. She didn't mince words, either, she was just cool. Me and June were like friends. So I think within terms of Billy's familial contacts or whatever, everybody respected that I got on so well with June.

His dad thought I was a "Turkish whore." That's what he referred to me as: a "Turkish whore"! I'm half Turkish. Imagine it was a play, right, and you've got the dad coming in and going, "Is that Turkish whore here?" You know, it's not real. Everything was really heightened. And this is interesting: nobody took drugs. It was all like shots of whiskey and cake. It was like we were living in 1962, not 1982. Everyone was definitely stuck in the sixties. Break out of the 1960s and all hell would come loose. It would be high treason.

Now the relationship between us is really good. I wouldn't do this if it wasn't. I always had "no comment," because I wouldn't say bad things about Billy, because I understand that we were both very young, and it was very complex. Billy and I both had complicated childhoods and we clung together. It was very dramatic, our relationship, and very passionate as well—and very creative. We worked all the time, very hard, which was really good for young people, doing their own thing.

I posted some photos of us the other week on Instagram. People asked me about it and they said, "Who took these photographs?" I said, "Billy took the photos: he's a really good photographer." Just another thing that he does. I wish Billy got more credit for all the musicians that he's worked with and everything. I'll tell you what: he's a really fantastic guitarist. I remember in *NME*, when he won Solo Guitarist of the Year or whatever it was and stuff [there is no evidence of Billy Childish ever winning an *NME* award for anything musical]. I don't think people understand how seriously he's taken in the music world, but he's always low-key.

The other thing with Billy: when they're with their bands, the moment they were supposed to go on *Top of the Pops* or whatever, they'd dismantle and change the name of the band! Every time! He always sabotaged his musical career. I think maybe that's similar to why he had multiple relationships at the same time, because he was scared of being on his own. So if one didn't work, the other one would. I don't know. But all I can say is that I'm sure that for Billy, looking back on that now, he wouldn't be proud about hurting people like that.

Billy Childish

"I love Tracey, but I'm not interested in any of her nonsense."

I'll tell you the way the relationship with Tracey is characterized:

we were at art school together and it was some sort of dual thing going on, which is not what it was like at all. This is what happened.

I'd been expelled from St. Martin's for publishing supposedly obscene poetry, late '81. I was meant to be at art school in London. My father had gone to prison for drug smuggling and I couldn't afford to go in and my mother had no money. I was also doing my poetry and my painting at home, which I got permission off the college to do, off my tutor.

The fanzines, I couldn't pay to get done, or the poetry magazines I was doing, and they were getting quite explicit. I knew Eugene Doyen, who had become the social secretary at Medway School of Art. He said, "Well, we'll pay for them, we'll do it through the college and they'll be done in the library." So they went to the library and the librarian saw them and said, "It's obscene," reported them to the head of the college, and took my work away. I was up in London, seeing my tutor, he says, "Where's your work?" I said, "It's been confiscated and they won't give it back to me." So he rings up Medway College and the head of Medway College was pals with the head of St. Martin's College, so the head of St. Martin's College called my tutor in and said, "What is this student doing in Medway when he's meant to be on his course? Why is he publishing obscene material at my friend's school?" And my tutor said, "I don't know." Then I was thrown out.

That was when I met Tracey. We were not contemporaries. I'd already done the Pop Rivets, I was already in the Milkshakes, we had made a few albums, done John Peel Sessions. The biographies say that me and her met at Maidstone College of Art, but the time line's totally out. We didn't meet at art college—I made records, played in groups, published books, and did all these things first.

I was a painter. I lived in Chatham, because I had no grant. I lived at 107 [Rochester Street]. Interestingly, Kyra's husband now, Chris Berthoud, his elder brother, Nick Berthoud, lived at

107, too. I used to paint at home, even when I was at St. Martin's, because I refused to paint in the college. So my paintings were all at this house. Nick Berthoud was friends with this girl who dressed a bit 1940s, made her own clothes, and was in the fashion department at Medway College of Design. She'd been round the house when I wasn't there, seen my paintings, and this girl was interested in becoming an artist.

The Medway Poets did a reading for Television South one day. I was subsequently banned from the broadcast, because I was considered unbroadcastable—it was confessional stuff. After that reading, there was a party in Gillingham. I went there and there was this girl with an amazing figure, 36-18-36, who talked to me. I asked her what her name was, she said, "Tracey"; I thought she said Rosie. She knew who I was. We walked back to 107 from Gillingham into this very heavy foggy night. She stayed the night but we didn't have any sexual relations, because I'm not someone who's very pushy. We slept in the bed, and she was content with that.

I then went on tour in Germany with the Milkshakes; I was still with my girlfriend Sheila Clark, who I did later marry. When I got home from tour there were about eight or nine long letters from Tracey; we used to call them "Tales of the Unexpected." They were all about herself, a biography. Steve's [Lowe] got the letters now. She lists all the things she likes and doesn't like—like, she wrote she hates swearing and will never swear. It doesn't include anything that she later said she was into, when she got famous. There's no Edvard Munch. I'm in there with Erte, who was a [Russian-French, art deco] fashion-artist guy. She might have had Egon Schiele, because she knew him through David Bowie—she was a big David Bowie fan.

I went down to Margate. She lived with her mother and her grandmother above a Kentucky Fried Chicken shop in Cliftonville. And we became an item. She used to write to me every day. She was 100 percent obsessed with me. I found her very attractive and I was also very attracted to the fact that she was so obsessed with me. But she was one of the most clinging, difficult people. I know how harsh that sounds, but I'm just telling you the truth. Sometimes I wonder if I just ended up going out with her because of my dad.

When I met Tracey, I was still doing my publishing, running Hangman Books as it was called. Tracey wanted to become a painter, or do art, so decided to walk out of the fashion course at Medway. She then applied to Sir John Cass in London to do a foundation and was living in Medway, not in Margate, in the basement where Eugene and Graham [Day, of the Prisoners] lived. That was 3D Castle Hill, a good mailing address. I wouldn't live with her because I was sensible enough not to. She was doing the administration for Hangman Books, writing the letters and sending out the books I made.

Tracey then got into Maidstone to study printing. She was into woodcuts, so we started making them. She wanted to do Hangman Prints, and she charmed the printers at the Maidstone College of Art, so we made some postcards. Now, Hangman Prints was Sanchia—who was a printmaker—Tracey, Sheila (my previous girlfriend and soon-to-be wife), and me. I mean, it didn't really go very far. We made a postcard each or a couple of postcards.

Then Tracey was sent to London to sell books, or these magazine things we did. I said, "Go to Compendium, go to Bernard Stone," I knew the bookshops now, "and you try and sell these things in London." If you've seen those photographs of her in red stiletto heels and a bathing costume, which we called her performing-bear costume, guys would just buy them off her straightaway. She sold stuff to Bernard Stone, became pally with him, and with Mike at Compendium.

They said to her, "These are very difficult to display, you need to do them as books."

How the hell do we do books? I had to think about it. Tracey said, "Well, the technicians at my art school said they could do it, we need a spine and they could do it in the summer holiday or the Easter holidays—we could do one." In the end, they did a couple. Tracey would go around and sell these things.

Ironically, I was writing about me and Tracey a lot in these books, which she absolutely hated. I was doing all this confessional writing, which is the other irony, because she hates confessional writing, or did—she got over that, apparently.

She was highly sexualized as a young girl, but not prior to our relationship. She was quite prudish, and absolutely focused only on me, which was great and terrible. I was someone who had been denied love. or adoration, had been told, "You're ugly and unattractive." So to be totally the focus of someone, someone who was really into sex, was fantastic. My problem was the psychology, and that is why I married Sheila, because I got on with her and I wanted someone I could talk to, because Tracey doesn't do intimacy in that way. She wasn't interested in true intimacy.

I didn't have a sexual relationship with my wife Shelia. I went home on my wedding night. I married Sheila to have someone to talk to, but also Shelia wanted a council flat in Brixton and had to be married to get it. I said I'd help out. I was also convinced I was going to die young and thought, well, it'd be good to see what being married is like before I do. I really was that seriously re-tarded. Part of it was also if Shelia had that flat, it was a bolt-hole I could go to, to escape this fucking sex-crazed woman that I was going out with! But as well as being a problem, the sex-crazed-woman bit was the attraction.

I never lied to Tracey. I believe in truth more than anyone. But she said that line to me, which I used as a title of a poem: "I'd rather you lied." She didn't want to know about anything to do with my true behaviors, or desires, what I thought. How can you have a real relationship with someone who'd rather you lied to them? So I wrote in notebooks instead and, of course, after months of saying she'd rather I lied and didn't want to know what was in the notebooks, she read the notebooks. I'd have told her if she hadn't asked me not to.

My mother June liked Tracey. She came round for Sunday dinner every week. Once my mother said to me, "You'll have trouble getting rid of that one," but June and Tracey were quite pally. June basically fed her for two or three years because June's very easy, a generous person in that sense.

Tracey tried to get me to live with her throughout this period. I was a very useless boyfriend, in the sense that I spent my time trying to avoid her. When we were playing up in London, for instance, Miki [Berenyi] turned up and would be down at the front of the Milkshakes. I said to her, "Have you come to save me from the Ottoman Empire?" because I used to call Tracey the Ottoman Empire as she's a Turkish Cypriot.

I don't see this as a "I'll put them all straight; needless to say, I had the last laugh!" I'm just telling you, because you can be quite sure that if I tell you something, that's what it is. This is like going into court, in a sense. If you're talking to someone like my father or Tracey, you're in the situation where you're talking with someone who is compartmentalized, but quite charming. But she was seventeen or eighteen, and I was twenty-one. Which is a big difference. You're young and you're both going through changes, but different ones. I understand that now.

We played in Belgium in '83 and I met Kyra. Kyra was fifteen when I met her: she was a schoolgirl, but there was nothing going on. I used to correspond with Kyra; she had a boyfriend who'd come along to the shows. Tracey was still trying to get me to live with her all the time, which I wouldn't.

Meanwhile, Kyra must have split up with her boyfriend. She was seventeen, I think, studying acting at the conservatory in Brussels, but she left, came to live in Chatham with me, and I split up with Tracey.

I remained friends with Tracey—we didn't have a sexual relationship—right the way through. If I was in London, I would go into the Royal College and see her sometimes, or go round to her flat.

I would go up to London and sell Hangman books, Hangman records, because now Kyra was doing the administration of Hangman. Tracey was still very angry about my confessional poetry and my language—the opposite of what she puts across now. But she was always on the breadline and I would often give her money from any Hangman records or books I'd sold. If I'd had a good day, I would give her twenty quid.

And we remained friends like that up until 1991. We went to an art thing which I hated. I was on the cover of *Artscribe* and Tracey said everyone was jealous: "People would give their eye-teeth to be on *Artscribe*." I didn't care. We met Sarah Lucas, who is quite funny; I don't like her art much, but I liked Sarah. She was the only one I liked out of those Brit Art people. Tracey tried to get me to go along to these things with Brit Art people, and I said, "I've avoided cocaine people in music, and I'm not about to start meeting them in art."

She got in with them anyway. She then met Carl Freedman—who happens to be my gallerist now—and Carl was her boyfriend. He was a writer for *Frieze*, and he was the one who told her to do confessional art. Tracey told him about me and Carl wanted to work with me then, but Tracey wouldn't let him.

I'd met Jay Jopling [Emin's art dealer; founder of the White Cube gallery] through someone else, so I knew who he was, and I didn't like that crowd. I was allowed not to like it and to have my opinions when she was doing this stuff, up until she was nominated for the Turner Prize [in 1999]. Then she rung up the house and told Kyra to "tell Billy he's no longer my friend." She didn't speak to me for ten years, until I had my major breakthrough as an artist, and she got in touch with me the next week!

She got straight back in touch with me, and this is how this craziness goes: She sent a letter to Steve Lowe at L-13, congratulating me and wanting to meet up, saying we've been friends for thirty years. And I thought, *What the hell? There's ten years which doesn't exist, which is missing, where I wasn't her friend, she wouldn't talk to me.*

And then she insisted that I go to an exhibition of hers in Margate. Initially I wrote back to Tracey and I said, "Fine, no problem at all, we can meet up, I was sorry to hear about Emin dying"—Emin was what we used to call her dad. I knew he had just died. So then I went down to this fancy garden party that they had at North Foreland of some film producer friend of hers—this was a party on her behalf—and her mum was there, I hadn't seen her in ages, and various members of the family, Carl, Jay Jopling. Tracey introduced me to them, said, "This is my friend Billy, we're friends again because he was so nice about my father dying." And this is what I mean: she will believe that, because she wrote to me, "Can we be friends?" and I said, "I'm sorry to hear about your dad." So in her mind, we're friends because I was nice about her father dying, but that is totally secondary. She will believe it, because Tracey believes her own delusions.

I didn't like not being friends with her because I like being friends with everyone. I don't do enemies. And I don't do things where I don't speak to people, but people do things where they don't speak to me, like my father, Tracey; there's a few people who do that to me because I'm not the person they require me to be, but I never send anyone to Coventry, because I think it's like primary school. But my family do it, Tracey's family did it—like her mother, I remember, didn't speak to her sister—they all do it: "We don't talk to them." It's absolutely unbelievable. And then they wonder why there's wars. Talking is all there is.

Since we've been in contact again, I keep her at arm's length. She's full of nonsense, and I'm not interested in her nonsense, or her obsession with herself, or how clever she thinks she is, or how brilliant she thinks she is. I love her—that's another thing. I love Tracey and care about her, but I'm not interested in any of her nonsense or hanging out or being part of any crowd that those people are like, because they're fucking idiots. The problem with me, you see, is a lot of people would only say that if they were angry and they didn't like the people. Whereas I'm not angry and I don't like the people. I don't mind that they exist, and I don't mind what they do, as long as I don't have to be involved.

The other thing with Tracey is, she didn't speak to me for ten years. Now, if Tracey says to me, "I didn't talk to you for ten years because you were a rotten boyfriend, you gave me VD, you're a fucking arsehole, and I was angry," right, which she could say, then you'd have the basis of, "Do you want to go forward as friends?" But no, it didn't even happen. So if it didn't happen, how do you go forward? I don't mind being blamed. It can be all my fault, because she can say, "It's all his fault, but I'm over it," and I go, "Fine, okay." Then, at least there'd be a semblance of reality, not this fucking fantasy world.

So many people live in this weird fantasy world where things aren't said and didn't happen and are not true. I'm happy for them to all do that, but I ain't doing it. For me, everything is the truth and the integrity of something, whether it be good or bad. What happened happened, and you can't lie about it, you can't change it. It is really dangerous and unsafe for me not to know what is happening. In my family, no one said what was really going on; that's caused me to require everything to be clearly designated, because otherwise it's dangerous. That might be the psychological reasoning behind my crazy output and my crazy requirement for facts and truth.

My paintings are made on deep canvas, on raw linen, and they have a frame left round the edge of them, which is painted round, and then it's bare linen.

Tracey, she comes to all my shows. She said, "What would happen if you didn't paint the frame on and you painted to the edge?"

I said, "It would be very much the same, apart from I'd have painted to the edge."

"Have you thought about *not* painting to the edge?"

"Yeah, I've thought about it, I do it sometimes."

"Hmm."

And then, next exhibition, same question; next exhibition, same question. I'm in New York and walking around with the sales team at Lehmann Maupin, and Rachel Lehmann says to me, "One of the girls asked about the way the paintings are done, said, 'Well, it's a big point of contention about why Billy does these frames'"; because Tracey was represented by that same gallery. And I said, "Well, it's not actually a point of contention, it's an obsession of Tracey's."

I'll tell you one of my new favorite Tracey stories. She came to my exhibition at Carl Freedman about six years ago, and Tracey was sitting opposite with Carl. She's getting a bit maudlin—she's talking to me about the old days. I can see she's upset. So I come round to sit next to her and chat. She's talking about how lonely she was, because Tracey can't sustain a relationship with anyone. I mean, I was with Kyra fifteen years, I've been with Julie for twenty-two, so despite all of my failings, I can maintain relationships! But Tracey gets very lonely.

So I've got my arm around her and she's crying on my shoulder. I said, "Well, Trace, you've got to understand that I did love you and I do love you, it's just I couldn't live with you because it was so terribly claustrophobic—it's just too claustrophobic, the way you are." I just had to come out with it. So she's sobbing and her head's down, and I thought, *I hope I haven't sent her over the edge*, because you never know with Tracey what the reaction will be. Slowly her face comes up, a big smile of joy spreads across her face, and she says, "That's exactly what Carl says." And you think, *Fucking hell!*

It's important to add that I don't admire or envy anybody's success; I pity them. Because it makes them all wankers. It never works. It always is less, not more. I don't know where the exception is. I don't see it. I've had a little, but it depends what you call success. I'd say I'm at the bottom of the top end. Before that I was nowhere. Neither places really bothered me too much. I mean, when Damien Hirst and Tracey were pretending they were outsiders, I said, "Well, I'll swap with you. You want to be outside, right, you go outside and I'll come inside!" They weren't keen on that.

But my success, all it meant was we live in a nice house and we have nicer dinner. My networking is not networking, because if I network and I say what I feel about things, it has a total polar-opposite effect. It's like Julie, my wife, says to me: "You're so much like you."

dolli bambi

don't be such a mambi pambi
you can stomach dolli bambi
she got pissed on turkish brandi
grew a mustache like a spanish grandi

dolli bambi - dolli bambi

feeling hot and feeling randi
i spent the nite with dolli brandi
she wobbled like a turkish candi
i woke up to a hand shandy

dolli bambi - dolli bambi

i climbed in her bedroom window
she was lying on her back legs akimbo
spouting bullshit like a margate bimbo
a furry arse like a sunkissed hindoo

dolli bambi - dolli bambi

she was born on beaches sandy
to a father brown as ghandi

To Ease My Troubled Mind

every song of hate I rote
was for love of that turkish scrote

dolli bambi - dolli bambi

Billy Childish (1995)

16.

Pictures of Billy (Billy, Oh Billy!)

Eugene Doyen was the treasurer of the student union in the aftermath of what came to be known at Medway College of Design as the "Pop Rivets Bloodbath" of 1978. The band were playing at the college that year when a huge fight erupted in the audience, with bottles of beer raining across the room. Claret everywhere. Afterward, the college announced it wouldn't be hosting any more events, so the treasury decided to redistribute its funds, the final stage of which entailed the student union giving away its money to anyone who wanted it. This sounded quite far-fetched, but many people turned up anyway with pitches for investment, like a bargain-basement *Dragons' Den*. Some came wearing special sweaters they'd made to promote a poetry book they wanted to produce. A feminist group needed money for meeting places and whatnot. Bands required cash to record demos, buy equipment, go on tour.

Doyen was unmoved. He said he didn't care what the feminists were saying, he was unimpressed by the poets, he didn't want to hear the bands. Just give them the money, he said.

That's when he met Billy Childish, who wanted to get his fanzines printed. Doyen took a look at Childish's secondhand jacket and thought he was one of those middle-class punks who dressed down. "Get back to your tea and bread and jam," he sneered.

Billy Childish smiled, recognizing a young man with a similar sense of humor. "Wholemeal bread," he replied.

Doyen said he'd help out with the printing.

The next time the pair met was when they bumped into each other in the Chatham shopping center. "We had a little argument," explains Doyen. "About Dada."

It turned out they'd both been reading the same book about the avant-garde art movement and disagreed whether the German artist Kurt Schwitters, of whom Childish was a devotee, was a Dadaist or not (he was, but not exclusively so).

"It's the kind of thing you argue about when you're eighteen," says Doyen with a sigh.

Childish asked Doyen if he wanted to come to his place on Ordnance Street for a cup of tea. Off they went.

Doyen had originally traveled down south from his home in Birkenhead dressed in a salmon-pink linen suit and hoping to become a "trendy London photographer." It wasn't long after arriving in the somewhat more salty environs of Chatham that he ditched the suit. "If I had a budgerigar that color, I'd strangle it," a stranger had growled at him in the street.

He hadn't lost the desire to become a photographer, however, and at the house on Ordnance Street he took some photos of Childish attempting to pluck a tune on a guitar. He'd just started to learn the instrument, but progress was slow.

"Ten years later Billy still couldn't tune it," says Doyen. "Which I think is a good thing; too many guitarists are technicians."

As he was shooting Childish, Doyen noticed that his teeth were chattering. The house was freezing. Could Billy turn on the gas fire, please? Childish laughed. They'd cut off all the plugs to remove any temptation to use the heating. "So that's how they were all doing, cash-wise," remembers Doyen.

Doyen wasn't shooting him for the money, though. He recognized immediately how striking Childish was, and how unusual the sixties-obsessed music and art crew who coalesced around him appeared, too. It was the dawning of the era of New Romanticism, of Spandau Ballet, Duran Duran, and Adam and the Ants, but here was a contemporary scene that seemed molded from a fifties kitchen-sink drama about beatnik outsiders. They appeared out of time, in a world of their own making. Looking at his first shots of Billy, he was even more convinced that he'd stumbled upon someone perfect for his stark black-and-white photography. Childish was magnetically photogenic.

Real recognizes real. Childish saw in those dramatic early shots that Doyen was the exact person he didn't know he was waiting for to document whatever the hell was going on here. He also liked having him around. They made an unofficial, un-spoken agreement that Eugene Doyen would be Billy Childish's mate, who also happened to always have a camera. He'd shoot his bands, his friends, and, increasingly, his life. For the next five years or so, Eugene Doyen almost exclusively documented the Medway music scene.

Nowadays, Eugene Doyen is billed as—ahem—Lecturer in Film Practice and Director of Education at the Department of Film Studies in the School of Languages, Linguistics and Film at the University of London. It's a highfalutin title, but Doyen is a no-tably humble and generous man. Sitting in the canteen of the ULU campus on Mile End Road in east London to talk about his old friends from Medway, he pulls from his canvas tote bag a ring-bound folder and a memory stick. The folder contains print-outs of some of his most relevant pictures for this book, while the memory stick is filled with hundreds of his photos. We can use whatever we want, he says.

"Billy has an unlimited license to use my photos without cost," he explains. "He can share as suits him and I'm happy to offer gratis to any projects that support him." This, in the field of music photography, is a highly unusual commercial position. I gratefully open the folder to take a look inside.

Doyen never shared a home with Childish, but he did live in the same Medway houses as Tracey Emin, first in Luton Road and later in Castle Hill with the Prisoners's Graham Day and others, the address that Emin did her administrative work for Hangman Books from.

"Billy was basically there the whole time, though he resisted officially moving in with Tracey," he remembers. "They were both wild, of course, very dramatic. But even then, to my mind, the two people who were going to be successful were always going to be Tracey and Billy. They both had a sense of money, as well as of getting things done. Billy gets up in the morning, he makes music, he writes, he makes a painting. Tracey was the same. They never stopped."

Childish was a powerful impetus on everyone who fell into the orbit of his productivity. Doyen explains, "He'd organize gigs for his bands, and for other bands too—he'd just say, 'We're doing this.' People would grumble because he'd take charge, but he'd get the gig, play the gig, get the money, and share it all equally in the pub after. It was the truest sense of that punk DIY thing you can imagine. He kept everyone busy."

He offers an example of Childish's all-encompassing creative drive. "Once he said to the Milkshakes and the Prisoners, 'Let's make an album together in one day, we'll do a side each.' So on a Sunday morning he gets everyone up, loads them into his van—he loved his vans—and drives them to Canterbury, and what's more, they're playing it live in front of an audience, so he's made sure all these kids are there too. He's gathered a roomful of teenagers in a studio to dance to rock 'n' roll music on a Sunday morning. And it was brilliant. Not many people have that force of personality."

This inspirational cajoling extended beyond bands to girlfriends as well. "Billy never had that attitude that many boyfriends have of, *You're my girlfriend, I do things, you don't*. He was the opposite: he was always pushing Tracey, or Kyra, to do things, organizing her creatively."

This was how his relationship worked with Doyen too. He'd call up Eugene and tell him he wanted to shoot a record sleeve tomorrow; he'd be clear on where to meet, what the style should be, what order they'd stand in, and where the locations were. "I'm a photographer's dream," says Childish now, "because I say, 'Why don't we do these pictures, I've got these hats we can use,' for example, and they don't realize I'm just using them to propel myself forward."

"Once," recalls Doyen, "he called me up and said he wanted to have the Milkshakes shot on the Junkers JU 88," the Luftwaffe bomber that came down during a Second World War raid on Chatham's dockyard.

"Meet us there at lunchtime," Childish requested one morning. "We've only got an hour." Russ Wilkins drove Eugene up there on his lunchbreak, accompanied by his stepladder so they could get some shots perched on the wing and by the cabin. Within an hour they had the shots for their next Milkshakes album sleeve, titled, with tongues typically in cheek, *The Milkshakes in Germany*.

"You'll notice that Billy never had this thing about being in the front: *I'm the singer or the front person, I'm the star.* No. The order was always democratic and the shape of the photo was the most important thing. It's what made the Milkshakes shots so good, really. They had such a strong visual idea and identity, always. Billy, Bruce, Mick: they were really good at graphic design, presentation. They're artists."

The most surprising commission Doyen received from Billy Childish had nothing to with his bands, however.

It was December 1, 1982, Billy Childish's twenty-third birthday. He called up Eugene and invited him on a trip to London "to buy guitar strings." Doyen could tell there was some kind of secret plan afoot, but he jumped on a train with Billy to Charing Cross and duly headed to a store to pick up the strings. Then Childish said they were going to go to Vauxhall to meet his ex-girlfriend Shelia Clark. He was going to marry her.

Clark was waiting at the registry office with a couple of her friends. Childish had only brought Eugene. The wedding deposit was taken care of, but they didn't have enough money for the rest of the license. "So we had a whip around," explains Doyen.

Doyen opens the file at the photo of Childish and Clark glumly standing amid the litter in the street immediately after their wedding. "Then we went for a Chinese meal and afterward caught the train home to Chatham, where Billy goes back to Tracey. She said to me: 'I didn't know where he was, I had all these presents for him.'" Doyen shrugs. "Six months later she found out."

He turns to a photo of Billy and Sheila posing in white vests in his bedroom, showing off their matching Hangman tattoos. Doyen points to a shot of Emin: "She saw their Hangman tattoos and said she wanted an anchor instead. Sheila's at the Royal College of Art now; she teaches textiles."

We leaf through the folder.

There's a set of Childish with his fists raised, in his family home in Walderslade, surrounded by his paintings. "The top floor was a studio space and that's where Billy painted for a time. As you can see, he's in his expressionist phase," says Doyen. "The fists, well, he had one boxing match that I saw, but he got biffed around a bit. Chatham's a very tough town, the Royal Engineers are there, it's just not the game to play in Medway."

There's a photo of Childish and Mick Hampshire sketching patients at Oakwood Hospital, which opened in 1833 as the Kent County Lunatic Asylum. Childish liked to go and draw there when it was the psychiatric wing of Maidstone Hospital and was even employed briefly as a porter before he was dismissed for telling the doctors how they could improve their care. It's a story detailed in his novella *The Ward Porter*, which was published in 2015 under the pseudonym of Odysseus.

"I only went to Oakwood once: a quiet space for people who have fallen apart, people who will probably stay there for the rest of their lives," says Doyen, adding that he owns a painting that Childish did of the hospital. He tells a story of the time the Milkshakes got lost in Maidstone's one-way system. The driver stopped to ask directions from a passerby, who wondered if they wanted the psychiatric hospital. Yeah, said the band, and the man offered to show them the way. When he got in, everyone inside the van convincingly pretended to be patients. He jumped out at Oakwood none the wiser.

We settle upon some of Doyen's many photos of Childish and Tracey Emin. "Impossible to take a bad one of them, they looked so dynamic. And every shot we did, it was never just a snap. It always had a purpose: 'We're doing a poetry book,' etc."

He remembers the first time he met her, when they were all together in an American-style diner. "She was very giddy and highly entertaining, saying things like, 'I only eat yellow,' and, 'I never go to sleep.' You could tell they were entranced with each other. Billy left without paying for his chips, though."

We flick through the Childish and Emin selection: some shot at the back of Bruce Brand's house in Luton Road; one on a sofa, with Childish's painting of a nude Sheila hanging directly behind them; shots of them together in his bedroom with "Tracey in her Dolli Bambi outfit," both bristling with animal magnetism; a photo of Emin laughing, with her front teeth missing . . .

"She had so many different stories about losing those teeth," says Doyen, chuckling. "Her brother knocked them out; she was drying her hair, got bored, and stuck the hair dryer in her mouth; she pulled them out because she wondered how it would look . . . Who knows what happened."

We look at some photos that Doyen took of Childish while directing two short films with him: 1980's *The Man with Wheels*, a tribute to Kurt Schwitters in which Childish is wearing one of his father's Edwardian suits; and *Quiet Lives*, a domestic drama starring Childish and Emin, with a violent conclusion.

Here's a selection of Childish with his close companion and collaborator Sexton Ming. They were in the Medway Poets, made surreal spoken-word albums together, did art projects, and were largely inseparable for over a decade, but now they're estranged.

"Sexton has a unique mind, a fantastic sense of humor; he was a bit like Captain Beefheart," says Doyen, as we look at a photo of Ming and Childish hitting a piano with hammers. "But life was very unfair on him. He looked odd, he hadn't been educated beyond school, he couldn't fit into society really. Who'd employ Beefheart? But Billy 100 percent was behind him: 'We're making music with Sexton. We're going to put exhibitions of Sexton's work on, we'll sell his work, sell his albums, put his poetry on.'"

Laughing at the memory, Doyen recalls a poetry event that the Medway Poets were at. The night had been intense and a little pompous and pretentious. The stage was empty, the house lights down. "Then Sexton came out, sat down at the table, and just said 'Poetry' slowly in a very deep voice into the microphone. The place collapsed."

We look at photos of the Milkshakes playing at the Hope and Anchor in London—"Such a joy live, the opposite of all the other bands at that time; it was a rock 'n' roll dance party, lots of laughter"—photos of other Medway groups the Delmonas and the Prisoners, and Childish snogging Kyra De Coninck on the Esplanade in Rochester, not long after she moved over from Belgium. There's a session in a pub with Childish, Ming, Sheila Clark, and various other pals documented, as well as various images that are the next shot along of album sleeve sessions you've inspected by all the local groups, as well as poetry collections. One of the best of these album photo sessions is for *I've Got Everything Indeed*, a blues session by "Wild" Billy Childish that was recorded in one day and released by his Hangman Records in August 1987 (art direction: William Loveday, sleeve: Bill Hamper). Childish is holding two guitars by their necks, smoking a cigarillo, and standing in front of an intricate cartoon mural of the sleeve that he'd painted on the wall.

"Billy invited me around to his rented house, saying he wanted to have a photo taken for the new record," says Doyen. "I take the photo and he steps away; the bit in the wall where he's positioned himself was blank, cut perfectly to fit in him and the two guitars. He moved out of the house soon after and just left the mural up for the next tenants."

There's a glorious photo of Tracey Emin having afternoon tea with Hilary and Sarah from the Delmonas, with Eugene himself sitting behind them, which looks like a still from the film *Saturday Night and Sunday Morning* set twenty-odd years earlier.

Then we come to a couple of photos of Childish's mum June, shot in her home when she moved to Whitstable. She's holding Doyen's focus intensely.

"Billy really supported June for twenty, thirty years," explains Doyen. "He did his painting down there every Sunday and we'd have lunch with her. He looked after her, made sure she was okay financially, and really encouraged her ceramics and pottery. He put a book out of her pottery!"

Eugene closes the file.

"The big secret I tell my students about work is this: you get up in the morning, you have a cup of tea, then you start your work and keep going . . . that's all there is to it. You put in a thousand hours a year. There's no shortcut. They think I'm mad, but that's what Billy did. He just did the work. Two hundred years ago, if Billy was shipwrecked on some distant beach and met a new tribe, his role would not be as the hunter-gatherer. He'd be the craftsman, the painter telling their stories. He's an artist. That's who he is."

Doyen slips the folder and memory stick into the tote bag and hands them across the table. "Good luck with the story," he says, and we step off toward Mile End Road, in search of the next chapter.

17.

Self-Portraits in Broken Glass

It is November 4, 2023, and the Medway delta glitches to the persistent boom and crackle of fireworks. Inside the Medway Little Theatre in Rochester, however, all is silent save for the sound of verse ringing out from the stage and, unusually, as this is a poetry event, hearty laughter.

The event is billed as "an evening of Medway poetry and folk," a launch for Billy Childish's new poetry collection, *self portrate in broken glass,* which is about to be published by Tangerine Press. Childish will be reading, as will his old Medway Poets sparring partner, Bill Lewis. After the interval, Childish will take to the stage with the Singing Loins to perform some folk shanties of his.

First, though, Wolf Howard walks onstage and, given that he is about two sizes too big to squeeze beneath it, awkwardly pulls up a chair to the desk at the front. He's all in black: black jeans, black polo neck, black waistcoat, and black beret. As a teenager in the 1980s, Howard—whose email signature describes himself as "Wolf Howard (Gentleman Amateur)"—was the drummer with the Daggermen, a modish Medway band who sounded a bit like early Kinks and often supported the Milkshakes and Prisoners. He started playing drums with Childish in the early aughts with the Buff Medways and has remained behind the kit for most of his subsequent combos. Alongside Lewis and Childish, he's a painter who was also one of the original Stuckists. He writes beautifully dry verse, too, poems that he delivers in a magnificently deadpan style, which frequently has the Medway Little Theatre in guffaws.

A couple of poems that he reads from his "small book" called *When Tramps Wore Suits* stand out. The first is about his unhappy experiences with computers, which are often hand-me-downs from Childish—"and when I get them I understand why they didn't need them anymore."

you ruin my life

if my computer were a person
i would slip a blade in behind
its windpipe and rip it forwards
i would stuff knives in each eye
and
twist them as if playing
table football
i would swing a sledgehammer
up into its chin screaming like a
javelin thrower
i would pound its face to a bloody
pulp
laughing as the muscles and tendons
split apart
then relish the crunch of bone
hardly noticing the blood from
my knuckles spurting out sideways
i would lie it down so its neck was
over the kerb and then I'd stamp on
its head
and then I would sit in my cell
for the rest of my life
wondering how I could have hurt it
more

Wolf Howard (from *When Tramps Wore Suits*, 2018)

Before the room has really composed itself, he delivers his potential hit single, "a nice short one" . . .

In the Paper . . .

Mr and Mrs Hargreaves
have announced today that they are to get divorced
he is 97 and she is 93
'we thought we'd wait until all our children were dead'

Wolf Howard (2003)

We welcome Bill Lewis to the stage next. Gray of beard and wearing a tan jacket, his meditative delivery is substantially different to that of Howard's. He has a shamanic vibe and uses shakers as a rhythmic accompaniment to some of his verses. He dispenses with them for "The Twentieth Century," which is more like a short story than a poem, though the mood remains that of a Greenwich Village happening circa 1966, albeit with a strong Kentish aroma:

The three bears come back from their walk. They live in a neat little cottage in the Wild Wood, which used to be very *wild* but now it's a nice neat suburban housing estate and everything is much tidier. They are horrified to discover their house has been burgled. Porridge has been eaten; furniture broken; beds slept in.

Baby Bear finds a semi-comatose blonde in his bed. He sniffs her. She smells of booze and by her dishevelled appearance he thinks she may have had sex. Much worse than this, someone has placed Modern Art in the centre of the room and you can't move without tripping over it. Father Bear is getting angry.

'You'd better take a look outside,' says Mother Bear.

Father Bear goes out into the garden. His mouth drops open in disbelief. This is the final straw! Someone, some vandal, has placed a very large Twentieth Century in the middle of the nice neat lawn.

'Who is responsible for this outrage?'

A man steps out of the shadows.

'It was I,' says Pablo Picasso, 'and I am not sorry.'

Bill Lewis (from *This Love Like a Rage Without Anger: Poems 1975–2005*)

This reading hints strongly at the humor and attitude toward art and the modern world that have seen Bill Lewis and Billy Childish through over forty years of friendship and collaboration. A few weeks before the event at Medway Little Theatre, I had an email conversation with Lewis about their long alliance:

Tell me about your background, please.
I was born in 1953. My dad was a shepherd and later a farm laborer. We were very poor and lived in a tied cottage on a farm in Kent. I left school in 1968 without any qualifications (I didn't even pass the eleven-plus), which made me smile many years later when I was giving a lecture at a university in the US.

I grew up in what was then a little village (now swallowed up by the local town). The village is bordered at the north of the village by a large wood called Oaken Wood and at the south by the River Medway. It features in some of my more rural poems.

In the early seventies, I was in a group of poets called the Out-crowd with my childhood friend Rob Earl. We met in a pub in Maidstone and read our latest poems out to each other and talked about literature.

I worked at several low-wage jobs, manual work, warehouses and shops up until 1976 when I had a breakdown and ended up in a psychiatric ward for several months.

When I got out, I decided I would not go back to working in

dead-end jobs. I'd always felt like a square peg in a round hole. I did my best to fit in and it was one of the things that led to my breakdown. I had always wanted to write and paint. I put together a portfolio of my artwork and decided to try to get into art college. I tried several but they wouldn't accept me without O levels. Luckily for me, in 1977 Medway College of Art and Design decided to let a few people in on the merit of their work. So, at the age of twenty-five, I became a mature student. I did a year but didn't go on to do a degree.

How did your path become entwined with Billy Childish?

I have often wondered how that happened. There just seemed to be a connection. We didn't hang around with the same crowd at college, but whenever we ran into each other we got on well. He brought out several photocopied fanzines and included some of my stuff in one of them. I also did the same and put some of Billy's poems in a magazine of mine. It was in the last few months of the final term that I invited Rob Earl over to do a reading at the college, and then Billy came over to Maidstone and read at an Outcrowd meeting. I think without knowing it then, we had formed the core of the Medway Poets.

What was he like when you first met?

The first day of college all the new intake of students were milling around and I noticed him watching all of us with that bemused smile on his face. I remember he was wearing a leather jacket and had short blond hair. I think he was as out of place as I was.

Tell me about the Medway Poets, please.

The Medway Poets really started to come together near the end of college and in the first months of 1978. A man named Alan Denman, who lectured in English at the college's Complementary Studies department, hired a room at the back of the York pub near Chatham railway station and started putting on cabaret evenings once a month. The York was a really rough pub, but the room was separated by a yard and had its own entrance. It was usually used for martial arts. Billy, Rob and I read at those, but we weren't yet a group. Later, Sexton Ming arrived and he and Billy hit it off and became good friends. A lot of the poetry was really bad but we began to realize that a few of us could do more and we formed a group. We hadn't yet got a name.

What was Billy's input? What was his poetry like then?
His poems at that time were very Dada-influenced. He admired Kurt Schwitters very much. Later, by the time we read at the Cambridge International Poetry Festival in 1981, he had discovered Bukowski and Fante. He was influenced by them, but what he got from them the most was permission to use his own voice. None of us were going to sound like Oxbridge types. I think Billy's Hangman Press books had an influence from Black Sparrow Press; those books were very beautiful to look at.

What was the dynamic between everyone in it?
It is sad that Sexton has now fallen out with Billy, they used to be so close. We all had big egos and we were young; it goes with the territory. Billy and I thought Sexton was a genius. He was so entertaining and funny in an offbeat way. I remember Billy saying that you never want to go on after him and I think that was true. Once the audience had seen Sexton we were all just 'Joe Normal.' Everyone I know who knew Sexton has a Sexton Ming story to tell. We all liked Rob but several of us, including Billy and Sexton and myself, didn't always get on with Charles Thomson. But I did respect Charles as a poet.

In those first few years we managed to put on a united front, though cracks soon formed. But when we were all performing our poetry to an audience, it was good and we were unlike any group of poets on the scene at the time. We still didn't have a name and when we got our first gig outside of Medway we met at Charles

Thomson's flat to figure out what the hell to call ourselves. It was me who came up with the Medway Poets but I now know it had pissed off a lot of other poets in the Medway towns. That was not my intention. I remember seeing a poster for some other poets in Chatham that read: 'We are Medway Poets too!' The river that gives our region its name seemed the only thing that we all had in common. We were all coming at poetry from different angles.

I'm keen to hear of any anecdotes from around this period you may have.

At one of the readings at the York, a poet from Cambridge named Richard Burns (aka Richard Berengarten), who at that time was writer-in-residence at the Victoria Centre in Gravesend, brought his entire poetry class over to the York. He liked a lot of our stuff and in 1981 he got us a gig at the International Poetry Festival in Cambridge. They put us in a huge venue that sat 2,000, but there could only have been about thirty people in the audience. A few years later some of us went back to Cambridge and read to much larger audiences.

At that return to Cambridge in 1984, I went to see Sexton's reading. He had an electric guitar and started his set with a song. It was his version of 'Wild Thing' but he'd changed the words. He hit the chord and sang: 'Virginia Wolf / You have small breasts / but I wanna know for sure.' The audience were laughing so much they were in tears. At another reading in a theater in Canterbury, my wife Ann found a wheelchair backstage and Sexton wheeled himself up to the microphone and did the entire reading in the chair; then got up and walked off stage at the end.

When did you meet Tracey Emin? What was your perspective on her relationship with Billy?

I first saw Tracey (without knowing who she was) when I was waiting for a train at Chatham station. She was on the other side of the track. I thought she looked interesting. I think that was several months before she met Billy. I don't know what to say about Tracey, except that they were two people who should not have been together.

You were a founder of the Stuckists, which included Billy for a time. Tell me about that, please.

The Stuckist experiment was a worthy attempt to redress what we thought was a fault in modern art. We wanted to go back to the beginnings of modernism and try not to take the so-called 'postmodernist' route, which in my opinion is a cul-de-sac. Art literally painted itself into a corner, then forgot to paint. I mean, how can there be such a thing as postmodernism when modernism is still alive and kicking in so many new forms? We saw ourselves as 're-modernists.' We thought that the Stuckists would be the vanguard of a re-modernist movement. What actually happened was a lot of groups formed around the world, calling themselves Stuckists, but there were some other re-modernists that emerged at the same time.

Billy obviously thought it hadn't achieved what it should have done, as he left after the first year. We did, however, accomplish some things, one of which is a return to figurative painting (which we were being told was dead) albeit in an imaginative form.

How has your relationship with him evolved over time?

I have always liked Billy, he and Rob Earl are two of my closest friends. I like Sexton too, but I haven't seen him for years. With Billy, I think one of the things that has bound us together is our fascination with the nature of reality. We often speak about that when we meet. We both feel that reality is stranger than most people think. Billy once said, pointing toward the bandstand in Victoria Gardens, 'If I paint that I have to make it look more like itself than the surface.' I'm paraphrasing him here but that was the gist of what he said. We are trying to see below the surface.

A long time ago, we both sat on that bandstand in the early

hours of the morning, passing a bottle whisky back and forth; and he told how he had seen a black panther on two occasions, once in the woods behind his house and another time in the town. We have a local legend about a big cat that haunts the area. We finished the bottle and Billy decided to paint a portrait of me, so we walked toward Rochester, taking a shortcut past the college and over Jackson's Field. Just as we got there we both heard a roar. We looked at each other and decided to pick up pace and see what it was. A circus had camped on the field and a lion had woken up in its cage and was roaring.

Many years later, I was having coffee with Billy's ex-girlfriend Sanchia Lewis in London and she told me that Billy had also told her about the black panther he had seen. They were driving through Germany at the time. They stopped for a toilet break and to stretch their legs. Just as they got out of the van they heard the roar of a big cat. Walking along the road, they saw the signs for a safari park with pictures of lions and tigers on it. Strange that should happen on both occasions of him telling the story. Coincidences fascinate me and I think they are little glitches in reality.

I know that you suffered a nervous breakdown many years ago—Billy suffered similar much more recently. Were you able to offer any counsel to him? What's the route out? And how does it change someone?

I don't think I counseled him, but when he talked about it I knew how bad it must have been. My breakdown occurred when I was twenty-five. It was awful, but in a way it was one of the best things that ever happened to me. It was more of a breakthrough than a breakdown. It led me out of one life into another. It was a crisis not only of the mind but of the spirit. I think Billy and I would agree on this. We are not religious but we both believe in something beyond our physical selves.

You've known Billy Childish a very long time. Tell us something we might not know about him.

You know, if you read his books you probably know more about him than he does. He is very focused on his work. He once told me 'it tethered him to the world.' I understand that, because being an artist is a total thing. You're born that way and have no choice in what you do, you just do it. He is very generous and doesn't take himself too seriously. He is one of the most truthful people I know and he is a bit of a trickster in the mythic sense. Trickster magic is strong, a necessary thing; it helps you deal with your shadow. Spirituality isn't all light and crystals. I think he is a spiritual person but some might not see that, because they don't understand what that means.

At the Medway Little Theatre, Billy Childish is about to reveal something about himself once again. Many years ago, he wrote a poem called "the every when," which described his life story with mirrored openings of each verse. Recently, his daughter Scout read the poem and told Childish that it's no longer authentic.

"She said that it's not true that I don't eat cheese, as the original claims," he tells the room, after reading his first version, "so I thought I'd better update it." Over the next ten minutes, he reads the rebooted poem. It's pretty much as good an autobiography as he could wish to deliver:

the every when

speaking as
a
man
whos
earlyist memory
is

being sat in front of a black and white
telivision set
unable to move
the screen alive with static
1960

speaking as
a
man
asked by
his bearded father
stood in toeless sandels
if he would like the police
to come and arrest him
1962

speaking as
a
man
whos legs erupted in
violent boils
then
named hop-along-cassidy
by
nana lewis
for
my
staggering walk
aged 2

speaking as a
man
who
in
the ice winter of 63

lay in bed
with his older brother
watching him vomit red-brown sludge and grit
onto white sheets

speaking as
a
man
sat by a window as
a
smiling snail
was crushed
benieth the blind boot of
a
laughing postman
in 1963
house number 159 named chiaroscuro
by my artistic father

speaking as a
man
mocked
and
named 'the smell' by
my
barstard
family
1965

speaking as
a
man whos
father left home
for a portly misstress
named ann wiseman

1967

speaking as
a
man
who has watched a lazy
flying sauser
revolving
in a clear summers sky
back garden 181 walderslade rd
1967

speaking as
a
man
who
wittnesed
9 ft
shaddow people
on
cursed land
with
the
vicars son
jonathan francise
lordwood juniors skool 1967-69

speaking as
a
man
who had
12 teeth extracted
by mister williams
family
dentist

gillingham hi st 1968

speaking as
a
man
told by his mother
that when
she
found she was pregnent
she
tried to abort him
'as all mothers do'
front room
large round table looking at the candleabra

speaking as
a
man
sexualy abused
over 4 consecutive nites
by norman
woodwerk teacher
and friend
of
the family
he later carved me a wooden crusafix
to
ward off wearwolfs
and
vampires
seasalter 1968 challet named 'como'

speaking as
a
man

who survived 3 near drownings
the great dains hotel 1968 camber sands 1969
the norfolk broads 1970

speaking as
a
man
whos path was crossed
by
a black panther
nr tunbury wood
visiting dave marsh
early 70s
approx 6 o clock
british summer time

speaking as
a
man
who bearly learned to read and rite
aged 14
1st book read
lord of the rings
jrr tolkin
walderslade 2ndry skool for boys
1973

speaking as
a
man
acosted by
a
real live goblin
(front garden benieth the fur tree)
walderslade 1974

speaking as
a
man who carved
'ork crusher' in icelandic runes
on a hand made club
smeared with his own blud
1974

speaking as
a
man
who lost his virginity
to t. h.
15 year old
girl of delewear
the
isle of spetses
1974

speaking as
a
man
punched on the the nose
by the
religious education teacher
mister boyce
walderslade 2ndry skool for boys
it mite have been
april time

speaking as a man
who read the dao de ching
and
studdied kung fu
tia chi

and
doaist yoga
in the back streets of chatham
1974-75

speaking as a
man expelled by
skool proctor mister shored
walderslade 2ndry
skool for boys
so
that
i wouldnt
be able
to sit my one exam
o-level art
easter
1976

speaking as a man
refused an interview at the local
art skool
due
to
my
lack of education
medway college of design
1976

speaking as
a
man
who carved
geronimos head
apprentice stonemason

the nuclear dumping ground
st marys island
1976

speaking as
a
man
who
placed his own hand on a granit block
and
smashed it with a 3 lb club hammer
her majistys dockyard chatham
february 1977 (aprox)

speaking as
a
man
convicted
of
shoplifting
a jar of country born setting gel
from boots the chemist
value 36 1/2 pence

speaking as
a
man
accepted
into
art skool 4 times
on the genius clause
as 'a student who lacks the nessissary qualifcations
but shows exceptional artistic ability'
1977-1980

speaking as a man

put on
probation
medway college design december the 1st 1977

speaking as
a
man
tattooed on the left buttock
with
the dadaist poem
i dont bother
with ideal i eat the apple with the peel
kurt shwitters
1887-1948

speaking as a man
commended by kurt schwitters
son ernst shwitter
'please send my kindist regards to mr childish'
marbrough gallery
piccadily
1980

speaking as
a
man
told by his painting tutor
that his attitude
was
no
way to go about getting a degree
who then
answered
'what would i want to get a degree for?
so i can teach students

to get a degree
like you do'
st martins skool of art
1978

speaking as a man who
walked out
of the painting department
st martins skool of art
1978

speaking as
a
man
sent benieth the machines
to clear
rotting fruit
by the bug eyed charge hand
pekham fruit packing factory
(employment 1 day)

speaking as
a
man
dissmissed from his job as ward porter
for
mearly
offering simple
advise
on patient care
to
dim-witted doctors
oakward mental hospital
barming nr maidstone
1979

speaking as
a
man
who
punched his father
clean down the stairs
to
bounce his
blond head
off the bottom slate step
upon reginald john hampers
release from prison for drug smuggling
1980 ish

speaking as
a
man
who played guitar and
sang
tuneless compasitions
on the boards of the star club hamburg
before it
being
torched on the instructions
of
consentration camp survivor
and sex pope of st paulie
reni durrand

speaking as
a
man
re-accepted on to
BA
painting

st martins skool of art
1980

speaking as
a
man
expelled from
st martins skool of art
by
the skool head
mister simpson
for publishing
obseen poerty
1981
(only friend peter doig)

speaking as a
man
offered
paid poetry readings
if
he would
omit
useing the words
fuck
and cunt
kent litrichar officer
john rice
gravesend adult education center
1981

speaking as
a
man
who told

john rice
kent litrichar officer
to go fuck himself
gravesend adult education center
1981

speaking as
a
man
accused
of
being not a poet
but
a pornographer
john rice
kent litrichar officer
1981

speaking as
a
man
who watched
micheal horovits
perading around
the pre reading swaray at
at
sir clive sinclairs mansion
holding his latest poetry collection
featuring
a
portrate of himself
by
david hockney
wearing the same shirt
as in the painting.

cambridge international poetry festival
1981

speaking as
a
man
ostrasised
by
poet
micheal horrovitz
for simply tapping
him on the shoulder
and
asking
- have you only
got
one fucking shirt
mate?
pre reading swaray at
sir clive sinclairs mansion
cambridge international poetry festival
1981

speaking as
a
man
worshipped by traci emin fashion student
medway college of design 1981
only later
to
be
designated
as
a man
of low

intelligence
little talent
and
petty
jellousys

speaking as
a
man
who confrmed
the above
when
viewing
micheal horovits
wearing the same shirt holding up the same book
and
smooching around
the royal dutch embercy
holding hands
with
the london poetry secuteriate
leaning in
- you have only
got
one fucking shirt!
the royal dutch embercy
london
late 1982
(congratulated by alex trocchie)

speaking as
a
man
pinned naked to the floor
by 3 police officers

the toe of
a shiny boot
in
his guts
being asked
- so you like riots do you boy?
you want to stab a police officer?
drunk tank
rochester police station
1983

speaking as
a
man
who relaxed himself on the dole for 13 years
whilest
similtaniously
travling the world
running a small press
and
record label
and
starting up a harem
all
at
no profit
1981-1994

speaking as a
man
born
of
an alcoholic
who himself was alcoholic up untill
age 33

who was then dry for 18
years
but then drank a
150 pound bottle champane
with his
wife
to see what it was like
2003

speaking as
a
man
who underwent 6 years
intence phycoanalysis
7veral 10 day vippassna retreats
spent
30 years practising yoga
and
can not abide
the
special voices
employed
by poets
teachers
or fucking yogies

speaking as
a
man
who was the apparent co-founder
of
an art movment which
he
imeadiatly left
upon seeing

their 1st shit
exhibition

speaking as
a
man
acused
of
plagurism
and
bitterness
by
previouss admirer
jack white
for grosse insolence and
not returning the massage
2002

speaking as
a
man
who now
eats cheese
was
married benieth
a volcano
in
the pacific north west
who
has had multipul past lives
as
violent pirat
shamen
crow indian boy
murderous sioux warrior

and
is guarded
in heven
by
the spirit
of
the crow
i
see that truth
allways
resides
in
the
birth
place
of
the every when

Billy Childish, from *self portrate in a broken glass* (2023)

After he finishes reading, Childish puffs out his cheeks with an exhaled "Fucking hell." He calls over to Michael Curran, who runs Tangerine Press.

"Mike, is all of that really in the book?" he asks. "Can we take some of it out?"

"Yes, it is," calls back Curran from the side of the stage, where the finished books sit in a pile on a table by the bar, ready to be sold during the break. "And no, we can't."

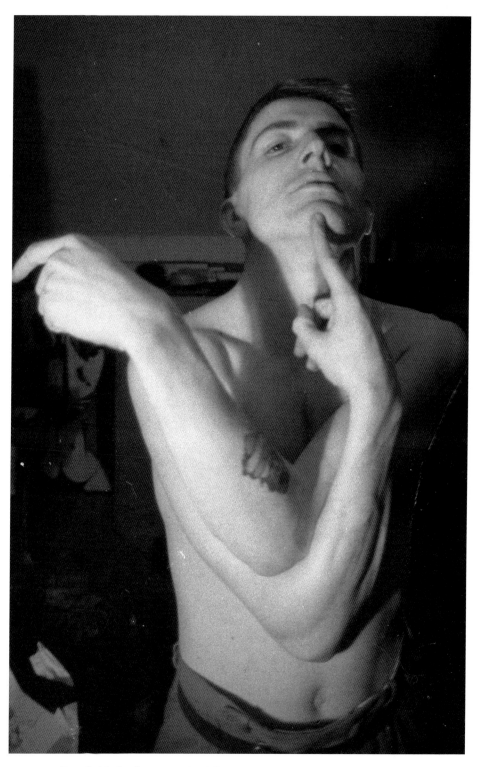

Billy Childish photographed for a painting, May Road, Rochester

Billy Childish photographed for a painting, May Road, Rochester

Mickey Hampshire and Billy Childish, drawing in
the dayroom of Oakwood Hospital, Maidstone

Billy Childish and Tracey Emin, Luton Road

The Milkshakes with a Junkers JU 88, Rochester Airport (L-R, on ground: Mickey Hampshire, Billy Childish; on wing: Russell Wilkins crouching, Bruce Brand)

Billy Childish photographed in front of a mural for the cover of *I've Got Everything Indeed*, 1987

Sheila Clark and Billy Childish on wedding day, Vauxhall, December 1, 1981

Left Sexton Ming and Billy Childish

Below Billy Childish with the Milkshakes, Hope and Anchor, London (Bruce Brand behind him, Mick Hampshire to his left, and Sarah Crouch watching from side of stage)

Bottom The Milkshakes and Prisoners photographed for the cover of *Thee Milkshakes Vs The Prisoners—Live*, September 23, 1984. (From left, kneeling: Billy Childish, Graham Day, James Taylor, Bruce Brand; standing: John Gawen, Johnny Simons, Mick Hampshire, Allan Crockford)

Billy Childish on Ordnance Terrace (Charles Dickens's childhood address)

Left Billy Childish and Sanchia Lewis in the kitchen of his house on Ordnance Street, 1980

Below June Hamper at home, early 1980s

Bottom Billy Childish and Eugene Doyen

18.
Kyra

"You think you know me
my secret intentions
but you never, ever been so wrong"

From "Secret Intention" by the William Loveday Intention (2023)

It is hard for people who love the work of Billy Childish—who think his mind is a precise tool for making sense of the human condition, who laugh loudly at his cutting jokes, his daring turns of phrase, and who admire his well-considered sense of place and humility, his powerful spirituality—to think too deeply, or even at all, about the way he behaved toward the women who loved him, and who he supposedly loved, for twenty-odd years of his adult life, between 1980 and the early part of the twenty-first century.

He was a cad. He was a scoundrel. He was a reprobate, a rogue. He was an absolute rotter. None of these words really do him justice. If you were, perhaps, the parent or close relative of one of his romantic partners during the madness of his love life during this period, a sharper description might leap to mind. We cannot skip over his behavior, of course. It's mostly all available to inspect in his work, anyway.

Let's just take a look at the no doubt tongue-in-cheek front cover of *I Am the Object of Your Desire*, an album released by Wild Billy Childish & His Famous Headcoats in 2000, as he entered the endgame of his shagging around (he possibly wouldn't appreciate that description, but we're all friends here and must speak plainly): There's Billy Childish in the center of the photo, leaning against a tree, lost in handsome contemplation. At his feet, gazing up at him, is Kyra De Coninck, still officially his partner at that time. To his left, smiling at his wondrous features, is Holly Golightly, Kyra's singing colleague in Thee Headcoatees and—though the precise timescale is foggy for those involved—Billy's sometime lover. And pawing at his right sleeve is Sarah Crouch, a third Headcoatee, who was resolutely not in any romantic relationship with Billy Childish ever, but whose presence may represent one of the other women Childish was in a relationship with then.

Seated around Billy's kitchen table, we're talking about his "harem" period. He says that everyone knew about it: he never had affairs; instead, he had multiple relationships at once. "Which," he admits, "doesn't solve any problems, I found out. It's a bit more honest, but I thought that made it all right. It isn't."

It's incredible that someone like Childish, who on many levels exhibits such emotional intelligence, could imagine that people might not suffer if he were to have multiple relationships at once. But he seemingly convinced himself that it was a possibility.

"It is just gross egotism," he says now. "I saw it as a bastion against the world. It's like, *How do I win? How do I feel all right, how do I work, how do I survive this?* It's very baby-fied, very immature, naive. I mean, you can understand it in the sense of being afraid of being alone, of desertion, of needing things in place that will keep me safe, but when I say you can understand it, I mean on an intellectual level. It doesn't create any excuse. You can say, 'Oh, yeah, that person really is messed up!'"

This comes up as we discuss his long relationship with Kyra De Coninck. With respect to most of the people interviewed as witnesses to his personal life, Childish likes to establish from the outset that what he says is the true version—because he doesn't lie: "If I say something happened, you can be sure it happened"— but he doesn't try to set any ground rules with De Coninck.

"Kyra's got a good memory, she's very clear about events. In terms of personal relationships she may not be as trustworthy as she could be, but she won't lie about what happened." With that in mind, we make the necessary arrangements.

Kyra De Coninck lives in Rochester, about half a mile away from Billy Childish, in a terraced house with her husband Chris de Coulon Berthoud, a social anthropologist, and their teenage daughter. She is a university lecturer in sports and exercise sciences, who provides sports massages to athletes at events and international championships.

Sitting in her front room, surrounded by her son Huddie's paintings, as well as some of June Hamper's pots of cats, we drink atomically strong coffee as she casts her mind back to that night at Ancienne Belgique in Brussels in 1983, when she first met Billy Childish as a fifteen-year-old, after he'd played there with his group . . .

Childish Witness: Kyra De Coninck

"Billy's constantly piercing balloons around him . . . He can laugh at himself."

I was blown away by the scene, by the clothes, by the music, by the attitude. The Milkshakes at the time had this group of fans who would travel with them on the ferry to Europe, who would then go to the gigs, often climb up on the speakers, drop their trousers. I'd never seen anything like it. Billy was so cheeky. I was flattered, because I was quite a serious teenager and my friend who I was with was the good-looking one, but Billy and I clicked.

Afterward, we wrote to each other for a number of years. Of course, we led very different lives: he was a lot older than me, seven or eight years, and when you're that young, it's a big difference. At the time, I was involved in theater and drama; I knew some of the authors that he was really into. But I didn't know anything about blues, I didn't know anything about rock 'n' roll. I was into very different music—I liked German punk like Xmal Deutschland—but we got on really well. We wrote to each other for quite some time. I think I've got those letters somewhere.

Then the Milkshakes came back to Brussels and I went to see the gig again. I came to England a few times to visit him, and one visit, he said, "Well, do you want to come and live here?" At the time, I'd finished my studies in Belgium, I'd started drama school in Belgium, and I thought, *Why not? It might last for six months, be really good for my English.* Forty years later, I'm still here. Never, ever thought that it would turn out the way it has.

I can remember being really scared of Tracey Emin, because, although they had split by the time I'd visited England, from our phone conversations when I was still living in Belgium I knew that it was very fractious, they had lots of arguments and fights. I can remember after a really big argument, her taking all of his books that she had printed at Maidstone College of Art and chucking them in the river. Then I met her, and while we were never close friends, we were part of the same group of people.

I was so shocked when I got here! I had traveled with my dad to Eastern Europe. We'd go on holiday to the DDR and Poland, so I'd seen different ways that people lived, and when I first came here, it really reminded me of Poland. It was so poor, people didn't look healthy, everything was crumbling and falling apart: really desolate. It was very bleak.

But it was also super exciting.

Billy would pick me up from the station and I'd sit in the van, we'd go to a gig with the Milkshakes, and it was all a world that I'd never encountered before. My dad's a taxi driver, my mum was an accountant, I'm not from a particularly exceptional family, but there was always literature or we'd go to exhibitions. There was an interest in the world. My family are very political, as well—my grandparents were communists—and I think I reacted to that, because it was about your role in society, about making it a better place. I think for me to go off and live with Billy, it was the furthest away from that, because everything was about him, everything was about the self. There was a disillusionment with wanting to change the world. I think that's what really attracted me about punk, and that's what really attracted me about Billy. His view of the world was so different from what I'd encountered in my family.

What I found here were lots of bands, lots of places to play. The spontaneity, the creativity, the energy of the place I really enjoyed. Everybody was on the dole, but they'd go on a tour in Europe in between two periods of signing on.

A few months ago, a friend of mine in Belgium came across the letters that I wrote to him from that period, and he said, "It's like you're describing this exotic island, because you were so fascinated." To him, it sounded horrendous, like I'd ended up in this hellhole where there was absolutely nothing and loads of desperate people. But for me, I thought it was absolutely brilliant.

In the beginning, it was Billy and me against the world. I really understood and took on board the sense of his fight and his struggle, his hatred for what he felt was double standards. I still feel that. It was his attempt at honesty. At the time, we were both really into Charles Bukowski. We connected through some of the writers that we both liked.

But our living arrangements were abysmal. Actually, my dad sent a detective from Belgium, just to check, because they were so worried about me. They went through our bins even, followed us. I read the letter that he sent to my dad: "There's no drugs and they pay their bills; the boy drinks too much, but she doesn't and they go on tour together a lot."

I was just eighteen. We lived in number 2 May Road, near here. I can remember in the bedroom there was snow on the inside, because it was very cold that winter when I moved here, Christmas '86. Lots of snow, and none of the houses had central heating. In Brussels, even in the 1980s, everybody had central heating. I saw the snow inside the window and thought, *That's wrong*. I tried to wipe it away and Billy got really angry. He said, "No, that's insulation, that means that the snow keeps the cold out!" It was cold enough in the bedroom for the snow not to melt.

I can remember a guy from the gas board coming to close down the gas stove in the kitchen because it was unsafe. I was crying and saying, "Well, how am I going to keep warm?" We had this electric cooker and I'd put the electric oven on, opening the door just to have a little bit of heat.

Bertie from the Milkshakes lived upstairs. He was in a jazz band at that time, so we would hear this funk and jazz coming from where he was practicing. He was only around for a few years, but we lived there until we moved to Boundary Road in 1995 or '96. It was a tiny house, covered in all of Billy's paintings; he was painting on wood then. A really manky bathroom and then next to it was a cellar space and that's where they would rehearse, where lots of the albums were recorded as well.

I was only allowed—this sounds ridiculous now when I say it out loud—I was allowed to have a TV, but the TV had to go back in the box when I was finished with it. It was a little portable TV that I was allowed to take out, watch a program, and then it had to go back in the box. Billy had his rules. I mean, he still does that—they watch telly on Apple TV on their computers, but they don't have a TV.

Initially, I could tell that he was drinking a lot. I probably thought, *I can change him, I can help him, I can make things better so he doesn't suffer so much.* It was kind of a rescue mission. But at the time, it didn't feel like that: I was in love, we were both in love, it worked really well, we got on really well, for years and years and years.

And then, I think things started to deteriorate. There was a dark period where he was very unhappy. I think he had a massive breakdown, but at the time, I didn't realize that's what it was. I thought it was normal. It's my first relationship, I had never met anybody with alcohol problems. I would try to make it work somehow.

I think that was the period he started having relationships with other women. He would be quite manipulative in how he would talk to me about it. He would kind of threaten me with the truth. He would say, "Yeah, but, you know, when I'm with her, it means that I can be a better boyfriend for you." It was a load of bullshit, but at the time, it was like, *Okay, he's being unpredictable, and really verbally aggressive with me.* So I thought, in my stupidity and naivete, *Maybe he's right, maybe that is how it's meant to be and maybe that is how we can work, because our bond is so strong and blah-blah-blah, and we do the books and the records together and we play music together and we have all this other stuff going on that makes part of our relationship.* At the time it was a relief, because I thought, *Well, actually, then I don't have to listen to him for at least another afternoon.*

He convinced me to such an extent that I always thought it

was my fault: *Oh, it's because I'm not enough, or I'm not this.* I would defend him to other people, though. I would do anything to protect the status quo. And there was also a really exciting part of being in a relationship with him. There was no fame at the time, so I can remember we used to take photographs of his paintings and I'd have these little slide sheets, going to loads of galleries all over London, months and months of doing that, trying to get an exhibition for him.

I basically dedicated my life to him and I never got any of the benefits! By the time we'd split up, that's when things started taking off, and all of a sudden people were very interested in his painting, writing, and music. Everything took off. I lived through all the grottiness, when people saw him as an anachronism, as somebody who was irrelevant, which of course only fueled the fire. That spurred him on.

He absolutely brought the creativity out in me, though. We translated *Cannon Fodder* by [Louis-Ferdinand] Céline together; that was a real labor of love. I'd never translated, my French wasn't perfect, but that was something that I would never have done if I hadn't been with Billy. I did do a little bit of drawing, but that was more under duress rather than something that I really wanted to do. The music, though . . . I was really interested in drama and performance, and that's what I really liked when we started Thee Headcoatees. I loved playing live, I loved going on tour. I felt very spontaneous and I loved doing things with a group of people.

Thee Headcoatees were Billy's idea. Thee Headcoats were rehearsing, and I think Sarah [Crouch] was doing some backing vocals, Debbie [Green] was there, because she was going out with Johnny [Johnson, bass], so they'd come down from London, Holly was with Bruce [Brand, drums]. So we were all there and Billy suggested we do some songs. I think he had the idea from the Delmonas—we all had a partner in the band, apart from Sarah, but she'd been in the Delmonas.

I can remember the mic dangling from the lampshade in the

kitchen; we would all stand around the table, rehearse, and sing the songs into it. I'd never done any singing before, so that was super exciting. We made five albums in the end, which I would never have done without Billy. People said, "Kyra, you can't sing!" "I know, it doesn't matter. It's punk!" There were tours in Japan, the States, and Europe; that was such a big part of my life, and particularly in the first few years from 1991, that was just incredible. Those first few tours, when we were Thee Headcoats and Thee Headcoatees playing together, were amazing.

The flip side, toward the end, was when we were separating as a couple and Billy started seeing Holly in the band. That was horrendous.

A lot of that went on when we were still together, the other relationships, and I started to plan escape routes. I applied to go to university, and for him that was a heinous act, that was one of the worst things I could ever have done.

I didn't just leave from one day to the next—I made lots of attempts to leave, but it was so hard. I also had a secret relationship with somebody else, who used to be in one of his bands a long time ago—again, trying to escape.

I did go to university in Sussex in the end, studied anthropology. I ran away. I secretly took over a flat from a friend of mine who had studied there. I literally packed my bag the night before, and then I just snuck out, went on the train, and lived in Brighton.

There was a number of years where I was then seeing someone else. I told Billy about that relationship and his first reaction was, "Why didn't you tell me before, because I let Jeannine [Guidi, who Childish first met in Hamburg in 1981 and saw intermittently] go to America?" I was like, "Yeah, that is, again, not the reaction I'd expected."

This other relationship finished quite soon after. I went back to Billy for a little bit. We hobbled on for a number of years, trying, but the big thing that came from all this was he stopped drinking.

We then started restrictive diets, a lot of focus on macrobiotic food. Lots of meditation, lots of yoga—he's still very dedicated to his health and to his well-being. He started seeing lots of therapists. I went into therapy as well.

We were going through a really rough patch again a little while later and we'd split up again. But we had booked a tour in the States, and so we did still go on the tour. By then he and Holly had started a relationship. It was right in front of me. And then I found out I was pregnant. Looking back at it, I must have been already pregnant before we got to America. Before the tour in the States, we went on tour to Japan, and I was sick as a dog. I can remember lying on the floor, just being so sick, getting up, performing, and then having to lie down.

I went to the doctor when we got back, because I thought I had a thyroid problem, and she put the sonar on. She said, "I think you're pregnant," and I said, "But I haven't had sex for sixteen weeks or something!" It had been a few months. Then she put the ultrasound on me and said, "Can you hear that?" It was a heartbeat. She said, "You need to get a friend to come and pick you up."

From my friend's house, I phoned Billy. I will never forget his immediate response. His first reaction was, "I will always be there for you and the baby. We will work this out." Because I'd thought, *Well, what am I going to do?* I was homeless at the time. I was thinking, *Do I start my new life in Belgium?* I had plans to go to India to study Ayurvedic medicine and Ayurvedic massage, because I ran a massage practice at the time. I'd made these plans for an escape route, but I couldn't then do that.

But he vowed, "I will always be there, I will support you, we will work this out, don't worry." I thought, *Okay, this is meant to be, this baby is so desperate to exist.*

The atmosphere in Thee Headcoatees was really bad with Holly, though. Holly and I have kind of made up since—I was in Berlin for a conference and we had a nice chat, made our peace.

But it was horrendous at the time. I was like, "You can have him, I don't want him, I've been with him seventeen, eighteen years, even with the baby, I don't want Billy anymore." I think she was very, very angry about it. We did do a few gigs when I was pregnant—but it was not good.

That last tour in America, when Billy and Holly were going out with each other, the atmosphere was awful. Everybody was so fed up with Billy and Holly sneaking off with label people and trying to make deals with them. I can understand it from her point of view: this was going be her big ticket, this was going to be her and Billy's breakout. They'd already made an album together,* but there were plans for more. They were to be the star couple rising from these ashes. It didn't quite work out that way.

During this time, Billy meets Julie and starts seeing her. I didn't know that then, but I did meet her in Seattle on tour; she was looking very glamorous in this beautiful Chinese dress. I just got this feeling from her, like, *Oh, I wonder whether she's one of his previous conquests?*

Eventually, Julie comes to live in England with Billy. I'm living just a few streets from here, me and Huddie. Billy and Julie see Huddie every weekend. I was still trying to run my massage practice at the time, as well. And Julie and I, we got on really quite well in the beginning, then there was kind of a split. I think it was probably because she needed to develop her relationship with Billy and I needed to develop my own relationships.

I can remember Billy saying to me, "Oh, you and Julie should do a band together," and we did do the A-Lines together. That was good fun and really important for me. Even though it had Billy's wife in the band, it was still a step away for me from Billy.

We are good friends, but we are nowhere near as close as how

---

* *In Blood* (1999): a late Headcoats album, credited to Billy Childish and Holly Golightly, which sounds like lust's ransom note. Each song—"Let Me Know You," "Upside Mine," "Step Out (of Your Dress)"—is a declaration of overpowering sexual desire, the voices of the pair entwined in lockstep randiness. It's one of Childish's best records, too.

we used to be when Huddie was a kid. Billy's status and recognition in the world has changed and she's a completely different character from me. Julie's had a very different experience with Billy. Similarities as well, but at a very different point in his life.

I know that right now my friendship with her is that when things get bad, she will always come to me. A few years ago, when Billy was in a really, really bad way with his breakdown, she came to me. I think his past is probably very difficult for her. Actually, my daughter and her daughter are good friends, too.

With the parenting of Huddie, I did the majority of it; then Julie did a lot of it as well. When Huddie was little, we used to go on holiday together, though, go camping. That was all for Huddie; so that Huddie felt loved. God, that all seems like such a long time ago—he's twenty-three now! Billy and Huddie adore each other. I'm glad it turned out that way. It wasn't always easy.

With Billy, you can see that his personality comes from his trauma and from everything that developed him, everything he fought against. But he's done it with a sense of humor. He's constantly piercing balloons around him. Whereas other people can have a very similar outlook, but they don't have that charm or wit about them. He can laugh at himself.

I think the difference now when I speak to Billy is he's surrounded by very different people. When I was with him, he was surrounded by people who would either not talk to him, or tell him that he's a pile of rubbish; that nobody's ever going to be interested in anything apart from the music, which was very niche, underground. There was a small group of people that absolutely worshipped the Milkshakes and worshipped Thee Mighty Caesars and worshipped Thee Headcoats, but that was it.

He's always had a fan base within music, but at that time never in art, hardly ever in the writing. His poetry was really derided.

Billy used to write these hilarious letters to people. I remember him writing to Richard Branson, saying, "Here's a poetry book, send me some money, how are the pickles going?" He used to write a lot to Page 3 girls—he was a member of the Linda Lusardi fan club and the Suzanne Mizzi fan club! He used to send them his poetry books. On our pinboard in the kitchen there were signed photographs of Suzanne Mizzi and Linda Lusardi. He'd read the *Sun* newspaper, which I always found odd. He'd explain it to me by saying, "I need to know what I'm up against." One of his big hatreds is of left-wing intelligentsia, *Guardian* readers, they are the devil—but they're his fans now, ironically; the ones that can afford his paintings.

He used to write to complain to John Peel too: "You never play my records." John Peel read out one of the letters that Billy wrote in; it said, "Here's a fiver, maybe you'll play my record now." And he'd stuck a fiver in. It was playful and I loved that.

You don't have to have done as much therapy as Billy has to realize a lot of his problems stem from his parents. I really liked June. That's one of the things I find really sad—she died during COVID and I never got to see her. She had a complex relationship with Billy. Billy and I would go there every Sunday to have dinner. I think she never really recovered from the trauma of having a volatile—well, violent—relationship with Billy's dad. She was quite a recluse. She was very indecisive; she often relied on Billy to make decisions, but then would fight those decisions as well. She was really creative, like all the family. I have a few of her pots.

She was funny as well. One of my favorite stories with June was when she said, "Oh, this policeman came round and he was looking for cocaine!" I think this was something to do with Billy's dad. "I let him in and he was looking in the house. He said, 'Oh, you have to be really careful, you know, because even if you touch the powder, you can get addicted.' So I said to him, 'Oh, it didn't have that effect on me when I last had cocaine!'" I was really fond of June.

I met his dad a few times. That was a really big thing—that Billy reconnected with his dad, at the time. We went to Hayling

Island to visit him and to visit Hugo, who was a tiny little boy. But that has always been really complex. I think the key to a lot of what drives Billy, what repels or fascinates Billy, is about his dad. He was such a destructive person. Billy never had time with his mum and dad together.

His dad is a really disturbed person. When you meet him, you get a weird feeling off him. Billy will hate me for saying this, but he's got that intensity that Billy has, but he has it in such a distorted way. I reckon Billy's dad sees himself as some kind of elevated person, somebody who we should all bow to, that he was never recognized for the genius that he was. His children never figured in his life. Even when Billy obviously started to get these markers of success, his dad never acknowledged that, was always very dismissive, and would talk about himself, what he had achieved. Really horrible.

We saw his dad when Huddie was born, went to meet him at Victoria station. I can remember I had Huddie in my arms and he didn't even look at the baby. He was just talking about himself. A very, very disturbed person. I'm glad Billy found a different path.

Exhausted from De Coninck's testimony but still vibrating from her coffee, we say our farewells. When I explain that my next appointment is with Sarah Crouch, aka Ludella Black, her former colleague in Thee Headcoatees, Kyra kindly offers to walk me across town to Crouch's ceramics studio on the edge of the Medway.

As we march through the backstreets of Chatham and down Jackson's Field above New Road, I think about Billy Childish's memories of the back end of their relationship.

Finding out about Kyra's affair was the jolt he required to stop drinking, which he realized was badly out of control. He was becoming as selfish and as unreliable as his father. So he quit: "First whiskey, then I weaned myself off beer slowly over six months, and I didn't drink again for eighteen years."

When he was eight or nine, Childish used to decant his father's whiskey into a dash of Coca-Cola and bring it into school to help him make it through the day. Breaking that partnership with whiskey in particular was significant. He tells me, "My health improved—for example, my migraines eased away. I stopped the harem games too."

His "harem" wasn't all local; that would have been impossible to maintain. It consisted of women in Japan, America, Europe, London. "My bastion against the world, scattered across the nations." But it had to stop, and so it did.

Kyra, says Billy, had another affair, or perhaps he suspected she desired to have one, he's not sure and doesn't care, and that was enough for her. She wanted a proper separation. She requested they do marriage counseling as their exit interview. They were in this for a year, explains Childish, adding that Kyra didn't bring up her most recent desire for an affair. "At the end of the year, the counselor said, 'I see that Billy wants to be together but you don't, you want a separation.' So we agreed to separate," he recalls.

"Then she said she wanted a reconciliation." Childish says he suggested that if she did therapeutic work on her psychological state, he'd consider it. He says that she wasn't willing to invest any more time in that, so they split.

"And then I had a fling with Holly for several months. In the midst of all that, Kyra says, 'I'm four months pregnant.'"

This understandably threw a wrench in everyone's works. "Holly got very, very upset and annoyed about that. I had actually told Holly about the last time I ever slept with Kyra, because I tell people stuff and I don't like lying, but I don't think that was taken into consideration in the moment."

Holly Golightly initially did not respond to requests to put her side of the story across. She now lives in the US, working with horses in California by day and making music by night, and her reluctance to revisit this period was understandable. Prompted, however, by a final email, she got in touch with this simple comment:

"I have never spoken about Billy in any interview I've done, or even privately amongst friends really, and I don't feel the need to start now. I am really grateful for all the amazing experiences we shared back then. I loved being in the band and look back on those days with genuine love and fondness for the most part. It is something I will always be thankful to have been part of."

In the white heat of the pregnancy-news explosion, with all its implications of professional inconvenience and seismic personal revolution, Childish decided he needed to continue his journey of inner development with increased vigor. He'd take advantage of the fact that Thee Mighty Caesars were regrouping to play in Las Vegas soon, by heading out into the Nevada desert to undertake a vision quest retreat . . .

Up a flight of stairs, in an old warehouse overlooking the Medway, Sarah Crouch has a large whitewashed studio for her ceramics, where her partner of over forty years, Mick Hampshire, also paints. Their creations fill every available space and it appears like an ideal spot to work. "I love it here," she says. "Been here for yonks—it's cheap and look at it: perfect!" She worries that they may not be here much longer, though. There are developers sniffing around this waterside location. For decades, the reason why so many art students stayed on in Chatham and its neighboring towns after graduating from Medway College of Art and Design was the fact that it was located in a run-down area with high unemployment and, crucially, affordable housing and studio space. But, encouraged by the high-speed train link, developments are rolling down through Rochester at a fair lick. Even crumbling old Chatham High Street may get a daub of fresh paint one day.

Crouch leads the way to the water's edge, where she lives with Hampshire on a well-appointed and homely houseboat. Mick has no desire to relive the old days, when he was Billy's front-man foil in the Milkshakes, but he shares an email address with Sarah—she replied saying she'd be happy to talk about Billy Childish instead. She's known him since 1980, after all. She has seen every side of him.

"Billy was always the same," she says. "You knew it was going to be all about him every time. He was very dapper, he liked to be heard. He had a presence. You could see it in him: *Yeah, he'll go far with that ambition for success!*" She laughs. "That's actually one of his lines, but it's very true."

She speaks about him with the wary, exhausted affection of an old but not hugely forgiving friend. She says they've had plenty of ups and downs. "He's not very patient with me—so if I irritate him, that's the end of the conversation. He irritates me too, but it's only his opinion that counts, so we clash a lot."

It's been a long and tricky relationship, she says. What they have in common is a similar sense of humor and tastes in art, clothes, and music—"I can't stand Bob Dylan, though." She is, however, a fan of Billy Childish's music on the whole: "I'm always very happy to do any work with him; I love singing his songs. Playing with him live has always been good. It's just if we have a general normal conversation, it can get a bit heated. That's the same with Mick and him, which is why he doesn't do talking about Billy much."

She sang backing vocals on a few Milkshakes songs before joining the Delmonas with the other wives and girlfriends of the band. She recalls the Milkshakes years as being madly fun for the most part. "At the height of it, it was such a fantastic laugh. Tracey and I would get all dolled up and be happy to be on the arms of the two most handsome men in Medway. It was lots of drunken dancing with your friends."

She and Tracey Emin were tight throughout, until the Milkshakes appeared in 1984 on *The Tube*, Channel 4's Friday-evening music show, alongside the Prisoners, Tall Boys, and Stingrays in a special live sequence about garage bands. She says that the label people at Big Beat, who were putting out an EP of the four groups, colluded with producers to push Childish and Emin to do the interview, while the other band members were relegated to onlookers. Afterward, Crouch was furious. She felt protective of Mick, but also believed that it went against the band's collective ethos. She told them so and walked off.

"I got really angry. As I was walking down to Chatham, I could hear Tracey clattering behind me. She went, 'Sarah!' I said, 'I can't talk to you, Tracey, I'm too angry!' She wouldn't leave it: 'Sarah!' I turned around and shouted, 'You prostituted yourself on the telly!'" Crouch bursts out laughing, then sighs. "We fell out for a good few years after that."

After the *Tube* performance—or maybe before, in truth—she realized that Hampshire's heart was no longer really in the Milkshakes. He just wanted to play fun rock 'n' roll shows in local sweatboxes. It had all become a bit showbiz for him. Plus, he hated being lumped on nights with psychobilly bands such as Guana Batz, whose fans spent the whole gig thumping each other. "After one gig at Klub Foot or one of those rockabilly nights, he was really down: 'They'd probably prefer it if I just farted into the microphone.'"

Compared to the end of Thee Headcoats and Headcoatees, however, it was a mellow and happily mutual uncoupling. She explains, "The end of Thee Headcoatees was absolutely horrendous." Like the Delmonas before them, they were the partners of the boys in Childish's band. But unlike the Delmonas and the Milkshakes, Thee Headcoatees went on tour with Thee Headcoats.

She continues, "When we started, it was such a scream. The four of us got on really well. It was like us against the men, we had our own private jokes and so on. We had really good times and a lot of the gigs were brilliant with us and Thee Headcoats. We were lucky to have done so many great tours, but the last one in America . . ."

What Crouch describes sounds like the storyline from a cokey Fleetwood Mac documentary, rather than two good-time, sixties-styled, garage-punk groups from Kent who wore deerstalkers as props. "It should've been a fantastic tour, people were really excited to see us, but instead it became all about Billy and Holly," she says. "I was sharing a room with Kyra, while Holly and Billy were suddenly all loved up together after years of moaning about each other."

Bruce Brand, meanwhile, was sitting uncomfortably behind his kit each night, stormily brooding. "Bruce was grinding his teeth throughout, because he was still in love with Holly—it hadn't been so long since the end of their relationship. And even though Kyra had told me she was ending the relationship with Billy, I found out that she's pregnant with his baby."

The final straw came at the airport awaiting their flight back from the US. "That's it," announced bassist Johnny Johnston. "I'm not doing this anymore. After years of Billy moaning about how controlling Holly is, suddenly she can do no wrong—I'm out."

"I think Bruce gave a little cheer," says Crouch, chuckling. "He might have done that when Mick left the Milkshakes too. It was so dramatic. If only we'd been successful: the tabloids would've loved it. Billy was too controlling as well. Everyone was calling him 'sir' behind his back and I think if it wasn't going to be fun, why bother?"

Occasionally, Crouch will get up alongside De Coninck and sing favorite old Headcoatees songs like "Wild Man" and "Davey Crockett" when Childish plays live. She loves doing that and she has a good relationship with Julie, Billy's wife, meeting her for lunch from time to time. "We go round to their house for drinks too," she says, "but I always say to Mick we're only stopping for an hour, because otherwise there'll be some sort of row. We can all laugh and get on, but Billy's very self-absorbed and it can depend upon what mood he's in."

Sarah Crouch kept a Milkshakes scrapbook when the band were still together and gets it out now on the floor, stopping to point at reviews, old gig tickets, and photos. "Aw, look at my handsome boy," she says, pawing at a picture of Mick holding the microphone and grinning in some forgotten nightspot.

He's not retired, though. Sarah will join Mick Hampshire when he takes his garage combo, the Masonics, featuring Bruce Brand on drums, on tour or plays in local pubs. He also paints prolifically, "but he has no real interest in selling them." He does as much music and art as he ever did, but he also takes jobs that allow his hobbies to remain just that: the fun thing he enjoys in his spare time.

Sitting on his houseboat with his adoring long-term partner, their artist studio within a stone's throw, it's like looking through a window at a life that could've been Billy Childish's, had the dial shifted a fraction in his head. Mick went down one road when he left the Milkshakes, while Billy followed another. What if they'd stayed on the same track and both headed for a steady life of personal, quiet satisfactions?

"Billy's wired differently to Mick," says Crouch dismissively, with a shake of the head. "He's after something else."

From: william claudius
Date: 8 September, 2023
Subject: billy—should we . . .

---

mite be fun to do 'i didnt get where i am today with out saying no'.

bbc film early 80's
i think cbs 90's
celbrity big brother
etc

From: william claudius
Date: 6 October, 2023
Subject: should we mention the things I've turned down?

---

big brother
reading with alan ginsburg
supporting chuck berry
supporting the sonics

From: Ted Kessler
Date: 9 October, 2023
Subject: Re: should we mention the things I've turned down?

Will do, of course.

19.

Billy Graham

It's 1983 and the Milkshakes are playing in St. Albans. They're sharing a bill with the Tall Boys, post-rockabilly types fronted by Nigel Lewis, who'd previously played double bass in the Meteors, maniac rockers from Middlesex with a group of hooligan fans who followed them everywhere, causing aggro. Gigs with the Tall Boys could get rowdy.

Thinking about it, it might not have been St. Albans. But then again. A lot of those double bills with rockabilly and psychobilly bands were the same business in a different room for Billy Childish: the Milkshakes would play, and their fans would dance while loads of big geezers around the edge stood, arms crossed, watching. Then the psychobilly band would play and everyone would bundle in, punching each other. Or vice versa, if the Milkshakes won the toss and went on second.

As the Milkshakes were playing in St. Albans, the fire curtain came down. They'd overrun their slot, refused to leave, and the venue had called time. Childish was walking from the stage when one of the Tall Boys's crew—was it Nigel himself, might have been—shouts over. "Oi!" he calls to Billy. "Oi! Give us a hand!" He's rocking the massive PA system, but it's too heavy to budge on his own. Childish looks around the fire curtain into the audience, who are still gathered hopefully in front of the stage. He shouts at them to move out of the way. And then he joins the Tall Boy in rocking the PA. With one final huge shove, it comes crashing down, through the curtain and smashing across the dance floor. Mayhem.

Everyone starts picking bits of the PA up and hurling them across the room. People are swinging on the fire curtain. A fight breaks out. The police arrive: time to leave.

Back in Medway, a representative of the Milkshakes calls the venue in St. Albans asking innocently about payment for their recent performance. Fuck off, comes the reply. You smashed up our PA. You owe us money!

Affronted, the Milkshakes's representative replies: That was nothing to do with us, that was the Tall Boys.

We have your guitarist on video pushing it over.

Oh.

The riot police had to be called and a policeman was injured by a knife in the disturbance. It's all in the local papers.

Oh.

The news is related to Billy Childish, who writes it all down in his pocket notebook under a heading of "Riot in St. Albans! Policeman stabbed, big fight, smashed up venue: must get local paper" . . .

Sometime after, Childish is on a night out with Graham Day, front man of the Prisoners, in Rochester. Graham and Billy get on really well, better than most in their two bands. Day lived in the same Castle Hill house as Tracey Emin at the time, so they're always knocking about, looking for fun diversions when not playing gigs or recording.

The pair are walking down Rochester High Street, drunk. They have spent all their money in the pub, but at this stage in Childish's drinking career, being happily drunk is nowhere near enough. He wants more, though both of them are now out of funds.

They pass Topes, a fancy wine bar and restaurant near the castle. Through the window, Billy can see the place is shutting down soon. There's just a couple of diners in the back. All the booze is on display at the front.

"You wait here," Billy tells Graham. "I'll get us a bottle of whiskey."

Graham Day raises a skeptical eyebrow.

Childish walks right inside Topes, leans over the bar, and grabs a bottle of whiskey.

As he does so, he's grabbed from behind by an employee and pushed against the counter.

"All right!" shouts Childish. "I'll put it back!"

The voice behind him grunts, "No you don't! You're not escaping."

Childish replies that he's not trying to escape, that he'll put the bottle back.

They wrestle for a moment or two, Billy still pressed against the counter. As they do so, Childish knocks the till off the counter with his elbow. The till smashes on the ground.

Not again . . .

Presently, the police arrive and Childish is bundled into the van. Graham Day is sensibly nowhere to be seen. Back at the police station, Childish is stripped and thrown "bollock naked" into a cell, in the drunk tank. After half an hour or so, during which he's sat shivering in this freezing, empty cell, three policemen return. One is holding Childish's notebook.

"What's this?" he asks, waving the notebook.

"It's my—"

"It says you like riots! Do you like riots, sunshine?"

"No, it's—"

"It says you want to stab a policeman! Do you? Want to stab a policeman, hard man?" One of the cops puts a boot in Childish's face, hoping he'll react.

Billy Childish doesn't flinch. He tries to explain that he was writing about something he read in a newspaper from St. Albans . . . Eventually, the three police leave the cell.

Hours later, they return holding two new items: Childish's UB40 card, showing he's unemployed, and his savings book from the Anglia Hastings & Thanet Building Society, which he had opened in the name of Kurt Schwitters and used exclusively for the Milkshakes's accounting. On one hand, he's signing on the dole. On the other, he has a bank account full of money. And the account is in someone else's name.

"Who did you nick this off?"

"I didn't steal it."

"Who's this Kurt Schwitters, then?"

"Well, you know, he's an avant-garde Dadaist."

"Where is he?"

"He's dead. 1946. Died in the Lake District, killed himself after he'd been interned on the Isle of Wight."

"Then how come you've got his bank account?"

"It's not his, it's a band bank account I'm just holding."

One of the policemen prods Billy's back with his boot. "What's this you've got written on your arse, boy?"

Childish laughs through his shivers. "It says: 'I don't bother with the ideal / I eat the apple with the peel.' It's one of Kurt Schwitters's poems."

"Who's Kurt Schwitters?"

In the morning, a policewoman opens the cell door, holding Childish's clothes. "You picked the wrong coppers to get nicked by last night," she says, handing over his belongings. "Now, clear off."

For the five hundred or so teenagers from the 1980s who passionately believed that the Milkshakes were the Beatles in Hamburg and the Prisoners were the Small Faces in Soho, the news decades later that Billy Childish and Graham Day were enjoying a Monkees-meets–*Withnail and I* lifestyle together during that same period comes as both a revelation and a validation of our young fantasies.

Sitting on a bench outside the Rochester train station, sucking on a colorful disposable vape in the summer of 2023, Graham Day revisits their friendship. "Billy and I got on particularly well," he says. Many of the others in their circle, however, found him intimidating. "Billy's got a nasty wit on him. He takes the piss out of people, but it's not always lighthearted. It can be really cutting. People were scared of him."

Over the years since both the Milkshakes and Prisoners split in the mid-1980s, Day has been in a couple of groups alongside Childish. It's interesting that despite Graham Day being a skilled guitarist blessed with a powerful vocal range, Billy Childish has not sought to employ either of these talents.

"In Thee Mighty Caesars, he asked me to play drums," says Day. "I told him I'd never played drums."

I know, said Childish. That's the point.

"Billy has got this thing about wanting things to be crap, which I understand, but I struggle with it . . ." he takes a hit on the vape, "on a technical level." As it turned out, Childish was right. Thee Mighty Caesars's brutally basic garage rock was very good fun. Day admits, "It's probably one of the favorite bands I've been in, I loved it."

He thinks there are a couple of reasons for this. First, having spent years at the front of the Prisoners, it was enjoyable to find himself sitting at the rear, bashing away at a new instrument with no real pressure to write or perform. And there was also an element of revenge involved.

He explains, "Thee Mighty Caesars was before the 'Billy Childish' emerged. He was just Billy still then, so me and John [Gawen, the other Mighty Caesar] would gang up on him, take the piss, and get our own back for years gone by."

What does Graham mean by "the 'Billy Childish' emerged"?

"During the Headcoats days, he put a lot of work into being successful," Graham says carefully. "When you don't see someone very often, then you bump into them in the street and they start talking to you as if they're being interviewed—I used to find that very disconcerting."

During the Milkshakes and then Thee Mighty Caesars, nobody ever wanted to know anything about Billy Childish or any of his groups. Sometime during Thee Headcoats's lifespan between 1989 and 2000, his profile grew, in part due to his books and paintings, but mainly just through the sheer weight of his musical releases and performances. He'd put the hours in, playing gig after gig after gig, recording and releasing, recording and releasing. Then, in the early aughts, when fashionable bands like the White Stripes emerged from the US and started name-checking him—because he was a cool underground garage, blues, punk, and beat artist, with this massive, largely uncharted catalog, as well as having a very strongly honed personal style—his profile morphed into something new. He became an influence. He had status. He was a legend. Who could have seen that coming?

"Billy got so used to speaking about himself, and because people really wanted to know about him now, I understand it," continues Graham. "But in his determination to be himself, he's created this thing, and I don't think he can ever come out of it, you know?"

Despite this, when in 2004 Childish needed a new bassist for his Buff Medways—named after an extinct breed of local chicken that Keith Gulvin hoped to reintroduce—he turned to Graham Day. Day jumped at the chance: "I love being in other people's bands when I don't have to do anything other than just play."

He was in the band for a couple of years, contributing to one album, the excellent *Medway Wheelers*, whose title track describes June Hamper's cycling club when she was a young woman. It drew good reviews in the mainstream press, and sold reasonably well too. But that was it for Graham Day. He was by then a fireman and couldn't commit to tours abroad. There were gigs planned in Australia and he'd never get the time off his job for them.

"I told Billy this and he very dramatically said, 'Oh, that's the end of the band then!'" remembers Day. "Of course it wasn't. He just got his wife Julie in on bass and changed the band's name, as usual." And so the Chatham Singers were born; they grew into the Musicians of the British Empire, and now the CTMF; it's all

Billy Childish with Julie on bass and Wolf Howard on drums, though.

Graham Day, like Mick Hampshire, continued to make music as a hobby with his bands the Gaolers and the Forefathers, among others, all the while building a career in the fire service. He retired a couple of years ago in his early fifties at the top of the tree: Senior Divisional Officer of Kent. Now, with time on his hands, he's part of a reformed Prisoners. "Funnily enough, Johnny [drummer] was the keenest, maybe because he was so mad in the old days and just wants to try and enjoy it like a normal human being," he says with a laugh. "He's had the most settled adult life out of us all, too."

Graham Day doesn't see Billy Childish much nowadays, even though they live near each other in Rochester. They didn't fall out. It's just . . . well, what is it?

"He's really sweet, Billy, a generous guy. He's quite fragile in a way, and I think we've moved away from the time when it was awkward to be with him. I'm always glad to see him . . ." The "but" hangs heavily above us. But . . . Billy Childish has worked so hard at working so hard that maybe some old sparring partners feel left behind.

"Putting everything into his poetry, his music, his art, into 'Billy Childish,' I think that's come at a cost to him. I think he might be lonely, because it's easy to alienate people without realizing. We—all his old friends from round here—we all do music things to enjoy doing them. He doesn't, I don't think. He works. It's made him famous, made him successful, but he's also alienated himself from his friends."

This is surprising. In almost every conversation with Childish, he regularly refers to many specific people, who he describes as his friends. He certainly has more friends than his biographer by the sounds of it.

"Yeah, we're all his friends," says Day now, "but will we invite him to our birthday party? Probably not." He shrugs. "Billy finds it very easy to hold court—sometimes people just want to have a bit of a laugh without that kind of stress."

If Billy Childish is someone he wouldn't invite to his birthday party, it's hard to imagine the pair making music happily together again.

Graham Day looks at me as if I'm crazy.

"I definitely would!" he says, chuckling. "I love playing music with Billy. Anytime."

He just has to call.

20.
But I Know What I Like

There is an old music press cliché—usually delivered by some
resolutely unlistenable band early in their career—that goes, "We
just do what we do, and if anyone likes it, it's a bonus." Rarely
is it true. Given a chance, we all want to be loved. Toiling away
unnoticed in the dark forever, less so. All flowers bend toward
the light in time. It's nature. It doesn't necessarily entail "selling
out"—whatever that precisely is—but it might mean a few small
compromises in delivery, a collaboration with somebody, kissing
an arse that's going places and can take you along. At some point
in a career, if it's going to have any longevity, an arrangement
with a particular devil within your chosen field must be entered
into, no matter how minor. Everybody you have ever heard of
in music, art, or literature has done it (and they all have a tale
of regret to tell about it). That is, everyone except for Billy
Childish.

He really has done what he does for over forty years, and if
anyone liked it, it was a bonus. For most of that time, they did
not like it, and sometimes that annoyed him a bit, but it never
remotely changed the course he was on, because he felt that was
sort out of his hands. He was just doing what he had to, and all
that he could do. He doesn't so much follow his muse as obey
its every command; otherwise he will wind up in the equivalent
of the Oakwood psychiatric hospital, where he used to sketch
patients in 1980. He is the definition of an artist—which, ironically, is the one term he hates and totally rejects. He has always
made exactly what he wanted at that moment, always released it

independently, and has never done anything to please anybody who could help him.

Nearly all musicians employ publicists to deal with the media, for example, even on a basic inquiry level. The first time I contacted Childish, in 1989, I called the number on the back of a Hangman-released record of his and he answered (on my third try). Even in the modern era, you can drop his Damaged Goods label a line and they'll run it by him, then give you his number to organize a chat directly.

In music, the sheer volume of stuff that he's released, the number of gigs he's played, has given him visibility. Decades of music, with over 150 albums out there, meant that someone had to like some of it. Over time, a number of people did like his music, because some of it is brilliant—but you have to put the time in to find the good stuff. He's buried it. And he doesn't release all these records so you can collect them and complete the set. He's very dismissive of vinyl completists, who he compares to children collecting toys from cereal packets. He actively tries to sabotage them, as when he released three Spartan Dreggs albums in 2012: the only way to get the third in the set—for free—was to send in a token cut from the sleeve of each of the other two, thus damaging those sleeves. That made him happy.

If Billy Childish plays a gig in London with one of his groups, 400 people or so will pay to come along. Maybe more would pay, a few thousand, but we'll never really know as he only ever plays small venues, because he's trying to make the gap between stage and audience as small as possible. A pub basement in north London is his equivalent of playing Wembley Stadium. That's how he knows he's arrived.

The novels and poetry books barely make a dent. They're rarely reviewed, they come out with minimum fanfare, published in small batches with great care by tiny presses—including his own. You really have to seek this stuff out. He published his novellas with L-13 secretly, under a pseudonym, and left the copies in libraries and on trains. What chance does this leave the collector or fan of his writing?

And has any of this dimmed his output? No. During the course of interviews for this book, Childish regularly mentions a book he's writing, a novel called *All the Poisons in the Mud*, but then another day will reference two or three books he's working on in collaboration with Antonia Crichton-Brown—a university student he met when she was working in an art shop—and I lose track of which he's talking about. It's impossible to keep up. He's there in Medway, churning it out, obeying his muse, attempting "careers in a year" in all of his disciplines. For a period, he copies me into some of the dozens of emails he sends his poetry publisher, Michael Curran: each will contain a new poem. Sometimes he's written two poems a day and fired them out to his publisher immediately upon completion. Curran merely replies, "Received and logged."

His painting followed a similar trajectory, and for a long time was probably the least successful of all his disciplines. Nobody was interested. Yet it was the one he most doggedly followed, painting every Sunday at his mother's home in Whitstable and then, starting over a decade ago, on Mondays at Chatham Dockyard too.

But before then, he painted from childhood. At Oaklands Infant School he won second prize in the school's art competition for a painting he did of Mote Park and its ducks. Whenever anybody subsequently asked him at school what he wanted to be when he grew up, he'd reply, "A painter." "But nobody ever asked me what I wanted to do."

For a while in the early the eighties, when he was in bands touring, after he'd been kicked out of St. Martin's for publishing poetry zines they considered obscene and for refusing to paint in the college, he took to painting only in the summer. He painted really intensely for two months, producing two or three hundred pieces each time. He decided this was unsatisfactory, so he

developed the habit of weekly painting instead. Let's take a ball-
park guess: he must have produced, what, four or five thousand
paintings? Many are lost or destroyed. Some he gave away. A few
he may have sold, but there were no really significant sales for
decades. Nobody was remotely interested in Billy Childish's paintings, even though he painted under the name William Hamper
until the nineties. He'd tell the gallerist that Billy Childish had
never painted, it was all done under his family name (as they are
a family of painters, after all), but they usually just credited them
to Billy Childish. It didn't really matter. Nobody bought anything
anyway.

There was a time, in fact, in the eighties when he was so down
on his luck, so poor, that he'd go to Chatham High Street and
sketch for coins. He would sketch you for a couple of quid. Maybe
some kind passerby has one of those drawings somewhere? Possibly. If so, it might be worth trying to find it.

In March 2022, when Christie's put Billy Childish's painting
called *toward a shore* up for auction, it had a reserve estimate of
between £30,000 and £50,000. It sold for £163,800. At over three
times its estimate, it was the best price realized at auction by his
work since his commercial breakthrough in 2010. But it is by
no means an outlier. Today, his paintings regularly sell for five
figures. In 2020, his US gallery Lehmann Maupin showed his
Wolves, Sunsets and the Self exhibition in South Korea. Four of his
paintings sold on the opening night for around $30,000 each to
buyers from South Korea and the US. A big and unusual deal
for a British figurative painter on the international stage. As he
explained to the *New York Times*, "It was an overnight success that
only took forty years."

For a very long time, he just did what he did: now everyone
likes it and he's receiving his bonus.

"Nick went to the Royal College and Slade," June Hamper told
Sean Hughes for his unfinished Billy Childish documentary,

comparing her two sons' trajectories in art. "He did everything the right way and Billy did everything the wrong way." But Billy's turned out to be the right way, after all. Nobody is spending that kind of dough on Nichollas Hamper's paintings.

Billy Childish sits on the sofa at the end of his kitchen, pondering his overnight success that was forty years in the making. He's feeling a bit light-headed because he hasn't eaten for forty-eight hours. He's fasting.

"I've done five-day fasts in the old days," he says, "with colonics and whatnot."

Nowadays, he tends to go on twenty-three-hour fasts for a period of two weeks, before moving on to forty-eight hours. "The body starts recycling dead cells and crap," he explains, "does some repair work. And you get down to fighting weight too, of course."

He closes his eyes to focus upon his art breakthrough. Painting, he often says, is his main job; the central focus of what he does. He's at his most clear-eyed when discussing it.

"People think they deserve certain things, that talent is a way through to what they deserve," he begins. "That's why you get so many bitter musicians, because talent doesn't amount to much." He's willing to accept that talent's useful, critical in some respects. "What is more critical, though, cynical as it may sound, is God's luck. Chance. Everything hangs on the journey you take and who you meet on it."

He believes his success in the art world is all anybody need observe as proof of this.

"I've never tried to achieve anything. I'm unusual like that. I've never tried to crawl up anybody's arse." The closest he's ever come to ingratiating himself with someone in a position of power to further his own creative endeavors is when he sent John Peel a fiver to play Milkshakes records on Radio 1, but that was more of a prank than payola or even currying favor. Besides, it didn't work.

Childish's journey of chance in the art world really begins when he met a Canadian student at St. Martin's in 1980. He was named Peter Doig and he and Childish got along very well, certainly compared to Billy's interactions with anyone else at the art school, which were nonexistent. He thought they were all idiots, and they didn't like him much either.

One of the things he and Doig both agreed on was that Edvard Munch was a great artist, and that Vincent van Gogh was a magnificent painter too, arguably the greatest. Neither opinion, surprisingly, was popular at St. Martin's School of Art in 1980.

Doig was also into Chuck Berry and rock 'n' roll, as was Billy, so they'd go looking for old 45s in the market stalls in London together. Doig gave Childish a copy of Charles Bukowski's short story collection *Tales of Ordinary Madness*, introducing Billy to the writer who arguably made the biggest impact upon him, leading him down a path to John Fante and indeed toward the idea that writing books could be something he might be able to do too, based on these guys.

Childish gave Doig a tape of some early Milkshakes songs in turn. He liked it, but maybe less than Billy liked Bukowski. When the Milkshakes played a pub on Museum Street near St. Martin's, Doig came along.

Time passed, but the pair remained friendly. Sometimes, Doig would come down to Medway to play ice hockey, "being a Canadian," and they'd catch up.

When Thee Headcoats started playing gigs, Doig would come along to watch them. After one gig, he asked if Childish would like to do an exhibition at Cubitt Street, the artist collective he was a member of in Clerkenwell. By now, Doig had won a couple of prizes and earned a notable profile—later, in 1994, he would be nominated for the Turner Prize.

Sure, said Childish. Doig suggested that they team up with a young curator named Matthew Higgs to put it together. This also sounded fine to Childish. So in March 1994, Billy Childish had a three-week exhibition at Cubitt Street curated by Matthew Higgs and enabled by Peter Doig. Thee Headcoats played at the opening and Sarah Lucas joined Tracey Emin and other Brit Art pals in dancing along. "Suddenly Tracey was proud of me again," says Billy. "She is whenever she senses I may be 'making the most of my potential,' as she calls it, but not so much when I'm not, I suppose."

A little time before then, a German guy had come over to do a piece for a fanzine about Childish. His name was Tim Neuger and his main job was working at the Esther Schipper Gallery in Cologne. Childish had suggested they take pictures for the German fanzine standing on the propeller blade of a Messerschmitt 109, with a Union Jack flying above it. Neuger didn't mind. Childish knew then he was all right. Neuger subsequently wondered if Billy would like to be part of a group art exhibition he was putting on at Esther Schipper. Of course, replied Childish. Happy to.

"Over time, Tim Neuger came into quite a powerful position of running neugerriemschneider Gallery in Berlin," says Childish. "Pete Doig became an internationally acclaimed artist and Matthew Higgs became the director of White Columns Gallery in New York. They'd all been told they were fools for liking my work, but in 2009 Matt came over to London and said he wanted to do an exhibition of my paintings at White Columns." Childish thought this was a very good idea.

Later that evening, Higgs had dinner with Mark Sladen, who was the Director of Exhibitions at the ICA, which was in a bit of a rut at that moment. What, wondered Sladen, was Higgs doing in London? I've just organized an exhibition with Billy Childish at White Columns, said Higgs. Quick as a shot, Sladen wondered if he could nab Childish to do one at the ICA too.

"In the space of a few days I suddenly had my first solo exhibition in New York, at White Columns, and my first solo exhibition at the ICA," explains Billy.

Was this Billy Childish's big breakthrough as an artist, at last? It was not. The ICA show passed with barely any fuss, other than a lukewarm review by Jonathan Jones in the *Guardian*. "I challenged him to a boxing match," Billy remembers. "But he declined."

On the night of the opening of the ICA show, Tim Neuger had a flight canceled in London and, having heard from Matthew Higgs about Childish's exhibition, returned to central London to attend the private viewing.

On seeing Childish's paintings, Neuger immediately offered Billy a show at his Berlin gallery. Then, a couple of months later, he proposed they kick things off with a solo presentation at Art Basel.

"I said sure, even though, me being me, I had no idea what Art Basel was."

Art Basel, an international annual art fair staged in Switzerland, is exactly the event that most low-profile painters wish to be shown at. In 2010, it was attracting at least 50,000 visitors over the week that it was on. For a largely unknown painter like Childish, having a solo show there was a significant opportunity. Other than doing the painting, though, he'd had no hand in engineering the opportunity. God's luck.

The show he put on was called *I Am Their Damaged Megaphone*, and much of the work featured in the exhibit was based on the Swiss modernist writer Robert Walser, who the likes of Hermann Hesse and Franz Kafka (and Billy Childish) cited as an important influence. Walser was prone to wandering at length through the countryside, as well as hallucinations and schizophrenic breakdowns, and on Christmas Day 1956, all three of these elements collided when he died on one of his mazy perambulations in the grounds of the Swiss hospital he was confined to. He was found dead of a heart attack in the snow. Childish, in researching his life, decided to paint a series of images based around Robert Walser dead in the snow.

Childish only really likes using good oil paint with vibrant colors: the room hummed with his hallucinatory expressionism. The paintings, it was noted by some art commentators present, seeing his work for perhaps the first time, bore a resemblance to those of van Gogh and Munch. Of course they do, said Childish. As with the music he makes, or the books he writes, his lineage and influence is plain. "There's other traditions in there," he told a reporter at the time, "but I do think van Gogh and Munch are two heights of modernist work and more cutting edge and relevant than a lot of cutting edge and relevant work there is now."

The sold-out show was an enormous hit. Bianca Jagger bought one of his paintings.

"Someone asked if I would like to meet this lady Bianca Jagger. I said okay." There's a brief, sweet moment on YouTube of the pair sitting at a table in the middle of the opening-night hubbub, with Billy pouring Bianca a cup of tea: "I said to her that I'd be mother. She was a very nice lady." However, she let Billy know that he was pouring the tea incorrectly. "I replied that since she'd been hanging out with boys from Dartford, maybe *she* didn't know the right way."

After the huge success of the Art Basel show, Rachel Lehmann of the noted New York gallery and art agents Lehmann Maupin got in touch. She'd seen his show and wanted to meet with him.

"I was intrigued," says Lehmann. "I went to visit him. I saw a very original, almost old-fashioned gentleman, charming, witty, and, in his own way, revolutionary in his attitudes."

The more time she spent with him and his work in England, the more convinced she was by both. She told him she wanted to represent him in the States.

"He's a very, very emotional painter. He doesn't sit in front of the canvas with a plan or a theme—in a way it's his own invented style, which to me feels like playing music. It's filled with melody." She asked Billy if she could look after his work and he said okay, as he liked her too.

She says, "He's very loyal and a wild, wonderful human being, but he's absolutely not strategic. He just doesn't care! He does his own thing entirely."

This, she adds, will not be a problem. "He is commercially successful, we have several museums buying his work, which is already a huge recognition." But she believes that will not be the extent of it. "I'm sure he's the kind of artist who in two, five, or ten years has a major retrospective in one of those museums. When that happens, it'll be hard to cope, because the interest will be overwhelming and we need to protect him, right?"

Childish agrees with this last point. "You should protect yourself from success," he says.

He considers his big art breakthrough. Maybe his style changed a bit, but he didn't do anything to force that. He just started making bigger oil paintings on larger canvas, that's all. He followed whatever he follows when he's painting. It's tempting for him to say that what happened was that *he* happened. But that wouldn't be true, either.

"All it really is, is that people who liked me came into positions of power," he decides. "I really like that. The important thing is not to think you've earned it or deserve it." It was just chance.

Huddie Hamper, Billy's son, once asked Steve Lowe if he was his dad's secretary.

"Listen, son, your dad works for *me*!" Lowe growled jokingly, in the style of an old-school mogul. Lowe is a polite, well-spoken Englishman with a finely tuned sense of humor, honed in that immediate postpunk era when statues were there to be kicked over, not polished. Nevertheless, he was only half kidding.

"I don't want to work for anyone," he told Huddie, who ironically does work part-time for Lowe at his L-13 base. This was also what Lowe told the German gallery when they suggested he be given a wage rather than a commission for Childish's work.

Lowe explained to Huddie exactly what he does with Billy: "I help your dad out. I organize his exhibits, log everything he does, publish some stuff, help with ideas, planning and so forth."

"Yeah," replied Huddie. "Sounds like a secretary to me."

Sitting at his desk in L-13, a labyrinthine basement beneath a nondescript office block in London's worker-bee Farringdon, Lowe is having a think about how he became entwined with Billy Childish in 2003, as well as just what it is that they get up to together.

L-13 is located on the site of a former clockmaker's and the warren of worktops and various art projects seems to have been placed on top of the former business without clearing it out first, with a new layer added on top of the last with each new art or graphic project undertaken. It appears gloriously chaotic, but also somewhat organized. There is a very good, almost magical atmosphere and juju about the place, considering there are no windows.

If you look up L-13 online, it is self-described as: "L-13 Light Industrial Workshop and Private Ladies and Gentlemen's Club for Art, Leisure and the Disruptive Betterment of Culture." This sounds like a thorough description of what they do. However, the next bit of the "About" says:

> We Are Not:
> The L-13 Light Industrial Workshop is not a gallery, a publisher, nor do we represent artists. Neither are we a real Ladies and Gentlemen's Club, a Light Industrial Workshop, and we most certainly are not an art collective.

Hmm. This begs the question, what is it that L-13 does? Luckily, the website also answers this:

What We Do:
We develop projects both ambitious and diminutive, publish
books, make prints & other artwork editions, convert impractical
artistic visions to reality, promote a playful polemic spirit, irritate
and offend some delicate souls in the big bad world of culture
and politics, and work with other galleries and organisations that
exhibit and support L-13 artists.

The website lists "the key artists currently active with L-13":

Harry Adams [which is Steve Lowe and his long-term creative
    partner, Adam Wood]
Jimmy Cauty
Billy Childish
Jamie Reid

On the floor by Lowe's desk are a load of KLF posters that I'm not
supposed to see yet. (Or am I?) The anarchic electronic music duo
had a string of massive number ones after emerging in 1987, before
machine-gunning the Brit Awards with blanks and deleting their
entire back catalog in 1992, then burning £1,000,000 on the island
of Jura in 1994. Subsequently, they've been rarely sighted, but these
posters advertise a world tour scheduled for the year 2323.

"So, a little way off," says Lowe briskly. "But it will happen,
we're putting everything in place for it."

The idea is that people buy tickets now and pass them down
through the generations until the year arrives. There's an elab-
orate physical ticket that you can inscribe and leave behind for
your descendants. The show may be hologram-based, but who
knows what technology will exist, or how they'll wish to present
the KLF in three centuries.

The duo are doing this to help fund a pyramid they're building
in Liverpool, made of bricks filled with people's ashes—that story
is probably worthy of another book all in itself.

One half of the KLF is Jimmy Cauty, with whom Lowe has worked since 2004. The other half is Bill Drummond . . . who Lowe also works with, but only with the building of the pyramids. So he doesn't appear on the list on the L-13 website.

"No, well, Bill is probably among the most prolific artists I know," explains Lowe. "But he does his own thing and doesn't always make it easy to follow, which is fine."

The KLF 2323 project is a fair distillation of what L-13 does: an impossible idea brought to life for fun with great panache, including some tangible product and an outside chance of maybe making some money. This is the kind of art world that Steve Lowe likes to be involved with, because, by and large, the art world is not at all for him.

While he was growing up, he hoped to be involved in either animals or art, with art winning out by the time he got to the end of school. He studied fine art at Byam Shaw in London, then went to Belfast to do an MA, but left just a month before finishing the course, having completely fallen out of love with art. "I didn't go to a gallery for maybe fifteen years after Belfast," he says.

He'd started a band with his girlfriend, alongside art school mate Adam Wood, and found playing live more exhilarating than "doing boring art for boring people." Looking back, he realizes that a contributing factor was that he'd been studying fine art for nearly five years, which was way too long: "I could've become a doctor in that time."

Playing in a series of "largely unlistenable" punk-influenced bands required him to make some kind of living, so he worked in a secondhand bookshop and dealt in rare books on the side. He had a flair for this and wound up with his own bookshop near Euston, on Woburn Walk. When he got a little extra space below the shop, he used it to house a collection of punk posters and whatnot.

After a cataclysmic breakup, he decided he needed to change

his life. He didn't want to grow old as a rare book dealer. So he and his business partner decided to open an exhibition space, just for a change of vehicle. They put on a show of Situationist stuff. After the show ended, the editor of *Art Monthly*, Andrew Wilson, asked Lowe if he had any plans for the space. Lowe did.

His business partner had recently befriended Billy Childish. He'd go down to Chatham and raid his bookshelf, acquiring copies of the first Hangman titles that Childish published with Tracey Emin and the like, and then flog them online. Lowe looked at what the books were being sold for, compared to what they'd been bought for, and he got in touch with Childish.

"You should be getting a bit more for these books," he told Billy.

To which Billy replied, "Well, do you want to help me sell these books of poetry we've published?"

Those were the last Hangman books that Childish published— three hardbacks in a case with a painted cover. Lowe took them on and did a good job of selling them. Billy was pleased.

Someone mentioned to Lowe that Billy also painted prolifically and an idea formed. Lowe says, "I hadn't really seen any of his paintings, but I was interested in his position in culture, as somebody on the margins of the mainstream, with a high degree of integrity and singular voice. To be honest, the painting was the thing I was the least interested in after the music and writing."

Now, Steve Lowe told Andrew Wilson that whatever exhibition he put on next, he wanted to avoid fine art. "Actually," he continued, "I'm thinking of putting on an exhibition with Billy Childish."

"Well, if you do an exhibition with Billy Childish you'll be avoiding fine art!" replied Wilson.

Years later, Wilson denied ever saying this to Lowe. "Billy's a wonderful artist," he insisted instead.

That first exhibition they put on of Billy Childish's work in 2003 was called *We're All Phonies*. This coincided with an article in the *Guardian* under the headline "Tracey Emin Stole My Ideas," and the release of a Buff Medways LP, *1914*, on Graham Coxon of Blur's Transcopic label, so the exhibition got a fair amount of attention.

Before it opened, Lowe told Childish that he didn't know anything about selling art, but he did know how to sell books, in particular items bundled together. So he suggested they make limited-edition prints, a 7" single, a chapbook of poetry, as well as a small-run box set of the stuff. Selling smaller items like this at an exhibition makes them more affordable, rather than shelling out for an expensive painting.

The tactic worked. "We sold lots of books, did really well with all the other stuff, and, actually, sold quite a lot of paintings, which Billy was very happy with, because at his last exhibition he hadn't sold a single picture."

Lowe remembers how dismissive a lot of people were of Childish's abilities and credentials as an artist during the exhibition. The *Evening Standard* critic present said that "one thing Childish will never be known for is his painting," while a friend from the music world suggested Childish was "a fucking nightmare to work with." Lowe resolutely refuted these criticisms, saying he'd always found Childish a delight and had no doubt he was an accomplished artist.

In reality, he wasn't very absorbed by Childish's paintings at that stage. "My mum paints and they reminded me of her expressionistic stuff," he recalls.

It was at this point that Lowe made an important decision about his future dealings with the art world: "People are very fixated on the product, the final thing. I decided at that point, *Well, if I'm going to have to work with artists, I'm not going to start making judgment calls on what they do, whether I like it or not; it's more to do with whether I think it's done with integrity and has some level of importance, whether to them or to other people—it's nothing to do with whether I like it.* I try not to get bogged down with personal preference."

This is the last thing you expect someone involved in working with artists to say, yet it is also entirely logical and probably good advice for anyone toiling alongside creators in any genre. It's like being a music A&R person in reverse: just help them do what they want—no creative insights, thanks. The musicians know what's best for themselves. As such, it's got a touch of the Billy Childish about its lopsided philosophy.

"He's much more fundamentalist in terms of what he thinks is good," says Lowe, considering this comparison. "He'll have a definite opinion on what is good and what is bad; I don't have that. I would say I'm less in love with art than Billy, I'm more anti-art than he is, but also a lot more forgiving of artists. Billy's so outspoken, too. I'm not. People get into trouble with Billy when they disagree with what he says and then think it's their job to convince him that their position is better than his. I always say he can have as much rope as he likes!"

The only two bits of advice Lowe ever gave Childish when they started working together was to avoid talking about the Stuckists "because they're a very limiting, negative energy," and not to mention Tracey Emin anymore. She already had enough attention without Billy adding to it. "Not sure how much of that last bit he took on," Lowe says.

Given that Lowe has not been Billy's secretary for the last twenty years, and he's definitely not his agent (though he does collect commissions), we try to work out how best to describe his professional relationship with Billy Childish. We eventually settle on *collaborator*, though he says neither of them are big on job titles.

He continues, "Billy's really charming, really loving, but he's a demanding person. Billy is the center of the universe, and if you work with him, you have to understand that your role is to do what Billy does, not for him to do what you do. I'm a good collaborator, I like working with people. It's weird, because I've got a towering ego, and so does he, but somehow the egos are different enough to get along without conflict."

One of their greatest collaborations started with a phone call from Billy to Steve.

"I want to do a poster," he told Lowe.

Okay, great, we'll do a poster.

"You're really going to like this: put *art* and then put *hate*," he instructed Lowe.

Lowe did this, then he added the Hangman gallows. "Now put *national* at the top," said Billy. Lowe added *national*. Lowe read it out: *national art hate*.

Childish: "Now put *week* at the bottom."

Suddenly, they had a "National Art Hate Week."

Oh, this is really good, thought Lowe. *Let's put the date in: 13th to 20th of July, 2009.*

Then Lowe said that if they were going to do a National Art Hate Week, they couldn't do just one poster, they'd have to do a whole series. So they did—they started making loads of posters, and the three other L-13 artists, Jimmy Cauty, Jamie Reid (best known for his designs of the Sex Pistols's records), and Adam Wood got involved in making them too. Soon, Billy thought it was getting a bit too satirical and silly—"mine and Adam's influence unfortunately"—so he brought it back to the border of what was acceptable and unacceptable. "That's when we did the Auschwitz signs and it got a little dark," says Lowe.

They put an Art Hate exhibition on at Cork Street Gallery in Mayfair, which included a *Jews Against Art* poster featuring a hung swastika with the Star of David . . . "I've got Jewish heritage," says Lowe. "I thought, *My God, I hope my mum doesn't see this.* And we also did the Artschwitz poster. Adam and I had done a campaign for the mayor of London, where we said, 'Bring back the smoke-stack.' With this, we turned the Tate back into a power station, powered by burning art. So that got adopted into Art Hate, and then it appeared on a poster behind the Auschwitz-style gates that Billy had come up with: *Art Brings Freedom*. Then Adam came up with the title *Artschwitz* and we pissed ourselves laughing about it, but very nervously."

One of the L-13 regulars came up to Lowe during the Cork Street show and said it was probably the most offensive thing he'd ever seen. Lowe replied that it's very difficult to have something that's not offensive when you're trying to be offensive.

He shrugs. "We're from that generation who thought it was our job to go out and really push people's buttons."

There isn't much art hate going on at the Carl Freedman Gallery in Margate, except perhaps from the artist whose opening it is.

It's July 1, 2023, and the hipster art world has put on its finery and jumped aboard a high-speed train toward the south coast for Billy Childish's *looking at paintings* show which runs here for the next two months.

Upon entry, each invitee is offered a two-page catalog, the front of which carries a poem by Childish:

**obaying
the
painting**

it
would
be
most pleasant
to
paint the paintings
i
like

but
instead
i
have
to
obay
the
silent
command
and
paint
the painting
i
paint

It's a bit of a scrum inside. Some people are chatting in the three rooms, others are looking at Billy's massive landscapes and portraits: paintings of himself, his wife, his daughter, lots of glistening cliffs and water, some horses, and one of Billy with June Hamper looking at a painting of him, shimmering with the hyper-realist, trippy feel of all his oil paintings.

The urge to rip one of these beautiful works of art from the wall and take it somewhere quiet to properly admire it is strong—but impossible to execute. It is a lovely collection, though openings are particularly bad occasions in which to look at the work they're showcasing.

Julie and Scout Hamper stand in a corner, appearing a little uncertain about where they should be putting their hands, as does Wolf Howard with his son. Childish, in a big white suit and white-brimmed hat, is trapped near the entrance by well-wishers and old friends, yet offers a handshake as I leave. There's a meal later for attendees but I'm here with my young son, so we make our excuses. As we leave, Tracey Emin arrives with a group of social outriders.

The next morning, Billy emails:

Date: 2 July, 2023
Subject: billy

---

hello ted
i hope your well
and show was okay

i find those things weird

i saw traci face to face 1st time in 5 years - she is pretty nuts
she's so off target

- the meal after was bizarre

over grown toddlers in suits and trainers
eating big sweet afters like a child party

I said to Julie - I'm so over what other people think is cool (never
a paying member in the 1st place)

X

A month later, he sends me another email on the subject of art and his breakthrough:

Date: 8 August, 2023
Subject: an important thort

I think a lot of people imagine I'm an outsider raging at the gates
all that happened in art is that it came to be that I was asked to
do what I already do - but 'in doors'.
music would have been the same if they allowed what I do to be
in their 'mainstream' but music is very snobby
with its attitude towards recording sound etc.
writing as well is very dominated by university graduates - all

well and good - but all of their bodies like you to be pushed thru
their sieve. Funny. I escaped that and got into
the elite art world - more fool them

billy

There's chance. And there's God's luck, of course. But sometimes, if you wait long enough, you do get just what your talent
truly deserves.

Childish Witness: Wolf Howard

Childhood Childish fan; music, painting, and poetry accomplice across three decades . . .

"I'm still in a few bands with Billy."

I became aware of Billy when I was at school. I was about fifteen, because my friend Dave Taylor's brother was in the Prisoners, James Taylor. I got to know about the local bands, including the Milkshakes with Billy and Mickey Hampshire. One day, I was walking across a place called Jackson's Field in Rochester and I saw Billy coming the other way. I happened to have a gig that evening with my band, the Daggermen; I was the drummer. So I went up to him and said, "My band's playing tonight and they're brilliant, you should come and watch them." And surprisingly enough, he came along. That would have been about 1984. I went to the MIC club a couple of times when the Milkshakes and Prisoners were playing around then, too.

I loved his music. When I was at school, David introduced me to the Milkshakes and Pop Rivets. We used to have gym class, and we were allowed to bring our own cassettes in to play while we bounced on the trampoline. I used to play the Pop Rivets, Milkshakes, and the Prisoners. We used to bounce to them.

The first time I played with Billy was some recording around his house. I did a track that was on a Headcoats album. We were going to do a band together. We went out one night and got really pissed, me, Billy, and John Barker, who was in the Daggermen. We were playing what we called "pussy pool," where you'd put the cue ball somewhere away from the table and smash it, trying to get it onto the table. Billy said he wanted to start a band with me on drums and John on bass called the Youngbloods. We said, "We can't, because we're both working all the time," which ironically was the only time in my life I've ever worked!

Then he went home and wrote the song called "Young Blood," which he put out with Thee Headcoats. The lyrics went "damn your fucking work / I want to be a Young Blood!"

We didn't do that band, but I drummed in Japan with Thee Headcoats when Bruce Brand couldn't go—and Italy. We didn't rehearse or anything first. I went down to a place and played a cassette of their stuff, tried to drum along, but I couldn't hear it, so I went out there thinking, *I've got to bluff it*. We took it in our stride, really. By that I mean we got pissed on sake—Billy didn't, but we did, me and [bassist] Johnny Johnson. We got away with it.

The first band I was in with Billy was the Buff Medways, which—I'd have to guess this, as well—was about 1999 or something? Billy was quite a fan of the Daggermen—well, he's not a fan of anything, but he liked the Daggermen—and so he thought he'd still like to do a band with me and John from the Daggermen. We even did do an EP called *A Tribute to the Daggermen*. Me and Billy were very good friends, very close back then.

All of a sudden, there was a bit of a buzz about the Buffs. Obviously, he's always had celebrities, rock stars, into his stuff, but it seemed to be quite a trendy thing. It was odd. You'd get people like Harry Potter [Daniel Radcliffe] saying he liked it. You know how recently Billy's been all about Bob Dylan? Well, when we started the Buffs it was all the Who. Billy had suddenly discovered the Who. Before then he used to take the piss out of us for liking mod bands. The Daggermen had done "A Quick One" by the Who, and he slagged that off. He even slagged it off in our album sleeve notes! Then we're doing that very song in the Buff Medways. One of those Billy rules that only he's allowed to break.

We went through a few lineups. It started with John on bass, but he had a couple of kids. We'd go to America and he'd be really churned up inside, missing them, which is completely understandable. John had a real job, and that, coupled with two little babies, I think was too much for him. So he left and then we got Graham Day in, another good friend of ours.

One day while we was doing a gig, I suddenly thought, *Oh yeah, these two, Graham and Billy, meant a lot to me when I was a teenager.* I really enjoyed it. I think Billy may have struggled with what he thought was Graham overplaying, but, you know, Graham needs to express himself, whatever instrument he's on, so he'll take on a lead role.

We all got on well. Graham was a fireman at the time. He would do what we'd call it his million-hour shifts: he'd say, "I'm not off work till next Thursday," and it's Monday or something. Then we started getting offered things like going to Australia, and Graham would say, "I can't do it because of work." We got to a point, "Well, this is what we do, we can't *not* do it because someone else is doing something different." Billy was too scared to phone Graham and tell him, so he emailed him. We changed the band name to not upset Graham. Then we started up the new band with Julie on bass, called it the Musicians of the British Empire. Technically a different band, but we've done the same songs since I started playing with Billy, so . . .

Obviously there's a million albums, but when it comes to a gig nowadays, Billy's like, "Oh, we should do this song off this album, this one, this one, this one, all these new ones." We go through rehearsing them and they're really difficult for us, because we're not that good at doing stuff off the cuff, picking it up quickly. I'm a bit better than them two, I think—but anyway, it comes closer to the gig and it's the classic thing of, "Oh, no, I think we'll do the normal stuff." One or two might sneak in over a five-year period, but generally it's the ones that we were doing in the original Buffs.

I'm still in a few bands with Billy. I'm in the Chatham Singers, CTMF too, and the William Loveday Intention. I don't think there's any others. I might be wrong.

They're all different. The Chatham Singers are a laid-back blues-type thing. I play with brushes every song, and maracas, all that. It's really toned down. Billy will be sitting down, Julie sits down, Jim [harp] sits down, and we play places like Medway

Little Theatre, because we can get away with just doing it more quietly. I don't even sweat onstage. CTMF are a full-on band, probably my favorite because I can go a bit mad. The William Loveday Intention haven't done any gigs. The main difference with the William Loveday is Jamie Taylor is on the organ, so it's studio based. When we record with that band, it's Billy on guitar and me drumming, then he'll do the bass, and when Jamie comes in to record the organ, I'm not even there. I think as Billy gets older, he says it's more respectable to do this laid-back stuff—he's doing the Singing Loins too, which is all seated. He just enjoys it more.

Our relationship has changed with time. When we started off, I was very much into his stuff. I really loved his art and his poetry and the bands he was in; he was way above me in that sense. I'd look forward to his books coming out. And then in the middle of it, we were together everywhere I went. Billy came with me to the pub all the time when my friends would all be there. Billy had stopped drinking, so I think it was handy for him go out with me. It felt safe.

But he wore my friends down with a lot of piss-taking. It's Billy's thing. We'd go round people's houses and he'd say to them, "Oh, this is fun, isn't it?" You know, he's so sarcastic. "This is fun, isn't it, all enjoying yourselves, are you?" After a while, they stopped inviting me, because they knew he'd come with me! I found it difficult over time. So things got a bit more distant.

Then it ended up that I pretty much just see him when we're recording or rehearsing or gigging. I always like to see him and we get on really well, it's just become more distant. And we have families. Back in the day, we didn't have much to do apart from whatever we wanted—of course, Billy's busy all the time, but he always seems to be able to be really busy and have time as well.

I'm not sure how many friends he has. He says himself that he hasn't any. He'd say to me, "I haven't got any friends," and I'd think, *Well, I'm one!* I do feel for him over this; people aren't going to phone him up and say, "Do you want to go out to do this or that?" I guess it would only have been me calling him back in the day. As I get older, I look at my group of friends and I can feel left out from them, too. My friends still all go on holiday together. I don't want to go, but then I feel bad if I'm not invited.

So, I'm sympathetic. But you do have to prepare yourself for a time with Billy, because it's going to be full-on. It just is. It's going to be piss-taking, and you can very often not be in the mood for that. It's hard to react badly to it, everyone laughs along with it, but I think quite often that people walk off, thinking, *Fuck that, I'm not doing that again!* There's a lot of that involved in it.

I don't want him to feel without friends. I care about him a lot. Me and my wife went round a couple of months ago, we had dinner with him and Julie, and actually got pissed and stoned. It was a great night. He does occasionally drink now. Sometimes they'll have brandy or whatever. I drink so much less than I used to, and when I do a gig, I'm very capable of getting much more pissed than I should be before going on. And neither Billy nor Julie are used to drinking.

There was one gig in France where we all went on pissed. It was one of my favorite gigs, actually. Billy was getting tons of things wrong, and it was just really funny. Someone afterward accused him of putting it on, because he couldn't tune the guitar and all that stuff; I said, "Believe me, he wasn't putting it on!" Another gig we did was Billy's birthday, and they brought on a glass of champagne for us each while we were playing. The woman put mine down next to the drums, and as she walked off, she tipped it over. I was gutted about that. Anyway, Billy had his one and then he turned round and said he'd been sick in his own mouth.

Julie is definitely good for his well-being. I mean, I don't know what it's like round there, but when I see them, they get on generally well, and, because of his recent breakdowns and stuff, she's his rock. I saw him having a breakdown in America recently; she says all the right things: "We won't do the gig, don't worry about it, everything's fine." I was sitting there, thinking, *Hold on, I need this money*—ha!—but he sorted himself out in time for the gig anyway. She gives him the space he needs.

I was one of the original Stuckists with Billy. We were in a bar somewhere, and Billy and Charles Thomson were talking about this art group, we'd be about figurative painting rather than the Brit Art thing—did I want to be in it? I said, "Yeah." It was probably 1998. I didn't pay much attention to it. I just go along with stuff. Then came the manifesto. I had a quick look through it; you know, normal Billy stuff. Then there was the first show in Shoreditch or wherever. That was really exciting; there was a buzz about that. My uncle went to it, he's rich and he bought up loads of paintings, he bought one of mine, 1,500 quid or something—you know, we had crazy prices because I didn't really know what was going to happen. It turned out that was the most successful one we had! I remember afterward Billy saying that my uncle should have bought one of his.

It was all quite a nice thing to be involved in, and we had group shows, but we had some strange people there, in the Stuckists. I was definitely against the conceptual stuff, you'd see it and go, *Oh, for fuck's sake, what a waste of time that is.* So I agreed with all the manifesto. But I had to leave in the end. I kept getting invites to go to the National Gallery dressed as a clown or hold up placards or whatever, and I never wanted to do that. Billy had long gone by this stage. I thought, *Well, what am I in it for?*

Charles said to me, "I want to donate paintings" to the National or the Tate Modern. He said, "They have to take them, apparently, and they might throw them in a skip or something, but they have to take them and then we can say we've given paintings to the gallery." I thought, *Well, a: I don't really want them just to go in the skip; b: I wouldn't feel that proud having one next to the other paintings, because I don't like them.*

I phoned Charles and he tried to talk me out of it, but I wouldn't have it. That was about 2006. I was in them for seven years or something. I'm still fond of them all and I'm happy to show with them. But I just carry on with my own paintings. Funnily enough, I did a painting the other day which is a bigger one—you know, like Billy's doing big ones—because I thought it might be a bit easier to paint big. Someone just coincidentally gave me a big old canvas that was made by the same people that make Billy's ones. That was really good fun. I was just getting it framed and then someone bought it, so that makes me want to buy bigger canvases.

I've been to both of Billy's shows that he's had at the Carl Freedman Gallery in Margate. I've been to his dockyard studio and I'm always impressed at the scale of it. It's brilliant, but even more so at the gallery. It's just that silence with this big old thing on the wall. My favorite was Julie swimming near a waterfall— just brilliant. And I loved the horse-sitting-down one.

His style seemed to me to change completely out of the blue. I don't know how that happened; I don't know how he suddenly got into the really big ones. A lot of the old style I really like, but this thing he does now on big canvas—for me, it's hit and miss. Some of them I think are really brilliant, and then there's others that are impressive, but I don't feel much more beyond that.

I feel bad, because he's given me six or more paintings over the years—I've only got two left. I remember, when people started selling them, thinking, *Oh, that's rotten.* I said to Billy, "That's rotten, isn't it? You should just keep them." Then I couldn't pay my rent a few years later, and, you know, I've got my son. I said to him, "I'm going to have to sell them," and he helped me, but I did feel bad. They were birthday presents. I wish I hadn't, but that's life, isn't it?

There certainly could be a day where he says he doesn't want to play music with me anymore. He has said that he wants to stop for a number of years. Things have changed for me in that respect, too. It used to be really exciting if a record turned up. They virtually mean nothing to me now. I go round Billy's, he goes, "This one's come out." I go, "Right, anyway . . ."—it's like that.

Gig-wise, we rehearse a lot more than we used to. We can do five or six rehearsals for one gig. I view that as staying fit. It's a workout where you don't feel like you're exercising, because it's fun. I used to hate rehearsing—as did Billy—but you adapt yourself.

A new thing for me is that my wife comes to most of the gigs now too. I was the one who would go to see bands but never took a girlfriend with me. I kept it all quite separate. Then when I met Kerry, she really wanted to come and be involved, and for the first time in my life, I wanted someone there. So that makes playing more enjoyable, because it can get difficult with Billy and Julie: they're a sarcastic, piss-taking machine. It helps for me to have somewhere else to go after the sound check. It's nice to have a break from them.

21.
Saucy Jack

Billy Childish has a fail-safe test he applies to people he thinks initially are all right. That test is: *Let's wait and see.*

What will this person be like when they start putting people on the trains? he always wonders. *They might seem okay, but what happens when they are given a cap, a list of Jews, and a train to fill? Will they put that hat on, before checking people off their clipboard and onto the trains, sighing, "Just doing my job, sorry"?*

"That's how I rate my friends," he says.

Consequently, when you first meet Billy Childish he is always very polite, quite cheeky and friendly, chatty, but nevertheless can appear a little standoffish as well. Like he's not entirely committed to you yet. He's just waiting to see.

When the White Stripes first came to London in August 2001, there was a huge buzz around Jack and Meg White's duo. The stars had aligned for them in a way they rarely do for unknown independent acts on their third album. After years and years of sludgy new-metal being served by the American rock music scene, suddenly the Strokes had released a couple of zippy, new wave, classic-sounding singles, played some packed dates, and, oh, what's this? There's this extremely photogenic blues-rock, garage-pop, brother-sister, husband-wife duo from Detroit, too? And they're coming over in August to play some dates to support their just-released third LP, *White Blood Cells*? Two unknown bands doing something different with a similar aesthetic adds up to an exciting scene, in music press terms.

White Blood Cells is a good album of theatrical blues-rock. It was reviewed enthusiastically and at length by the British music press, with features and cover stories planned by everyone from *NME* to the *Face*. The atmosphere around their London show on August 6, 2001, at the tiny Dirty Water Club in the Boston Arms, Tufnell Park—where Billy Childish and Thee Headcoats had a longtime residency—was hysterical. Normally, it was very easy indeed to just walk into the Dirty Water Club, wander up to the stage, and have a drink and a dance. The White Stripes's show sold out in advance and Kate Moss was on the guest list, which was unusual.

Booked well ahead of all the accompanying mania, the White Stripes's itinerary included staying on Bruce Brand's floor. They knew Brand through the network of international garage rock masons, and while he was at it, Brand also helped them get in touch with Liam Watson's Toe Rag Studios in Hackney, where Childish and co. sometimes recorded, so that the White Stripes could lay some music onto vintage tape, too.

Jack White must have been a knowledgeable fan of Billy Childish because, rather than asking him to support the White Stripes at the Dirty Water with the well-oiled and often raucous Headcoats or Headcoatees, he suggested that Childish perform a solo blues set. One for the connoisseur.

That sounds like a recipe for total disaster, thought Childish. *Playing a solo blues set to a room filled with wide-eyed* NME *kids rabid for the latest hot new band. Good, I'll do it.* He always loves a disaster.

"Luckily for me, the audience was very polite," he remembers. "They didn't know they were meant to ignore me."

While he was over doing local press and radio interviews, Jack White spoke enthusiastically to all about Billy Childish and his music. Big fan. When *Top of the Pops* asked the White Stripes to perform "Fell in Love with a Girl" live on TV, Jack White suggested to the BBC that they bring Billy Childish with them and that he'd paint onstage while they perform.

No way. You have got to be kidding. Forget it.

In protest, Jack White wrote *B Childish* in big letters on his forearm for the performance. "Who's Billy Childish?" people would ask Jack White. "Well . . ."

After Jack White got back to the US, he called up Billy and told him he'd like to have him perform with him on the *Late Show with David Letterman*.

Childish replied, "Well, that would depend on whose song we do—yours or mine."

"That didn't go down very well with Jack," he recalls.

One blowback from all this Jack White patronage was that US *GQ* decided they wanted to run a big profile of Billy Childish. That hadn't happened before. "It's an American-man magazine," explains Childish. "It was very big over there, apparently. The editor said he was a fan and this writer came and had a chat with me."

To help their readers along the path to Childish's work, *GQ* asked Eddie Vedder of Pearl Jam why he loved Billy Childish. "Eddie said some very nice things, comparing us to the Hollies or Buddy Holly, that type of thing," notes Billy. They also asked Jack White, who, perhaps smarting from the Letterman snub, replied, "I don't really know who he is."

It was obviously a joke. *GQ* didn't see the funny side, though, as they were kind of doing this big Billy Childish profile because Jack White had made such a fuss about him in the first place. So they asked Childish what he thought of the White Stripes and, as we have established already, Billy Childish cannot lie.

"I can't listen to that stuff," he told *GQ*. "They don't have a good sound . . . Jack's half into the sound and music, but then he wants to be a pop star as well, so you've got a big problem. We're aiming to close the fifteen feet between us and the audience; they're trying to expand it."

When the *GQ* article fell into the paws of a particular American man, he was extremely angry with what he read. So Jack White took to the Internet, as all avenging angels must. He wrote on the White Stripes's official website:

Billy Childish, Meg and I feel sorry for you. It must be lonely sitting in all of your garage rock bitterness Billy. You know children, when you take someone else's music and put your lyrics on top of it, it's still called plagiarism. Something Mister Childish hasn't learnt yet . . . By the way Billy, we didn't have to have you play with us, and we didn't have to mention you in interviews, we were just being polite in a foreign land. But you're welcome anyways. The bitter garage rocker . . .

Wow, thought Childish. *I must have annoyed him! He really doesn't know me.*

Billy picked up the phone to have a chat with Jack, reassure him it was just meant as good-knockabout fun. He wanted to apologize. When he called the number he had for him, he was told he could not speak to Jack White, nor should he ever call again.

So, instead, Billy also took to the Internet:

Though I have undoubtedly angered Jack White, I think it's a bit nasty of him to accuse me of plagiarism merely because his former admiration of my work was not reciprocated. It all smacks of jealousy to me. I have a bigger collection of hats, a better moustache, a more blistering guitar sound and a fully developed sense of humour. The only thing I can't understand is why I'm not rich. Yours sincerely, Billy Childish.

PS. I always stay well within the music industry recommended guideline of never plagiarising more than 50% of my material. But no matter who my influence may be, I would never stoop so low as to rip off Led Zeppelin.
PPS. I hope I've gone and offended Led Zeppelin now.

It might have been different in a boxing ring, but Jack White was never going to beat Billy Childish in a roast: too many hours in the back of vans touring with the Milkshakes, Mighty Caesars, Headcoats, and Headcoatees. That Medway needle is sharp as a filleting knife.

That's the end of that, thought Billy Childish. And it was, nearly.

Then, many years later, Childish awoke to a flashing light on his answering machine: "Jack had rung up in the middle of the night and left a very drunken, apologetic message."

Childish asked Ian Ballard at his label Damaged Goods to find out if it would be okay to release it as a 45 single. Ian didn't hear back.

Childish decided to call up Jack White himself, tell him it was all water under the bridge now, there was nothing to apologize for: "As you know, I like to be everyone's friend."

Once again, he was told Jack was not available to speak to him and he shouldn't call this number ever again. So that really was that.

Billy had waited, and then he saw.

A Song For Kylie Minogue

People think they know me but they don't know me
People think they know me but what do they know?
People think it's certain but it's uncertain
The only thing that's certain is I just don't know
I just don't know

Here's a song for Kurt Cobain
They asked if I'd ever met the man
I said I'm not really sure did he have blond hair
And they look at me like I don't even care
But I'd have been happy just to say hello
Is it really my fault that I just don't know
I just don't know

To Ease My Troubled Mind

Here's a song for Kylie Minogue
She's only tiny, so I've been told
She rang me up—she's quite polite
And I'm polite too so we got on all rite
She asked if she could use my poetry
I said help yourself girl—it's all for free
It's all for free

Here's a song for that strange boy Beck
the strangest one that I've met yet
He said he dug my sound would I call him in LA
I said as long as I do the singing and you just play
So I dialed him up on his scribbled number
a voice on the other end sounded like thunder
Where did you get this number?!
Where did you get this number?!

People think I'm bitter but I ain't bitter
People think I hate but that just isn't rite
I just don't dig the sounds but this I've found
If you say what you don't like it end up in a fight
You'll end up in a fight
Yeah, you'll end up in a fight

People think they know me but they don't know me
People think they know me but what do they know
People think it's certain but it's uncertain
The only thing that's certain is they just don't know
They just don't know

   Billy Childish for CTMF (2016)

Billy and Sheila, 1984
Woodcut print

Stood at the end of the bed, 1984
Woodcut print

Self-portrait, 1984
Woodcut print

Man with guitar, 1993
Woodcut print

man being devoured by the snakes of his, 1992
Woodcut print

Despair, 1985
Woodcut from Oakwood Hospital series
Initialled *BH* for *Bill Hamper*

Kyra, 1993
Woodcut print

Red squirrel, 2003
Woodcut print

gallows hart, 1994
Woodcut print

Self-portrait with spotted hank, 2006
Woodcut print

Juju with Braids, 2006
Woodcut print

Hangman Books shop poster,
circa 1984
Woodcut print

*BLACK THINGS HIDDEN
IN DUST,* Phyroid Press,
1982

Monks Without God, 1986
Woodcut print for
book cover

*Poems to break the harts
of impossible princesses,*
Hangman Books, 1994

Tear life to pieces, 1985
Woodcut print for
book cover

will the circle be unbroken,
Hangman Books,
1983

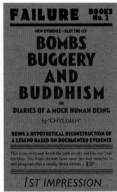

*THE IDIOCY OF
IDEARS,*
the Aquarium L-13,
2007

*Where the Tiger Prowls
Striped and Unseen,*
the Aquarium L-13,
2008

*BOMBS BUGGERY
AND BUDDHISM,*
L-13 Press,
2010

Hand-stamped book
cover, 2008
Collection of poetry
under the name
Charles Hangman

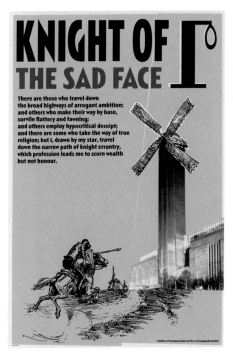

British Art Resistance Placard, 2008
Sign painting on board
91.5 x 61 cm

National Art Hate Week Placard, 2009
Sign painting on board
90 x 65 cm

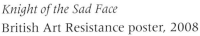

Knight of the Sad Face
British Art Resistance poster, 2008

National Art Hate Week field poster:
Program of Events, 2009
Distressed print on paper with collage
elements and rubber stamps

Artschwitz Tate Death Camp, 2010
The worst ART HATE field poster ever
Distressed print on paper with collage
elements and rubber stamps

I'd Rather You Lied, 1983
Oil on hardboard
122 x 61 cm

drunk, 1998
Oil on canvas
91.5 x 61 cm

Holding Huddie, 2001
Oil and charcoal on linen
122 x 91.5 cm

Man Stood on Rock, 2008
Oil and charcoal on linen
35 x 25 cm

FAR LEFT
The Offense, 1984
Oil on hardboard
60 x 40 cm

ABOVE LEFT
hangman gallows,
2003
Oil on nailed
timber with wire
42 x 31 cm

LEFT
St John's Church,
2005
Oil and charcoal
on linen
91.5 x 61 cm

neck twister, 2007
Oil and charcoal on linen
122 x 61 cm

girl with plaits, 2007
Oil and charcoal on linen
122 x 61 cm

LEFT
self-portrait with wife, 2013
Oil and charcoal on linen
122 x 91.5 cm

BELOW
in the frozen meadow, 2013
Oil and charcoal on linen
275 x 183 cm

RIGHT
man with jackdaw, 2017
Oil and charcoal on linen
152.5 x 122 cm

BELOW RIGHT
the artist and his mother, 2020
Oil and charcoal on linen
183 x 122 cm

walker, 2023
Oil and charcoal on linen
91 x 91 cm

mt tahoma, 2023
Oil and charcoal on linen
275 x 366 cm

22.

Demons

People think they know him, but what do they know?

According to two of Billy Childish's oldest friends, Keith Gulvin and Steve "Button Nose" Simmons, he's more or less identical in temperament and attitude to the Steven Hamper they grew up with, larking about as teenagers on archaeological digs or milk trains; you would have to interrogate both Keith and Steve for a very long time under the harshest conditions to squeeze out a bad word about Childish from either.

Then there are the exasperated former close music colleagues from the 1980s through the early aughts who knew him when Childish was a daft bigmouth, someone, as he'd jokingly describe the fame-hungry, "who would go far with that ambition for success" if only he was any good at one thing; they have now watched as that ambition in recent times has been realized tangibly with the kind of commercial appreciation and critical recognition that convinces people to write books about you. It's been suggested by some of them that he's playing the role of "Billy Childish," but they've got his number.

There are the former lovers and partners, for whom he will always be preserved in the outrageously dramatic, often shocking arc of each romance. These witnesses can't really conceive of him as he is now: midsixties, happily married and living in a commanding house at the top of the hill, empathetic, eccentric, solvent, wildly creative, open, honest, gentle, and sometimes quite fragile; a demanding man in many ways but never needy, always able to laugh at himself. That's the character that those who orbit him closely today describe; and his main collaborators in this modern era of being Childish are loyal for good reason. He brings warmth, even if he requires emotional commitment (and time) in return.

People think they know him, but what do they know?

Billy Childish doesn't watch TV. He doesn't go to the cinema. You won't find him at a football game, or a cricket match. He doesn't play golf or tennis. He's not a collector of vinyl (or stamps), and he's never paid any attention to what's in the charts. The only time he listens to the radio is if he puts on Radio 3 when painting on Mondays.

Instead, he's been on a long quest to feel better, to heal, and to know himself properly. He's taken a lot of spiritual expeditions in his spare time—which is quite often the same as his work time. These have included, but are not limited to:

TAOISM: which he studied under his own steam while a student at Walderslade Secondary Modern for Boys, where he also experimented with macrobiotic diets, neither of which were typical choices for a B-stream student there in the early seventies. "I took a lot of that Taoism into punk rock," remembers Childish. "I sent Johnny Rotten a letter once via Glitterbest [Malcolm McLaren's Sex Pistols management company] with a recommendation to use a verse out of the *Tao Te Ching* in a song, and I got a reply back from a minion saying it was hippie rubbish—which seemed a bit unfair!"

VIPASSANA MEDITATION: "These are ten-day silent retreats: a really big turnaround for me. I was very interested in Vipassana after I read a book on it, and then a friend of mine found out that they did Vipassana around the world. So I felt compelled to have a go. It's very straightforward: ten days, ten hours of silent meditation each day, no eye contact, no eating after noon. There's instruction but you can't be a member, which I like."

BUDDHISM: "I used to go to the Western Buddhist Order, and they're a real number, those guys." [The reputation of Sangharak-shita, founder of Triratna Buddhist Community (formerly the Friends of the Western Buddhist Order), became mired in grisly allegations of sexual abuse and coercion after his death in 2019.] "Meetings were held in an old drinking den of mine in Rochester, a hotel. You can get some meditation and teaching there, but the spiritual materialism and the elevation of gurus is not what I'm looking for, in the same way I'm not looking to elevate people into pop stars. The only people who require a guru are people who think they're not good enough, that they need someone else above them. I formed a thing called the Friends of the Enemies of the Western Buddhist Order in response. Western Buddhist Order are such a drag. They all have Buddhist names they're given when inducted, so I copied that in the Friends of the Enemies of the Western Buddhist Order—I was Venereal Itchy Scrotum, Wolf [Howard] was Mighty Boulder, my friend Steve was Welsh Wind Bag Primus, his brother was Welsh Wind Bag Secundus, Julie was Punk Rock Is Knock Knock, a Norwegian lad I know was Bjorn Yesterday, Kyra was Toy Gun Grandma . . ."

VEDANTA: "If you look up Vedanta on Wikipedia, it's described as a philosophy, but true Vedanta is just about the truth. It's awareness revealed in the minds of men. It's older than Buddhism and very plain-speaking. What I really like about it is that you can't become a member. Everything is taught by scripture. Its main argument is, *You're perfectly all right: we'll prove it.* It's a long, long process to prove it, but essentially it's that there's only one thing here and that's awareness. But you want the true Vedanta; get the wrong bit and you're in trouble, like getting the wrong bit of Christianity. There's a guy called Dayananda [Saraswati], he wrote a book called *The Value of Values.* That's a good place to start."

* * *

There was a moment a few years ago, just before the turn of the new decade, when Billy Childish was not perfectly all right, of course. He had a nervous breakdown, maybe more than one. He thinks it was sparked initially by the suicide of his friend's brother, "Welsh Wind Bag Secundus," the day before. It was, he says, "very bad." Those who witnessed it agree.

"I started getting these involuntary movements and high, high anxiety. Weeping. Unable to communicate and insane pacing, like totally hyper." He shakes his head and repeats himself, still shocked at the memory. "Totally hyper."

He continues, "I had a few bouts and then Julie got me up the hospital. I was put on quite strong serotonin-uptake inhibitors, but I didn't like how they made me feel."

Within a month or so, he started weaning himself off the drugs, which was not recommended. Normally, it should be a gradual process of reducing the dose over a couple of years, he says. Instead, he tried hypnotherapy, cognitive therapy, and "naturals," but he had several episodes subsequently and then another much more serious relapse, which required him to briefly renew his acquaintance with the prescribed drugs—but he once again came off them quickly. Subsequently, he's relied on various other therapies to keep moving forward.

Having had the breakdown, though, he lives with a new wariness. "I obviously experienced things that were similar to the breakdown earlier in my life, but didn't know then where it led. Now I have a fear of the click when it happens fully, because I have felt it . . . but I know too that you come through it."

One of the biggest tests during the breakdown for him and his wife involved not alarming their daughter Scout. "Huddie saw me in the middle of it, when I was making these weird involuntary movements, and I imagine that was upsetting," Billy says, but Scout was kept in the dark about specifics of her dad's illness, which, for someone like Billy Childish who does not believe there should be any family secrets, was a stress in itself.

Childish has undertaken several years of intense psychotherapy, but postbreakdown, the most regular form of therapy he experiences other than yoga is transformational breathwork, which he undertakes each week with therapist Rachael Hudson.

"It works very much on a physical level," Hudson explains by Zoom. "It works on a mental, emotional level, and for some people it also works on a very spiritual level, because it connects us to pure life force, which is our breath."

Speaking with Hudson, who is understandably hamstrung by client-confidentiality issues as to exactly how much she can say, it's clear that she gets as much out of working with Childish as he might get from her. She knows the modern Billy Childish: "I adore him. I love his energy. I love his unrelenting unwillingness to filter his life, and . . . if I'm allowed to say these things, I enjoy the element of him who chooses to live life on his terms. I enjoy that he controls his narrative. I know nothing about him that he doesn't want me to know about him."

We talk about the need or desire that Billy Childish has to let the world hear everything about himself; that as soon as you first meet him, he's right in there with some eye-opening personal revelation—rather than, say, a conversation about the weather or the English cricket team.

"My perspective," she says in vague agreement, "is that he might well want to get the most shockable things about him out in the very early days, to ascertain if you're big enough to see him for who he is." He likes to wait and see, as we know. Hudson thinks once he's accepted you, that wait is worth it.

"I think he's a very unique human being," she says. "I don't think he processes the world in the same way as a lot of people do, and that's original, it's refreshing, it's needed, and it's brutal at times; but there's also this sense of love that comes from him toward life and toward those he values, who are special to him. I really love the way that he speaks of those in his life who he loves."

I wonder if she can describe what specific response her breath-work with Billy produces. She can't, of course. But she does say this instead: "Some people report—myself included—experiencing a kind of bliss-like connection to an energy that is greater. I, for instance, have heard people describe their experience with ayahuasca, and that sounds very similar to something I've experienced through the breath. The only drug is the life force of the breath, though."

This is interesting, because in 2009 Childish went on two ayahuasca retreats. They were significant. He'd never taken LSD previously "because nobody offered it," so he didn't have any frame of reference for the hallucinatory experience at the core of ayahuasca: "I've never done hard drugs, but all these other people there doing ayahuasca were space cadets!"

He found the experience intense and, in some respects, life-changing. "I saw some very dark stuff and some very light stuff. It's probably a fifty-fifty split, but the dark stuff was very dark indeed."

The most intense visions he had on the ayahuasca trip were demonic; that is to say, he saw demons.

"I've seen flesh-and-blood demons," he says seriously. "In ayahuasca it's very easy to discern what's in the mind and what's in front of you, concrete. I saw a demon as close and as clear as you are." Childish puts his hand across his kitchen table, and with that the air sucks from the room. "Seeing demons was very impressive, but they were mundane and not scary. They were sort of sad and dark. And I do know a lady who could see demons regularly on the street, she could see them in bars, and they sit in people's energy field, drinking off people . . ."

Once you've seen demons, he says, you sense them. They're everywhere, he thinks. He feels them at certain gigs, and sometimes he feels it most acutely when people step toward him before or after a show, trying "to absorb something from me."

And yet he was surprised that the demons appeared so clichéd. "I was looking at one, thinking, *I'm prepared to believe that there's demons, but I'm not prepared to believe they look like demons out of a fucking Middle Ages manuscript!*"

He continues, "Then I realized, *Well, why not?* How would this energy manifest itself and why would it look any different to me?"

One day, a couple of weeks after his ayahuasca retreat, Childish was at L-13 in Clerkenwell where Adam Wood (who paints collaboratively with Steve Lowe as Harry Adams) was working on a reproduction of a painting from the Middle Ages. In the corner, there was a little demon with a pitchfork.

"God, they've got that exactly right," said Childish, out loud to himself.

"What?" replied Wood.

"Oh, nothing," muttered Childish, closing the conversation.

"Apart from to Julie, for about seven or eight years I didn't tell anyone about the demons," he admits now. "Nobody outside my closest friends know about it now, so it's a bit weird that I'm telling *you*."

The most significant spiritual interlude Billy Childish has experienced, however, was not that demon-infested ayahuasca trip. It was the vision quest he went on in a California desert in October 1999.

At the time, he was at a crossroads, physically, spiritually, and emotionally. He had split with Kyra although she was pregnant with Huddie. His relationship with Holly Golightly was also ruptured, and Thee Headcoats were breaking up too.

Childish was due in Las Vegas to play a gig with a specially reformed Mighty Caesars, but given all the unresolved chaos in his life, he decided he'd arrive there earlier to try to seek some kind of order in his life through a vision quest.

"It's an American Indian spiritual quest for direction in your life," he says. "You get guidance from the other side. It involves a certain amount of fasting, a sweat lodge, and then going out into the wilderness alone without eating." Billy bats away any suggestion that this sounds intimidating, dangerous even. "My stuff was really lightweight. Some people build it up over years and years; they can do lots more fasting and alone time."

Before he went out into the desert, he got in touch with a woman from Seattle he'd met on tour there a couple of years earlier. She'd come to see him play subsequently in her hometown on that last Headcoats tour, but he'd largely ignored her due to the fact that he had enough drama going on with Kyra and Holly at that precise moment. Now he called her to apologize and explain his situation.

After his vision quest had ended, Childish stood on the nearby dirt-track crossroad, and he waited. He'd given out precise details, so he had faith. He took out a flute he had on him and started playing it, walking up and down in his baggy canvas army shorts and white vest, tooting away.

Eventually he made out a dust cloud approaching through the heat haze. From within it, a car emerged. He lifted up the sign he'd made above his head, and grinned.

THIS WAY! read the sign. *JULIE! THIS WAY!*

23.
Nurse Julie

After Billy got into Julie's car, they drove. She'd already made one long drive across California to pick him up, but now they embarked on an epic journey in the opposite direction. They drove to Route 101, then alongside the Pacific coast, heading north from Southern California. Time was on their side, so they spoke at length without interruption.

In truth, this was their first real opportunity to do so alone.

A couple of years earlier, in 1997, Julie had come to see Thee Headcoats play in Seattle with her boyfriend at that time. Afterward, Billy had approached her. "He was incredibly handsome and very charismatic," she recalls, "so I was quite pleased."

They swapped addresses and went their separate ways. Over time, she'd receive records and books from him in the mail, and she'd write back. She was in the Stuck-Ups, a punky new wave band she played drums for, but it was a hobby more than anything. She worked at Amazon. She wasn't music mad like some of her friends, one of whom was a bit of a Billy Childish nut who got her into his back catalog.

When Billy said he was coming back to Seattle on tour with the Headcoats and Headcoatees, Julie was pleased. She was single now, so she was looking forward to seeing Billy Childish in this new light. However, the night was a great disappointment: he was preoccupied and distant. "He pretty much ignored me, but I was like, *Que sera, sera!*"

Then he called, explained in basic terms the bind he found himself in and why she should drive out to meet him at the vision quest at the opposite end of California. Almost without thinking, Julie booked time off work and drove down, stopping to see her family en route. When she got to their home, she told her dad, "Yeah, I'm on my way to the desert to meet this guy who's unlike anyone I've ever met. I'm going to pick him up and then drive back home to Seattle with him . . ."

"They were like, 'You're going to do WHAT?!'" she says now, laughing at the impetuousness of it. But she felt madly compelled to do so.

Julie drove them first to the poet Robinson Jeffers's famous home, Tor House, on the coast in Carmel, California, and then up to see the mighty redwoods, stopping in motels along the way. As they drove, they spoke. Billy Childish told Julie Winn everything. And then Julie Winn told Billy Childish everything.

"By the time we got out in Seattle, it was, *Okay, I think this is going to be a thing*," says Julie, with deadpan understatement.

"When she picks me up from the vision quest, that's it," confirms Billy. "That's love."

Thee Mighty Caesars played in Las Vegas a few days later and Julie followed Childish down there. "I remember meeting her," says drummer Graham Day, "and thinking, *Hmm, not Billy's normal type! Bit more of a rocker.* But she seemed nice."

The pair further solidified their new love affair in Vegas, hanging out with the Caesars and some of Julie's friends, who'd traveled along to hang out and probably run the rule over this dude. Yet in the back of both Julie's and Billy's minds, a clock ticked ominously.

"When he left, I was crying at the airport—like in some crummy movie," says Julie. "I was so gutted, just standing there, like, *Oh my God, what just happened?!*"

And more to the point, what would happen next?

While I wait for Julie Hamper to make it downstairs to the kitchen to fill in the gaps, I sit chatting with her husband. Unusually, Billy

Childish is a little tongue-tied when talking about Julie. "It's very difficult to characterize our relationship. I mean, like, she's the girl for me!" He has a think about what she's like. She loves ballet, she's been doing a lot of that recently. She really enjoys watching sports, particularly rugby, snooker, and tennis. She knits from time to time. He scratches his head. "She's a bit of a lone wolf." He offers an example.

Julie plays bass in CTMF, the band Childish fronts with Wolf Howard on drums. Childish used to badger Julie to write some songs for them. She was unconvinced: what would she write about? Billy suggested her brother, her mother, some mean old boyfriend. Oh, okay, she said. She then wrote and sang two lovely songs that bookend 2019's *Last Punk Standing*: "It Hurts Me Still" and "The Used to Be."

When the album was released, several of Childish's music friends told him how much they liked her songs. "You should let her do more," they said.

"She's only written those songs because I made her," he replied.

"Oh, it's the man behind the woman again, is it?"

Childish rolls his eyes now. "No, it's that JuJu doesn't think writing songs is important or adds value to her. I guess that's one thing that's very similar in us: I don't care what job you do or who the fuck you think you are. You could say that for Julie too."

The other thing they have in common is that Julie was certain after Billy left the States in 1999 that they would stay together, even though his ex-partner was due to give birth to his son two months later in a different country on the other side of the Atlantic Ocean.

They spoke on the phone often. Then, in January 2000, a month after Huddie was born, Julie came over to England to meet him (and Kyra). Afterward, she returned home to Seattle. She and Billy attempted to have a long-distance relationship by phone. It was not a hugely satisfactory state of affairs for either of them. So Julie tried to explore the possibility of Amazon relocating her, perhaps to England. Not going to happen.

Billy came over to visit her. Julie came over to visit him twice. On one of these visits, they decided to get married, because if they didn't, the relationship would probably fizzle out. They wanted instead to cement things.

In September 2000, Billy and Julie married in Madrona Park, on the shore of Lake Washington in Seattle. Julie wore a 1930s dress and Billy grabbed a secondhand suit from a shop the day before. Billy's friend Johnny Brewton from the small press X-Ray Books was the best man.

Then Billy returned to Chatham and Julie stayed in California, where she continued to work at Amazon until her prayers were finally answered and, in January 2001, she was let go from her job. She spent the next few months propped up by her severance pay, playing with the Stuck-Ups—for whom Childish would produce their eponymous debut album later that year—and practicing her ballet, "doing my own thing." She visited her family for a while and then, in June 2001, she flew from San Francisco to England to live with her husband happily ever after—release the white doves into the sky, play the closing-credits music as they smooch in a disappearing heart-shaped logo . . .

"I'd never had that level of stability before," she says now. "He had a house, he knew what he wanted to do, and was on this path. He was offering me this huge amount of love, interest, excitement, creativity . . ." She raises a shoulder nonchalantly, which is how she describes most things, good or bad. "So it was very nice."

It was very nice, but it was also very complicated. For the first month, she felt unreal, like being an explorer on a gap year, because, despite whatever the Medway Council would like to tell tourists, Chatham has very little in common with Northern California. "My friends and family were all saying, 'If you want to come back, just say because we'll help you, we'll sort it out.'"

There were environmental-adjustment issues to overcome, but there was also a more significant emotional hurdle. "I had to navigate an ex-partner and a small child." She shrugs. "There was a lot going on at the time."

When she'd previously visited or he came to see her, Julie could be a separate presence in this new family dynamic. She could also be an understanding voice on the phone. Now she was a permanent part of the equation.

"I don't think Billy really expected how much love he would feel for his child, and then have a new partner arrive. A lot of that time, I was trying to negotiate with the fact that, *Okay, so I know that this person is now number one and I'm not* not *number one, but I'm not the main focus here.*" It was a challenge, but Huddie lived with Kyra, and so, while Julie knew it was a priority for her to be a part of Huddie's life, "It wasn't hard graft on my behalf."

"The only thing I had to do," she says, "was to check my ego a little bit. And I liked Kyra."

Before she'd even come to live in the UK, Billy had been very clear that if she was going to be part of his life, she'd have to meet Kyra, meet Huddie, and make a leap into this new family dynamic. It was this or nothing, which she understood and accepted.

She met Kyra alone for lunch initially, which was a bit weird for both of them, but they got over that. After all, Julie was not a reason for the breakup so there was no need for friction. She explains, "I could feel empathy for Kyra's situation and I realized that whatever I was struggling with, her world had shifted monumentally. So I tried to be supportive but not too . . ." She pauses to laugh. "Trying to just be a balance, like, 'I can be your friend, but you and I both know that there's this thing in between us, so I can come as close as I can and try to help as much as possible.'"

If it hadn't been for Huddie, Billy imagines he may have moved to America to be with Julie, but that was out of the question. "Huddie's known Julie all his life," he says. "Julie's nickname

JuJu comes from him lying in bed with Kyra, going 'JuJu' about Julie."

As is typical, Billy suggested that Julie and Kyra form a group together, so they did: the A-Lines. Julie learned to play guitar and Kyra sang. They were, of course, a garage rock band who played quite a few gigs and put out an album. It was good fun. "We've had times of being close, but family dynamics shift all the time," considers Julie. "Generally, we get along fine. It was important that they had a good situation for their kid."

Two of the greatest songs in Billy Childish's catalog—two definite top ten hits in another universe—were actually written and sung by Julie Hamper: 2019's "It Hurts Me Now" and 2023's "Traces of You." They are both filled to the brim with a resigned, precise melancholia, and to know where they come from tells you something fundamental about Julie Hamper.

Unlike Childish, Julie did not grow up in a house filled with painters. "My father was in the military for twenty-five years," she says. "I grew up on air force bases and then, because my parents are interracial, when he retired we moved to California, because that's where they felt that they'd probably be most welcome."

Her dad became a postman, a job he had for forty years, while her mother, previously a housewife, became a nurse. "We would have all those sixties and seventies records playing, which I liked, but we were really, really not a creative family. I was not going to art galleries. I was a party girl. I wouldn't have even thought that a life could be creative . . ." She raises an eyebrow. "I think Billy finds my lack of interest in art or poetry vaguely amusing, because I do not give a shit." He has tried to encourage her creativity, "but it's not my thing. I don't have the drive to sit and do it."

When Billy suggested that she write a song about her mother or brother, however, he located the impetus in her.

"I still have some of the issues that I arrived with, but I have matured quite a lot here." She pauses. "I was thirty-three when

I got to England, but in reality I was kind of preserved in my early twenties because I lost my mother in a car accident then." Naturally, this event was devastating. "That really trapped me in a particular space. My family life dissolved after that and I must have had ten years of PTSD. I think the stability that I found here with Billy, who is a very mature and thoughtful person, allowed me the time to grow up. It helped a lot."

You can hear the enduring agony of this, the attempt to reach out through the dimensions to her mother, on the paisley-infused melancholia of "Traces of You," arguably the most melodically beautiful and moving song Billy Childish has been involved in recording.

She says that her mother's sudden death still reverberates through her every step, much as the song declares. "It's probably the defining moment of my life, and the most challenging thing I've ever experienced."

It has a rival, however. Shortly before Billy's breakdown in 2018, Julie's brother committed suicide—an event that Childish cites as a contributing factor in his own collapse. She says, "My brother killing himself had a huge, powerful impact on me, but it was a different thing to my mother. My brother was sixty-five, so I spent a lot of time thinking about him at that age, where he was at, you know."

You can hear the ache of her sadness and guilt at this event in "It Hurts Me Still," which opens with these lines: "I can't lie, it took me by surprise / I didn't see it hiding, in your eyes / I can't figure it out, no matter how I try . . ." The whole song is a hazy, tear-stained reflection of all the unanswerable questions loved ones of suicides are left with. "It hurts me still, and I don't know why . . ."

Then, in the depths of her mourning, Billy's mind went. "Billy's nervous breakdown was definitely the hardest thing we've been through. It coincided very much with my brother's suicide and was . . . very tough. Our relationship is always at its best when

Billy is a big, strong, powerful figure. So when he's not—and he wasn't for that year, obviously—then we struggle."

Even now, she says, the reverberations from his breakdown remain. "He tries really hard to mitigate, the best he can. He'll go, 'My mind's going.' So I tell him it's going to be okay because he's been here before and we work through it best we can."

Julie has a hunch about where Billy's anxiety comes from. "His mother was a real worrier, just an anxiety bomb, and that's an unfortunate gift that she left him with. I can see his mom in it very much."

Julie's relationship with June Hamper was, she says, complicated. "I have had many times not liking his mother at all," she admits. "She was a nice little old lady, but I didn't really like her that much. I mean, I could deal with her, but I didn't like her as Billy's mother."

This seems key to how Julie feels about people in Billy's orbit generally. She's protective of him. *Are these people good for Billy?* is an instinctive test she has.

She continues, "June was a very damaged person. So I could put up with her, and I liked her enough so we could get along one Sunday a week."

Despite being married to Billy for twenty-three years and bearing him a daughter who is now a teenager, Julie Hamper has only met John Hamper twice. "I don't think he said hardly anything to me. The only members of Billy's family I like are his nephew Sam and his half brother Hugo. But June . . . I didn't understand where she was coming from as a mother—"

Billy walks back into the kitchen. "What?" he asks.

"You're not supposed to be in here," replies Julie with a chuckle. "He just asked me about your family." She rolls her eyes.

"I took Julie to meet my father when Huddie was really young, and I brought my nephew along who was seven or eight, so he could meet him," recalls Billy. "John was asking about what we'd done, and when he heard the words 'Las Vegas,' he told this story of how he was asked to go paint one of those big casinos in the sixties when we were kids, and he said to us, 'Don't make the mistake I did!' Which meant don't make the mistake of not going. So typical, the exact opposite of what any parent would say, telling us to leave Huddie and move to the States . . ."

Billy says that his father didn't talk to his nephew throughout the meeting or look at Huddie. "He's a real strange boy," Billy says of John.

He nods and leaves the kitchen again. After he is gone, we pull up the hood on their relationship for a final time, take a look at how it's running nowadays. Billy Childish certainly seems to be a gentler person than he was twenty years ago. His wife should take some credit for that evolution, surely.

"Maybe," she says hesitantly. "We shifted into a family, with a kid; that's a major softening agent in Billy's life. You know, and age."

All relationships are hard, of course; they all take work.

"Our relationship has evolved," she agrees. "But the one thing that hasn't changed is he's a person who's really involved in his spiritual life, and he's had a deepening of his spiritual life. He's someone who is constantly working to understand himself better. In your life, you go from a place of *What's wrong? How do I fix it?* to *Oh, this is wrong, but I guess I'm just going to mitigate it*. He's always working on understanding that. His creative life is a big exploration of his inner life, trying to understand it and sort of express it and release it . . ."

All of which, she says, means this: "I think he's softer but I'm not going to put my hand up and say, 'Well, it's because of me!'"

It probably is, though, let's face it.

A little later, Billy comes back to the kitchen to embark upon a new interrogation. Julie is off to ballet practice soon. As she busies herself, getting her stuff together, I notice that over Billy's shoulder there are some fancy bottles of booze on a shelf—brandy and wine. Maybe the top of a champagne bottle. I ask how come they have alcohol on display if Billy's an alcoholic. Julie laughs quietly to herself.

"About twenty years ago," says Billy, "we had a bottle of very expensive champagne given and I shared it with Julie."

And you were able to do so?

"Yes."

I guess, I say, a one-off experiment for a special event is to be expected.

"Oh," said Julie, "he had a glass of wine last night with dinner. He occasionally has a drink if we have people over to eat, a glass of wine or something."

Can alcoholics do that, I wonder, have the occasional social drink?

"I didn't touch a drop for eighteen years," says Billy. "But now, with JuJu, I might do sometimes."

So now he can enjoy a glass of good red wine, or a nightcap of brandy, if he's with his wife or close friends, at home over dinner, or perhaps on holiday, and then not touch a drop for weeks?

"Yeah." He can drink in moderation socially. "I seem to, yeah."

I glance over at Julie, who has a wry little smile on her face as she leaves the room.

And there, at least, we have one tangible example of how being married to Julie Hamper has eased Billy Childish's troubled mind.

24.
Damaged Tangerine

Along with Steve Lowe at L-13 representing his art world dealings, Billy Childish works principally with two other people on his enormous creative output: Ian Ballard of Damaged Goods handles the bulk of his music releases, while Michael Curran of Tangerine Press publishes his poetry.

Ballard is a no-nonsense east Londoner who has released over 600 records on the label he started from his living room in 1988, and who has worked with Childish since 1991. Curran first published Billy's work in 2009, three years after starting Tangerine Press following an involuntary career change—from carpenter to handmade-book publisher. The pair have borne witness to two very different versions of Childish. Ballard was there for the desperate, chaotic 1990s Billy, in the cockpit during the messy demise of the Headcoats and Headcoatees; Curran met a more self-assured, sober Billy on the brink of the commercial breakthrough with his painting.

What they share, however, is absolute business independence. There is nobody bankrolling either, no other interests to satisfy. Childish gives them the work, they put it out. That's all there is to it and why they've all collaborated together happily for so long.

Ballard laid out his version of the Billy Childish story in the beer garden of a Leytonstone pub in the summer of 2023; Curran told his tale from Tangerine Press's south London nerve center.

Childish Witness: Ian Ballard of Damaged Goods

"There's nobody anywhere as prolific."

He's called Childish for a reason, you know. That's one thing I learned quite early on. Billy's said some terrible things about me in public. One of the worst was at a Headcoats gig at the St. John's Tavern in 1993. We were recording it for a live album, and he said, "This one's 'Fire.'" He went, "Yeah, this one's not for you, Ian; I know you don't like it because he's Black." The whole crowd looked at me. I just went, "Yeah, yeah," and shook it off. Imagine it now, if someone had taped it and it goes on the Internet.

I was going to his gigs before I met Billy. I'd seen the Milkshakes once or twice and then I saw Thee Mighty Caesars a lot. The Caesars really got me, more so than the Milkshakes. And I think I saw the Blackhands as well, the thing with the trumpets, the sort of reggae, soca stuff. I really liked that, but I loved the Caesars. It was more punk rock.

By 1988, I'd started Damaged Goods, but Thee Mighty Caesars had petered out at that point. There was a gig where none of the band turned up at the Dublin Castle. Billy was just sitting there on the stairs, so he did some blues stuff and then went home.

I'd never spoken to him, because I remember gigs where he and Tracey Emin were so drunk—Tracey especially—and they were fucking obnoxious. It's definitely a lot better if you don't meet your heroes when they're viciously pissed. But eventually I bottled up the courage. I took one of my first singles, by Slaughter and the Dogs, to a gig and I went up to him. He was sitting outside the Falcon, 1991. Thee Headcoats was just starting. He'd stopped one band and the next day another band starts, like it always does with Billy. I went up to him, gave him the single, and said, "I've got a record label, I come to your gigs, like your records and that." He was really chatty and nice. I said, "I'd love to do a single," and he went, "Yeah, what do you want?" That was it. He asked, "What do you want?" I went, "What do you mean?" He said, "Well, do you want to pick a couple of songs or something and do a single?" I said, "Yeah, you want to record something?" and he said, "Yeah." That was it. The start of thirty-plus years together.

So I picked a couple of songs and we did a Headcoats and Head-coatees split single ["Lakota Woman"/"Headcoat Girl"], which was DAMGOOD 1. That was when I realized that the original catalog numbers FNARR and YUBB were a bit silly. The Manics single was YUBB 4, so that was before Billy and I worked out that DAMGOOD's a good catalog number. So DAMGOOD 1 became the Headcoats and Headcoatees single. It got in the indie chart, which I don't think anything we'd done had before.

Billy went, "Oh, do you want another one?" and then before we knew it, they were doing a Milkshakes reformation for a Japanese tour, so I did the Milkshakes single, DAMGOOD 3. DAMGOOD 4 was the Headcoatees's "Davy Crockett" single, which was their big one—well, not big one, but one of the more important releases on Damaged Goods over the years. And before I knew it, DAMGOOD 7 was a Headcoats single, and you know what it's like—we're still doing it. We're up to DAMGOOD 600-odd. There's a Billy Childish single out tomorrow, actually. There is most weeks! It's a Guy Hamper Trio single. It's a monster, totally brilliant, because James Taylor's playing organ on it and he's a cut above.

We're still working together. We've never had an argument, we've never had problems about anything. I never have problems on Damaged Goods with most people. I'm pretty straight and mostly just put the records out. If people expect miracles, then they're on the wrong label. But if they want a good job and continuity, then they're on the right label.

It's a pleasure with Billy, it's still fun. Sometimes you get too many records from him. Lockdown was a bit tricky, accommodating him. He had nothing to do apart from go to the studio, and

Jim at the studio had nothing to do apart from have him going in. In some ways, it saved Billy's mental capacity, and also saved the studio going bust. Billy was down there pretty much every day for the whole of the first lockdown and most of the second. It was only because the studio shut down at Christmas that we actually got a little bit of a breather to release a few other records!

We meet up on a fairly regular basis, irregularly regular, but we talk on the phone all the time. I've had, God knows, ten emails today from him, because I've asked him: "Can you plug this art show, can you do this, can you answer a few questions for this interview . . ." There's a lot of coordination, and he's good as gold. He gets back to you on everything. He's more on the ball than every other band. He's constant. If you want him to do something, or you need a track for some old compilation, he'll always do it; he won't go, "Why, no." If you think it's a good idea, he'll go with it.

He's moved on from playing the Sir John's Tavern once a month, because that was the only way they made any money in the nineties and early noughties. They had to do a gig a month in London just to earn, or sell a painting, or swap a painting for a box of records so they could flog them. It was hand-to-mouth in the nineties, and I guess before that. But he constantly does stuff. I'm just talking about the music, but also the painting, the poetry, the writing . . . there's nobody anywhere as prolific. Possibly he does too much. It's very difficult, press-wise, because you're like, *Oh, another one for a new album review.* And some are better albums than others. There's probably one in four where you go, *There's some really good stuff on that, he's inspired.* Which is why I guess he keeps reinventing the name.

With the William Loveday Trio stuff, for example, when he first started doing the Bob Dylanesque stuff I was quite surprised, as he's never purported to like Dylan particularly. Then he's actually doing a whole album of Dylan covers, but better than the originals, and then he's doing three volumes of it. It's amazing, really, that he followed that all the way through.

When I first knew him, he was drinking a lot. And I mean, *a lot*. I used to say I drank a lot, and he'd laugh at me. He'd go, "So, when you get home, do you finish off a bottle of whatever's there and lie with it in bed and wake up with it?" Course not. He went, "You don't drink a lot." "Oh, okay." There were a few people around him who were all doing the same thing. I think it might have been about '93, something like that, he went to the doctor who said, "One more drink and you'll be in serious trouble." He actually took it on board and pretty much since then hasn't drunk, other than very recently he's had a tiny little nip. But it's completely different. He was just a monster. When he stopped drinking, you'd go up to him at a gig, chatting away, and he'd stick his fingers in your beer and suck them—just for the memory taste. Obviously, it ruined your drink. He was always really good fun, he was never a horrible drunk. He was just very boisterous, possibly too boisterous on occasion.

We went to Japan once with a bloke called Tetsuya from Vinyl Japan; four Headcoatees albums came out via Vinyl Japan. I went out there earlier because the Manics were on tour as well. So I saw the Manics one week, and then just as the Manics went home, Thee Headcoats arrived. I had a great two weeks in Japan, but very different as well, because obviously the Manics had Sony doing everything for them—lovely hotels, cars, and meals. Then Billy turns up and they're all in one tiny room with no windows.

The gigs were amazing in Japan, but Billy was very boisterous. I think it came as a bit of a shock, locally. Tetsuya would turn up; he was quite quiet and reserved. Billy would just jump on him and wrestle him to the ground in the breakfast hall. He got Tabasco once and poured it in his mouth, Tetsuya lying on the ground going, "Oh, Billy Childish."

The output has upped actually, the whole eight albums as William Loveday in under a year ended up as thirteen in a year—but we couldn't get them out because it took six months to get the vinyl pressed at that point. Maybe there's some legacy planning there, because I think he is worried about his health. I don't know if they're little things or not. I mean, Julie says, "Oh, he's all right." He'll end up like the Spike Milligan story that he loves to relate, about having *I told you I was ill* on his grave.

He's a big lover of Spike Milligan. He's got a similar humor to Milligan, Peter Cook, and early Peter Sellers. Have you heard any of the stuff he's done with Sexton Ming? There's a lot of sort of *Goon*-y references and Milligan. People do like those albums.

Sexton's out there. I was trying to put all the Billy and Sexton albums together into one double CD or triple CD, just so people could get all of it on something that's easy to listen to. It's not quite come together yet, and probably no one else needs it, apart from me thinking it's a great idea. A lot of records that I put out, I think it's a great idea and hope five hundred people will agree with me.

Billy's sales vary. With a CTMF album, probably a couple of thousand. On the more niche ones, it can be a thousand. The comps sell thousands, because loads of people find out about Billy Childish and then go, *Ah, how do I get further with this?* Which is why we did that *My First Billy Childish Album*.

I manage him on the music side—he's unmanageable, but I'm a buffer for him. Steve Lowe's there for all the art and whatnot. Julie's really good with him, she's not called Nurse Julie for nothing. I mean, she has sorted him out and got him on the straight and narrow, to a point, as much as anyone can. She's really blunt. I like Julie for that. She won't fuck about.

You asked if he's changed—I don't really think he's changed that much over the years. Probably a bit more serious than he was, but not really. He has his moments. It depends when you catch him, and if you join in the fun, he'll be as daft as arseholes. We've been together thirty-two years and it's still fun. And there's other labels that come along and do stuff with him, but to be honest it's quite good. Not to lose him completely, but you know, I don't mind the odd album.

Graham Coxon put out two Buff Medways albums after Billy had done the first on Hangman. When I first heard the Buffs, I was like, *Err, I don't think it's as good as the last thing you did.* I was wrong, because the Buffs were really good—well, I wasn't wrong, they were just different. I've grown to love the Buffs a lot more. Once I saw them, I was like, *This is brilliant,* but it took till the second album. And Coxon paid him five grand or something, which was more than I would have. I'd probably have given him three. After two albums with Graham, Billy headed back to Damaged Goods for the final *Medway Wheelers* album.

The big success with his painting is funny, because the art people don't know about the music, most of them. I went to an art thing where he was being celebrated and there was a meal afterward. Billy had to stand up and say, "Oh, and that's Ian who does all the records." *Oh, you do music?* It was that ICA thing where it broke for him. It just changed from two-bob paintings, selling them for three hundred quid, to Saatchi wanting to buy everything and things like that. Him not selling them to Saatchi was really cool. But his painting changed a bit then, his style changed. I didn't like it quite so much. I preferred the woodcuts, the charcoal stuff. Eye of the beholder.

It was amazing when it broke for him. All of a sudden, "Twenty grand for a painting? What!? I've got some of them!" It was brilliant.

I've done the first two albums with his son Huddie's band, the Shadracks, too. They're both really good albums, and there's another one due soon. Huddie's look is obviously completely Bowie in '77, '78 now. Saw him the other day and I was like, "Fucking hell, you've even got the same glasses, but you do do Bowie exceptionally well. You could be a model." He really could. I've known him since he was a toddler, which is quite funny, because that was from a previous life with Kyra, and then Scout's from the new life.

There was that Wild Billy Childish and Thee Headcoats album *I*

Am the Object of Your Desire—have you seen that cover? The cover said it all. That was the end of Thee Headcoats. Thee Headcoats stopped because it became a bit of a love triangle. I was in the middle of all that, because I worked with Holly [Golightly] closely as well, on her solo stuff. We were doing really well with Holly. I managed to circumvent it all by never talking to any of them about the other one. Billy would be like, "What's Holly say, then?" and I said, "Bill, I'm not getting involved, much as I'd love to sit and gossip." And Holly would say, "Has Billy said anything?" "Yeah, I like you all, you're all lovely, and I just want to carry on working with you all, and if I get involved, then it'll all cause friction and my opinion don't matter. I don't care."

Obviously, it was messy. Kyra being pregnant was a bit of a "Hang on, you're supposed to *not* be with Kyra!" That was the big moment. Holly was obviously upset . . . which is why she wrote such a brilliant album. Happy people never write good albums! Miserable bastards write great albums, and Holly's *Truly She Is None Other* is brilliant. Holly was very, very upset, it was a mess. They got it together while on tour. It was not good. It was Headcoatgate. I kept out of it all and ended up still working with everyone.

Childish Witness: Michael Curran of Tangerine Press

"The dyslexia is something you absorb."

I was a self-employed carpenter for sixteen years. About halfway through my carpentry career, I was getting a bit disillusioned with the construction industry and the lack of friends, money, that kind of stuff. I needed a creative outlet. Since my twenties, I've been an avid reader, so I thought I'd perhaps start a publishing company, and not just do that, learn to make the books myself, because I was good with my hands.

I picked up the bookbinding very quickly and then I started publishing in 2006. In 2013, I had a serious injury—I damaged my back and I lost all feeling in one of my legs for a few months; it was really awful, really painful. So I had to leave building. I'd been doing the books for about six years at that point. I was for-ty-three. I thought, *Well, I'll just dive into the books and see how it goes.* I never worried about it before; I just threw money at it when I had it. I did two books a year previously, but then I used my experience as a self-employed carpenter: *If I get the materials at the cheapest source and just rationalize everything, I could make it a viable business.* I stumbled through the first few years and then it started to make money. It makes a lot of money and then it doesn't make much money, the classic self-employed scenario.

I'd been aware of Billy Childish for many, many years. I got to know him through his poetry; I wasn't really too bothered about the music or the art—I mean, I loved the woodcuts, because they always went with the poetry.

That was always there in the back of my mind. About two years into Tangerine, I went along to an L-13 event in 2008, and introduced myself. Billy sent me poems to go in some anthologies I was doing at the time called *Dwang*, and they were all hand-bound limited editions and signed where possible by whichever writers were involved. Then he suggested, "Why not do a *Selected Poems*?" and that's the first book we did together, in 2009, *The Uncorrected Billy Childish*, of which there's multiple versions by Tangerine and also L-13. There was the Penguin art edition as well that we had to burn. [Penguin Books objected to the book covers for *Selected Poems* by Billy Childish, which were made in the style of their classic jacket design, so L-13 and Billy organized a book burning in Clerkenwell in January 2010. Footage exists online of the ceremony, including a ten-year-old Huddie lighting some copies in his garden.]

It was just before the ICA when suddenly everyone wanted to know him. It was extraordinary timing. I've been really lucky in my publishing, right from day one. I think people picked up on my desperation. I needed an outlet, an escape. Before it had been just drink, drugs, a shitty job, and nothing to look forward to except for a screaming foreman at seven in the morning to tell you what the day's events are going to be. I invested everything into it. The buzz line—well, I call it a buzz line—for Tangerine is "Publishing misfits, mavericks, and misanthropes since 2006," but that does include Booker winners, right the way through to complete unknowns. I do photo books as well.

We've done so many books with Billy now. He'd want me to say he's the center of my universe, and in terms of Tangerine Press, he's very important to me. His books are always incredibly popular. I would say the focal point for Tangerine as far as I'm concerned is probably Billy. It's very intense working with him, but it's actually a lot of fun. This is what I keep telling people, because if you say to someone, "I'm going to see a poet to go through their poetry for three or four hours this afternoon," they'd think you're insane, what an awful experience that must be, and it actually isn't.

We've done about ten books, I think. I go down to his house and sometimes we're just in absolute hysterics, because his poetry revolves around very personal anecdotes that are quite tragic in

many ways, but also incredibly funny, and then his stories shooting off that. I really look forward to them, because from a publishing point of view, we're getting the job done. He's the writer, I'm
the publisher, and we're going through a manuscript. I always
talk about the triangle of the writer, the publisher, and the work:
it needs to be separate. But with Billy, that happens very quickly,
because I think he separates himself from his poems straightaway.
There's always that wrench with writers, they don't want to let
their work go. I have to play the bad guy and then we get through
it and it becomes the work. But with Billy, he's already done that
himself, and that's why it's so enjoyable, I think.

He has no say in the design, he just suggests colors for the
cloth, but he leaves me alone, which is a great compliment, because he can be quite . . . not controlling, I think that's too strong
a word for him. But he wants to be everywhere. He's sincere.

It was just a relief to find a British writer of that open free-
verse style and honest, unafraid, verbose, but terse at the same
time, three-line poems, four-line poems, to pages and pages and
pages; like the new book, there's one [*the every when*] that's eight
pages long: an epic poem that sums everything up.

The dyslexia is something you absorb. I'm really good at spelling. I didn't read any books till I was twenty-one, because I was
always reading comics, but for some reason I could spell really
well. So going through the first book in 2009, he gave me the
manuscript and I put that in order. He said, "We'll just go through
it again and we'll put them into sections." And the dyslexia totally
turned me upside down, genuinely. I'd be sitting at traffic lights
in my car, and I'd think, *Is that a red light, is it the green light, is
that actually green?* because I was resetting my brain to not worry
about spelling.

When Billy originally sent me the Word document for the
whole book, which is very big, it's 200 pages long, there was an
autocorrect, so it corrected everything. I had to go through and
uncorrect *The Uncorrected Billy Childish*, which was sent to me

corrected. I'm still not good at that, because he wants it understood, you know, so there is an editing process, but it has to be genuinely in his voice. I get completely lost in it.

There's no contracts between us or anything like that; he's very trusting. Billy just lets it happen. It's such a relief in many ways, as a publisher, that you can say, "Yeah, let's do a book," rather than, "Okay, I need to do this, I need to do that, I need to talk to this person."

His books always sell out. Because it's generally very limited editions, this edition is 100 numbered copies with an art print in them, then there's 50 copies with the hand-colored portraits in there, so they're more expensive, and then there's a 10-copy edition for Rough Trade, but they're very expensive, they're 170 quid, the ones with the hand-colored portraits. The numbered ones are £50-ish.

The labor for me is very, very slow. I taught myself as a carpenter patience—I mean, you've got to be when you're a chippie on a building site, there's chaos around you, you're trying to hang a heavy new fire door in an old doorframe, and it can take hours.

So I've taught myself to be really patient with physical work, and you do have to be with bookbinding. It's very similar in many ways. You're dealing with wood, except it's pulp on this occasion, pulp pages. It is very labor-intensive, but you have to be calm for it.

I think Billy may have changed a bit with time, he's more regularly noticed now. But what hasn't changed is me wanting to publish him. We get the job done, but we have fun doing it.

25.
The Son and Heir

It's probably not an acknowledged scientific experiment, but you can nevertheless judge a person fairly well by how they treat their children and their animals. Let's test that idea.

Reginald John Hamper raised his children with a grievous lack of empathy, patience, availability, and love. By all accounts, he wasn't very caring toward June's cats or Billy's rescued dog pal Here-Boy, either.

His son Billy, on the other hand, has a close friendship with both his cat and his dog, and designed his life around his children as soon as they arrived, making sure that no matter how awkward or atypical any home arrangements may appear (e.g., father in touring musical acts, as well as outspoken, unvarnished memoirist; parents divorced before birth, etc., and so forth), there would be minimum reflected unease. His parental job, as he undertakes it, is to provide full-time love, security, and shrewd life guidance. It's a contrast with his own father, but not one that he's willing to claim is influenced by his upbringing in any way.

"I imagine that I am just able to feel nonromantic love in a way that John can't," he says. "I'm missing that heartless-bastard gene with my own children, luckily."

Despite carrying himself like an incredible ringer for David Bowie in his Thin White Duke period, Huddie Hamper is nevertheless an unassuming character. It's admittedly an opinion based on nothing more than sharing an after-work pint outside a pub in Farringdon one evening, but Huddie is a noticeably well-adjusted, mature, and gentle twenty-three-year-old man.

"For some reason, Huddie's got no sense of rebellion," says Steve Lowe, who's known him since he was three. "He's really easygoing."

When he was a teenager, Huddie—who by then was living during the week at his father's place rather than with his mother Kyra—would join Childish and Lowe if they had an exhibition in the US or Europe. Gradually, he became more interested in becoming an artist himself. "He'd come to the studio, and we'd help him out with his paintings," explains Lowe. That was when Huddie was fourteen. He left school two years later, took a foundation course in Rochester, and then studied Fine Art at Slade (just like his uncle Nick). "After he left college, he basically became his dad's assistant," continues Lowe. "Billy is a master delegator, the greatest: 'Well, ask Steve what there is to do.' He gets everybody working for him." Now Huddie works at L-13 on an irregularly regular basis. "I just keep him on his dad's stuff," Lowe says, "it's tidier. He's gradually picking up a lot of what I used to do, like helping Billy with designing record covers or posters."

It's incredible that despite not really talking to each other or mixing socially for decades on end, the male Hampers are all locked in quite narrow fine art pursuits; they're all so artistic.

"Autistic?" deadpans Huddie. "Yeah, I've been wondering about that for a while."

Painting as a career is a magnetic force for the Hampers. "My cousin tried to rebel against it," Huddie says. "He did an engineering course in a bid to escape, but now he's back, trying to put exhibitions of his painting on. I don't really understand how it works like that for us."

Huddie is not so much an apple that did not fall far from the tree, as a new branch growing out of the same root. At school, he was only ever interested in art and theology (arguably a remix of his dad's two main late-life pursuits); he dresses in a very familiar combination of vintage fifties and sixties styles; he even has a garage rock band, the Shadracks, featuring Rhys Webb of the

Horrors, who have released a couple of albums (produced by a B. Childish) on Damaged Goods and play minitours of Europe, too.

"Some people have been critical of him following too much in his father's footsteps," Lowe admits. "His paintings look like his dad's paintings, his music is very much in the same pattern."

Huddie agrees. "I think I just have similar tastes and some of the same interests. I have a similar style. Musically, there's stuff I like that he doesn't, but our painting is quite aligned."

Nobody is remotely uptight about this in the Childish solar system, which is a great neutralizing agent for angst.

"Huddie is very secure in what he wants to do and seems very happy doing it," says Lowe. "He's gradually finding his own voice, the band sounds more how he wants it to probably sound, the paintings are becoming much more his. He's not been in any hurry to prove himself or rebel against his dad. It just seems really easy."

The only statement that apparently wounded Huddie about all this came, inevitably, from within the family: "My uncle Nick left quite a rude comment on one of my Instagram posts a couple of years ago which I still haven't gotten over, because I thought it was very strange."

Under a post of a vivid painting from March 2020 of his father sitting near a tree with a beautiful pink sky behind him, titled *Man Sat in a Garden in Bekkjarvik*, and composed during one of the restorative European trips Huddie and Steve Lowe took with Childish after his breakdown, Nichollas Hamper wrote this: "When are you going to get your own style?" Quite apart from demanding a twenty-year-old art student in his second year of college have a fully developed, unique personal style (the painting looks a bit like a Munch, perhaps), at a time when an artist is in the very earliest stages of finding their feet, it's an oddly cruel thing to say publicly to a nephew he'd had minimal contact with through his own choice.

"He sent me some watercolors for my fifteenth birthday that I liked," ponders Huddie. "I went to visit him once in his house in France; that was very nice."

There was his stepbrother's wedding, too. Maybe a couple of other meetings? Whatever, he says. That's just what his dad's side of the family is like.

"I've only met John once, a couple of years ago, though I met him when I was a baby too but obviously can't remember. I saw him at Hugo's wedding as well. Apparently he likes me, though he can't know me really. He's old now, it's probably too late to bond, even though I was interested to know who he was when I was young."

He got on well with June, however. "She was a pretty nice grandma. She liked me and I liked her." He found her interactions with his dad odd, though. "She was always saying things I thought were designed to wind him up. She was aggressive with him in a way she wasn't with others." He smiles. "She always let me win at draughts."

Unlike his dad, Huddie grew up feeling engulfed by love. "I've always been really close to Julie, close to my stepdad too. When I was young we'd go on holiday all together, with my two half sisters too. I think compared to many of my friends growing up, I had a pretty perfect environment."

He's glad that his parents weren't together, in a way. It saved him going through an inevitable breakup later in his childhood. "Whenever I see them with each other, it's a bit uncomfortable. I can't believe they were together so long, because they really aren't alike at all."

When he thinks of those friends he had as a child, or even some today, he feels blessed to be the son of Billy Childish. "A lot of my male friends, when they were teenagers or young men, all their problems came from having bad relationships with their dads. We've never had any big falling-out—though that might be my character. I'm quite compliant."

Maybe their opposing personalities mean they fit together

better, though there are some issues. Huddie admits, "He's very intense, and he can be quite controlling in the way he likes things. My dad has his way of seeing the world and he wants people to subscribe to that." Nevertheless, Huddie does subscribe to the Church of Childish, so even this is not the kind of conflict it might be in many paternal relationships. They get along just fine. He paints with his dad on Mondays, he works with Childish's materials a couple of days a week at L-13, and in the remaining time he paints some more and plays music. It's a good balance, though he did leave the nest and move to London permanently to create some space between himself and Childish.

Huddie Hamper finishes his pint, offers a hand in farewell, and we watch him stroll down the street. He's off to meet his girlfriend, lolloping away from us in old Levi's hitched up elegantly, short leather jacket hanging immaculately from his shoulders: tall, slim, handsome, and free-spirited in these, his golden years. Unarguably one of Billy Childish's two greatest, most successful releases.

26.

Hanging from a Tenuous Thread (at the Victorian Ropery)

In September 2022, I started making a Billy Childish playlist. It was to comprise my favorite songs by him and his various groups from across the past five decades, something to focus my mind while I was thinking about his story. Soon, I had nearly seventy songs on it. I'd massively underestimated the task.

So I refined the rules of engagement: I'd pare it down to my favorite twelve Billy Childish "hit records in another universe," to mirror the kind of compilation album that would've informed every waking hour when I was a kid, like the Who's *Meaty Beaty Big and Bouncy*, a best-of that you can hold up in battle against anyone else's. Childish's labels routinely attempt to compile him and always end up with double albums. What if I imposed a numerical limit?

Taking the train down to Chatham one last time in the dog days of November 2023, I stuck the headphones into my ears. There are in fact fourteen songs on the "Hits from Another Universe" playlist of my favorite Billy Childish songs, but I remembered that there are coincidentally also fourteen on *Meaty Beaty Big and Bouncy*, so I can pretend that this was the plan all along.

As the train pulled out of Stratford, heading at soon-to-be-high speed toward Kent, I pressed play: forty-five Childish minutes lay ahead (just three more than *Meaty Beaty Big and Bouncy*, but Pete

Townsend was choosing from just six years' output, rather than forty-five). Here's what I heard:

"For She" by Thee Milkshakes (1981)

One minute and fifty-nine seconds of concise, unhinged love ache, written by a Billy Childish still reeling from Sanchia Lewis packing up and leaving him while the Milkshakes rehearsed in the front room below: "You're tearing me apart, when you say we should part / and I don't know what to, I don't know what to do!" he yowls, as an insistent riff repeatedly picks at the scab.

"I'm Out of Control" by Thee Milkshakes (1984)

As seen on prime-time Friday-night Channel 4's *The Tube*, the un-shakeable riff and chorus that hipped a nation of teenagers to the best garage band in the land, while simultaneously confirming to co–front man Mickey Hampshire that a spotlight this bright was not for him.

"You'll be Sorry Now" by Thee Mighty Caesars (1985)

Heartache turns to thoughts of vengeance on this brutally groovy subterranean missive. Possibly Billy Childish's best number to dance to—and rhythm-maker Graham Day wasn't even a drummer.

"I Remember" by Wild Billy Childish (1988)

Would there really be a home-recorded solo blues number in the pop charts of another universe? Yes, there would: "Well, I remember, all the things, all the things I did as a child . . . woah!"

"(We Hate the Fuckin') NME" by Thee Headcoats (1993)

Sadly, I misremembered giving this bitterly funny garage-punk letter of complaint "Single of the Week" in *NME*: I didn't review it. But I do recall Steve Sutherland, my editor, suggesting it should probably not be the answering-machine greeting while I was working on the *NME* Lives desk. One *NME* reviewer stormed out of the St. John's Tavern when Thee Headcoats played it and subsequently wrote a damning report of them. This still rankles Billy Childish: "I thought the *NME* staff would all be on our side. Surely everyone wants to poke their bosses in the eye?" Also includes the only occasion one-time squeeze Miki Berenyi can recall ever hearing Childish say her band Lush's name.

"Art or Arse? You Be the Judge" by Billy Childish & Thee Headcoats (1997)

What better way to further enrage Tracey Emin and the nineties Brit Art set than introducing your single about contemporary conceptual art with a telephone voice message of Emin complaining about the single's "puerile" intent. Medway mickey-taking epitomized in less than two minutes of punk bellyaching.

"Hurt Me" by Thee Headcoatees (1999)

Sarah Crouch was Childish's favorite singer in Thee Headcoatees: "She was really off-key and good." Here she vocalizes another love song about the demise of his relationship with Sanchia with a lovely, keening sense of despair and longing. "Holly arranged all the backing vocals on 'Hurt Me,'" remembers Billy. "She was brilliant with harmonies."

"Let Me Know You" by Billy Childish and Holly Golightly (1999)

I spun the bottle and it pointed to "Let Me Know You" from *In Blood*, but it could've been any of the songs. There's no explicit language on this album of hot and heavy rhythm and blues, yet the message is nevertheless oppressively randy.

"Troubled Mind" by the Buff Medways (2002)

The Who in 1965 but channeled through the perennial angst of a modern Medway man, with a little drum break lifted lovingly from Hendrix's "Fire": "I need you little girl . . . to ease my troubled mind."

"Punk Rock Enough for Me" by Wild Billy Childish & CTMF (2014)

Taken from one of Childish's best full-length albums, a kind of nature-infused pagan-punk set called *Acorn Man*, "Punk Rock Enough for Me" nudges out the title track by virtue of managing to conjure both a minimanifesto and a brief memoir from its lyrics.

"A Song For Kylie Minogue" by Wild Billy Childish & CTMF (2016)

In this alternative universe of mine, where lyrics are really important and the music is made by groups recording in nice wooden studios, playing with energy and a bit of soft reverb, "A Song For Kylie Minogue" is number one for months.

"It Hurts Me Still" by Wild Billy Childish & CTMF (2019)

Julie Hamper's bewildered message for her older brother who committed suicide, perfectly echoing the confusion and resignation of those left behind.

"It Happened Before (Will It Happen Again?)" by the William Loveday Intention (2021)

The epitome of Childish's recent Bob Dylan obsession, and his best approximation of that songwriting style, is this complete and utter dismantling of Tracey Emin over about five minutes of hilarious acid: "You said we'd been friends for years, but you didn't speak to me for ten / When you hear this song perhaps it'll happen again." Also features some very nice James Taylor organ parts.

"Traces of You" by Wild Billy Childish & CTMF (2023)

For someone who doesn't really feel very musically motivated or too driven to write songs, Julie Hamper is able to dredge up some deep, paisley-pattern soul: this song reaching out to her departed mother is a good place to close any show.

The skies above North Kent were closing in. As the train pulled into Chatham station, the playlist ended and the heavens unloaded their doomy cargo. Rochester may have all the Dickens-themed memorials and shrines, but Chatham has the more authentic Dickensian vibes. Walking down the chipped High Street in teeming, freezing rain, around the bus station, behind which a smattering of tents shook in the wind that blew in from the water beside them, I followed the Medway for half a mile, my umbrella as useful as a water pistol at the Battle of the Bulge.

Greeting me inside the gates of the Historic Dockyard stood Steve Lowe, inspecting his phone. It was a coincidence. Lowe was looking for Daniel Pfau, their artist liaison from neugerriemschneider in Berlin who was wandering among some of the huge, identical warehouses on the site, searching in turn for Lowe. I mounted the metal staircase rising above the old Victorian Ropery and entered Billy Childish's studio, following the ominous parping of Radio 3 toward Childish's voice rising just above it.

Billy was standing in front of a painting that Huddie was working on, giving his thoughts on how his son could rescue it. As they worked on it, I took a little tour of the room's huge canvases. There appeared to be quite a few recent paintings of the Sasquatch, also known as Bigfoot. I remembered Billy's breath therapist Rachael Hudson suggesting with a mischievous look in her eye that I should explore his interest in the Sasquatch with him, in particular what it may represent. When he finished with Huddie's work, I brought up the subject of the hairy mythical creature.

"What they represent," Childish said, "are Sasquatches. But I don't really talk about them."

Nevertheless, we spoke about the Sasquatch for quite a while. Childish says the Sasquatch is a bit like Bob Dylan for him. He wasn't attracted to either growing up, but sometimes "if you show a modicum of interest in something, then they come and find you." In fact, driving down to Canterbury with Julie the day before, listening to Dylan's song "Visions of Johanna," a thought struck him. He turned to his wife and said, "Bob Dylan is the best pop star who's ever been, isn't he? I didn't realize this before." Julie answered in the affirmative.

Similarly, he's grown more and more interested in the Sasquatch in his later life, but he is wary of talking about this on the record for understandable reasons. "It's a bit like the ghosts and the flying saucers," he says. "People want you to be weird. They want you to be mysterious and eccentric. I've read things about me where I'm portrayed as eccentric when in fact I've been very level and sane with them."

He knows that if we stand in front of this eight-foot painting of the Sasquatch he's made and spend a long time talking about it and its smaller two siblings nearby, then he'll come across as kooky. And Billy Childish is not remotely kooky.

"People also call me a know-all," he complains. "I specialize in *not* knowing things. I have never wanted to be involved in mending cars or amplifiers, for example. I never claim to be able to do things I can't—in fact, I sometimes claim I can't do things that I can, as this gives me more clearance."

He comes and stands a little closer to me, which he often does when a good line is approaching. "As far as Sasquatches go, I'll give you my quote: 'I don't need Sasquatches to exist and it's not my fault that they do.'" That is not the only quote, however. "I don't require there to be flying saucers, I don't require there to be Sasquatches—you know, there's very little I require, and if you talk to people who don't require things, that is a sign of sanity."

People who require things, he reckons, have an agenda, and while people with agendas can be interesting to him, he absolutely has no interest in agendas themselves. If you were to look into the Sasquatch without an agenda, to read about it, consider all the old research from across time about it, then you can have an informed opinion about the Sasquatch. It's a bit like one of his other musical favorites, Jimi Hendrix, who he believes very strongly, "about 95 percent certain," after spending a lot of time researching him, was in fact murdered and did not accidentally overdose as routinely stated.

"I don't need Jimi Hendrix to always be good or there not to be a lot of superfluous stuff within his music," he expands. "I don't need Jimi Hendrix to have been murdered, and I don't need Jimi Hendrix to have died of natural causes. When I look at what happened to Jimi Hendrix, I'm interested in what I find."

The best thing anyone can say, he suggests, when quizzed about the Sasquatch, or whether Vikings landed in North America, or flying saucers, or astrology, is not to say, "I don't believe in astrology," or whatever it is, but to comment, "I don't really know about that." That's what he says if someone wonders why they can't start their car, for example.

"When you talk to a journalist and they ask you what you think of a certain doorknob and you reply, 'Well, that one is really ugly,' the article then says you are obsessed with doorknobs," he says. "I bring this up because most people don't have huge opinions about doorknobs, but I do and so I answer, and then I become this freak in print, when in fact I just have an eye for some design . . ."

Steve Lowe enters the studio with Daniel Pfau. "Ah, doorknobs," he says. "And now you know his opinion on doorknobs."

Childish returns to his nearly blank canvas, the outline he's sketching. "Right, anything else from me?" he asks. "Or have we covered everything?"

"Were Sasquatches the final piece that you came down to ask about?" wonders Lowe. They weren't, but the Sasquatch conversation still continues for some time. Lowe compares what may be believed to be cranky mythical nonsense with, for example, some religious beliefs. "I was at a carol service at the weekend and the vicar was talking very seriously about the Virgin birth. I thought: *Does he really believe that an angel literally came down?* Because he was talking very seriously as if he did, whereas it does sound a bit nutty."

Billy considers this sympathetically as he marks his canvas. "People say they don't believe in other dimensions. But they die. People disappear and people appear. You've got radios with dials on them with different frequencies. If you were going to use your intellect, you'd say, well, frequencies are in nature, so why would frequencies be specific to one thing? It's a bit like cooking: how you make a meal isn't different from how you make a painting, because truth remains truth within everything."

I looked over at Daniel Pfau, standing next to Lowe and wearing the bemused expression of a man who'd accidentally dialed into the wrong Zoom meeting.

Billy thought a bit more about why Hudson suggested I ask him about Sasquatches. "In my breathwork you get a lot of past-life stuff and I've had a lot of connections within my past-life work with Sasquatches. Now, is there such a thing as past lives?"

I don't really know about that.

"Exactly. I could say I believe there is, but I don't require it to be so."

The conversation then moves onto much thinner ice. As I was writing this Billy Childish story over the preceding months, there seemed to me to be a clear divide between the people in his life and work today, people such as Steve Lowe and Rachael Hudson, Antonia Crichton-Brown, even Julie Hamper, who deal with him regularly in the here and now, and those from his musical Medway past. I sensed talking to former musical colleagues Bruce Brand, Sarah Crouch, and Graham Day an exasperated, exhausted, and dismissive frustration with him that isn't there with his current circle. But also, particularly with Brand and Day, a kind of longing for him. It sounded as if they missed him.

Childish has a lot that he could say about all that, but only so much that he can have printed, as "I don't want the world to know I'm that much of an arsehole."

He thinks of what he can say. "It's not personal. I just don't like music much," he begins. People want him to play gigs or, worse, go to gigs, but he doesn't really want to. Again, the "arsehole" clause means we'll paraphrase largely, but he doesn't want to be in a crowd of "gray-haired old cunts like me," he says, and continues, "Huddie plays with us and I feel for him, because he's twenty-three and the audience look like his grandparents or something. I come from a generation where old people at gigs were viewed with high suspicion—now they're watching me play." He invokes the "arsehole" clause and I promise to finesse. He notes, "People ask me to go see gigs and I'm like, 'I'm a fucking adult!'"

We turn to Graham Day in particular. "I love Graham," he says firmly. "We like each other a lot." He hopes to pick up Thee Mighty Caesars soon with him again, once they've both taken care of a few other commitments. "Did I tell you the story of the time we got thrown out of Radio City Music Hall in New York because of Graham?" he adds.

Billy Childish has a self-acknowledged habit of taking anecdotes "around the lake": when you are promised one story, you invariably take in several others along the way, often visiting distant, unrelated shores before somehow winding up at the stated destination. En route to Radio City, he tells us about some of the lovely dressing rooms the Buff Medways would be assigned when touring Europe, playing community centers and town halls: "I remember this one place in France, it was pristine. The organizers were chatting away to us, really friendly. As they were talking, I looked over their shoulder and Graham had drawn on the long, spotless Formica table with our drinks on it, a huge spurting cock." Despite his very senior position in Kent's fire service, Day's sense of youthful playfulness had clearly persisted. "This was about fifteen years ago."

Eventually, we take the anecdotal bridge across the lake to Radio City. In November 2004, Modest Mouse invited the Buff Medways to play with them in New York. On arrival, Childish, Day, and Wolf Howard were surprised by how formal and serious the arrangements in a grand old American venue like Radio City can be. They wouldn't be able to move from their assigned spots onstage, the fire curtain would be raised and lowered before and after their performance, there was to be no drinking onstage nor smoking anywhere within the building, and on no account could anyone touch any of the props loaded precisely around the stage in readiness for Radio City's fabled Christmas shows.

The Buff Medways played an enthusiastically received set. Afterward, for want of anything better to do, Childish found himself standing in the wings as Modest Mouse started playing. As he watched, he noticed Graham Day on the opposite side of the stage. He'd pulled out one of the minicars stored for the Christmas show and was now sitting in it, a lit cigarette in his mouth and a beer bottle resting on the steering wheel. "I could see he was trying to roll the car out onto the stage. I know he's a very naughty boy, so I nipped round to give him a hand."

As Childish arrived, Day looked up at him, blinking through the smoke rolling up his face, and shouted, "I can't get this fucking thing started!"

Billy gave Graham in the minicar a little push out onto the stage, though he's keen to stress that he was not in charge of the steering—that was Graham. Soon, they are in the middle of the stage of Radio City Music Hall in New York, weaving in and out of Modest Mouse in a miniature car that Graham Day is steering while puffing on a cigarette and clutching an open bottle of lager.

"I look up and all the security guards are on the other side of the stage, going . . ." Childish mimes a beckoning motion. "A really very attractive, tall, efficient Black man named Clinton who I'd had a nice briefing with earlier, he was in charge. That was when I realized that Graham was steering the car off the edge of the stage . . ."

Just as he was about to disappear off the front, Clinton stepped forward onto the stage, grabbed Day, and bundled him away, confiscating both beer and cigarette. "We were all frog-marched out of Radio City, the door slams behind us—and all our friends we've invited to see us are still inside." Childish rolls his eyes. "So, with the playing of live music, you're dealing with a lot of stories."

He turns back to his painting. "The thing I like about art is the painting, not the exhibitions. I don't like going to stuff." He can trace this back to childhood: "I've only ever liked three people at a time." Those present in the studio—Steve Lowe, Huddie, Daniel Pfau, painting accomplice Edgeworth Johnstone, and I—do some quick arithmetic, as he explains this further. "I don't do parties. I don't like crowds, which is why I've never been into football or any of that. It's why I gave up going to gigs when I was eighteen. I like to paint. And I like to be in a group with Julie and Wolf, because they let me drive the car and only step in if I'm about to hit a tree, and sometimes not even then. I can very occasionally still play a gig, but it's not my number-one dream."

One of the gigs that made him believe that he didn't really want to go to shows as an audience member anymore was, iron-ically, one in which he was playing—the infamous Pop Rivets Bloodbath at Medway College, back in 1979. He blames some punks from Rainham, who'd come down to smash the place up, starting with the bathrooms, which were completely demolished. While the band played, bottles rained down from the mezzanine level. "One embedded in the plaster wall behind the drummer's head."

There were fights breaking out everywhere, with blood already smeared across the wall. At one point, Childish could see some guy in front of the stage holding an empty glass. "I said, 'What are you doing, mate?' He looks up and says, 'Oh, it's all right, nothing.' Then he just smashes it into someone's head right in front of me, blood pouring everywhere, including out of his own hand. We've still got the blood-splattered set list somewhere. It was horrible; I'm really sensitive, but Bruce was crying backstage afterward."

Around then, he watched a gang of skinheads take a hippie-punk down the stairs and outside the Vortex to "muller him" at an X-Ray Spex show. That was the end of his gig-attending career.

It's important, he says, that I avoid stitching him up with his old Medway music pals. "I love them, I really do, I'm grateful for everything we did, but . . ." He has no desire to relive his nineteen-year-old life anymore. He had to go through an enormous amount of work to be a grown-up and he wasn't a happy boy anyway. He doesn't want to be an arsehole about it, though.

Billy's no longer nineteen, but it's November 27 and he will therefore be sixty-four in four days' time. He's arrived in a new portal in his life. We opened this book together on a call three years ago, discussing his multiple nervous breakdowns and their ongoing reverberations. How is he now?

"I've got this gum issue," he says, to my great relief. "Some kind of infection." He walks over to let me have a look inside his mouth. Pulling his lip down to show off his two gold-capped lower front teeth, he says, "These got a bit messed up. I had a big operation on them when I was fourteen, had them hand-drilled . . ."

Edgeworth Johnstone approaches. "I'm gonna shoot off now, Billy," he says. "I want to sort my holiday out." Edgeworth's plan is to go to Heathrow Airport tomorrow morning and see if there are any cancelations on flights to Bangkok. Apparently this is a good way of getting ahold of a cheap airplane ticket.

Childish looks skeptical. "Just come back alive, okay?" he

requests of his sometime painting partner, who is here by his side every Monday.

When they paint together, is Johnstone like the rhythm section and Childish the front man?

"No, I'm the guitarist, the singer, the drummer—rhythm is very important in painting. Edgeworth might play a bit of bass on it." Billy turns back to his canvas again. "Is there anything else we need to cover?"

I am forced to once again underline the keen nature of deadlines.

"Maybe we can do a second part," he suggests.

We both laugh at that.

"I find it impossible to moderate my honesty," he says, scratching away at his canvas. "I tell complete strangers stuff I shouldn't." He is uniquely open, it's true. "That gets me into trouble. It's that thing again where people imagine that their motive would be *your* motive." He shrugs. "I love truth, but not everyone is built for it."

We hug. I shake everyone else's hand and then climb back down the metal stairs and outside into the howling rain, tracing my steps back to Chatham once more.

The next day an email arrives from Billy Childish, with an attachment.

It's Julie Hamper's birthday and, as a surprise for her, Billy has compiled an album of the best songs she's sung or written with him, designed a cover, and released it on Hangman Records, via L-13. The album is called *It Hurts Me Still* and is credited to Juju Claudius, and the cover photo is of Julie holding a guitar, taken by Billy.

The accompanying blurb reads:

JUJU CLAUDIUS, aka Nurse Julie, is bass player and backing vocalist in song and dance groups: Wild Billy Childish and CTMF, the Chatham Singers, the William Loveday Intention and the erst-while MBEs.

Appearing alongside her husband Wild Billy Childish and Wolf 'Still Drumming' Howard, a highlight for many has been when Julie pens her own compositions, singing lead vocals and play-ing rhythm guitar (as well as on a few ditties by her husband). Hangman music techs have now gathered up 14 favourites for the edification of both the discerning listener and the three-chord pop enthusiast.

Jack Ketch, Ocean Beach, SF, 2023

It's such a lovely gift, I say.
"She's happy," he replies.
Really, that's all that matters.

Unknowable but Certain

A life and times, as noted by Billy Childish, with Steve Lowe. All factual errors are mostly accidental, occasionally deliberate, but always the biographer's fault.

1959 Born December 1 as Steven John Hamper, at All Saints' Hospital, Chatham, Kent. Second son to June Hamper (née Lewis) and Reginald John Hamper.

1963 Hears the Beatles, Bob Dylan, and the Rolling Stones. Smashed in the head with a toy scooter by his older brother Nichollas. Sees a bus stuck in the snow in the big freeze. Dances to the "Hippy Hippy Shake" with his mother in Nana Lewis's front room.

1964 Mimes to the Beatles in the living-room mirror with his big brother. Neighborhood pal Little Jeffery's family moves to New Zealand and the girls from the White House move to Australia. Eats pink sugared prawns with the youngest daughter on her front lawn on the day they leave. Finds out from Big Caroline that people die.

1965–66 Oaklands Infants School, second prize in the Kent Primary Schools painting competition: *Young Animals*. Wears his Beatles wig to school. Refuses to answer to any name other than Virgil. First place in the footrace at Oaklands Infants School.

1967 Lordswood Junior School. Father leaves the family home.

Makes the Dambusters paintings. Because of his undiagnosed dyslexia, he is placed into remedial class. Twelve teeth pulled out by Mr. Williams, the dentist. Almost drowns in the swimming pool at the Great Danes Hotel. First experiments with smoking, drinking, and sex, with Jonathan Francis, the vicar's son.

1967 On a July afternoon in a clear blue sky, sees a flying saucer hovering over his parents' back garden. His older brother and Paul Ravenscroft also present. Listens intently to his brother's Jimi Hendrix records. Raped by Norman, a friend of the family, while on holiday in Seasalter, North Kent. Makes his first sexually explicit drawings.

1969 Finds Here-Boy, the stray dog. First involvement with arson. Beats up a boy after school with Jonathan Francis. Is severely bullied over a six-month period by school headmaster.

1970 Fails the eleven-plus exam and sent to Walderslade Secondary School for Boys. Mother reads him *Lust for Life*, the story of Vincent van Gogh. Paints his first oil paintings.

1970–74 Mercilessly bullied by Michael Ravenscroft.

1971 School music report declares: "17%, Hendrix was not the only musician!" Nana Lewis dies.

1972 Mother diagnosed with TB. Father temporarily moves back into the family home. Sees the pop group Slade at Chatham Central Hall. First experience with marijuana at the London musical *Jesus Christ Superstar*. Paints the Jimi Hendrix pictures. Comes top of his class in the end-of-term exams, but he is not promoted, owing to his "eccentric behavior." Has a close encounter with a ghost in the driveway of his house.

1973 Forms the Walderslade Liberation Army, aka the WLA, with Keith Gulvin. Makes guns and black powder. First break-ins and vandalism/ecoterrorism. Dresses up in his mother's clothes and walks the streets.

1974 Major operation on abscess in lower jaw at the East Grinstead Hospital. Founds the MMRG—Medway Military Research Group—with Keith Gulvin, investigating and writing a history of the Medway fortifications. Mother comes out of the hospital. Family holiday in Greece. First bite of the apple with Theresa Horsey. Reads *The Lord of the Rings* by J.R.R. Tolkien and the Hornblower books by C.S. Forester. The MMRG starts restoration of New Tavern Fort, Gravesend, and illegally open the tunnels to the public, making £300 over the Easter bank holiday by selling the corporation's supply of Second World War steel helmets and gas masks. On a warm summer's evening he sees a large black panther walking in the woods behind David Marsh's house.

1974–75 Draws the illustrations for the first MMRG publication, *The Medway Forts* by K.R. Gulvin. Archaeological dig at first-century Roman kiln site on Upnor marshes with Ian Jackson. Finds Heinkel He 111 German bomber engine. Begins writing his own sea adventure featuring Captain Benjamin Hamper. Spends the summer camping at the spring on Farmer Tibble's land in Aylesford, mapping an ancient stone circle with Keith Gulvin. Starts regular drinking.

1975 Punched in the nose by the religious education teacher. First studies in kung fu and tai chi. Reads the *Tao Te Ching* by Lao-Tzu. Comes second in the Kent Schools under-18s Canoe Slalom at Canterbury, Kent (three entrants only). Winter walking in the Snowdonia mountains with the Kent Mountain Centre. The MMRG start illegal restoration of Fort Amherst, Chatham. Sees a goblin grinning up at him from under the fir tree in his parents' garden.

1976 Leaves Walderslade Secondary School for Boys. Applies to the art foundation course at Medway College of Design, but is refused on the grounds of lack of qualifications. Starts work at H.M. Dockyard Chatham as an apprentice stonemason, makes 600 drawings in "the tea huts of hell." Attends the Stockwell College of Building as part of his apprenticeship, while living with his brother in a squat in Chalk Farm, London. Hears "Anarchy in the U.K." by the Sex Pistols on a jukebox at the University of London . . .

1977 Purposely smashes his own hand with a club hammer, leaves his job, and declares he will never work again. Sees the Jam. Gives up tai chi and embraces punk rock. Sees the Damned, the Clash, the Buzzcocks, Johnny Moped, X-Ray Spex, Eater, the Unwanted, the Boys, 999, Generation X, Wire, Siouxsie and the Banshees, Richard Hell, Johnny Thunders, ATV, the Adverts, the Sex Pistols, etc. . . . Spends a day fruit packing in Morden, Kent. Accepted into the foundation course at St. Martin's School of Art, London, on the strength of his drawings (as a student who lacks the normal entry qualification but shows outstanding artistic potential), but refused a grant and instead attends Medway College of Design (as a student who lacks the normal entry qualification but shows outstanding artistic potential), where he is put on probation and refused a certificate of completion at the end of his college year. Publishes *Chatham's Burning*, the first of a series of punk fanzines, which include *Fab 69*, *Bostick Haze*, *The Arts and General Interest*, and *The Kray Twins Summer Special*. Adopts the name Gus Claudius, but is promptly renamed Billy Childish by his friend Button Nose Steve. Writes first lyrics and nonsense verse. Falls in love with Rachel Waller. Makes first collages and is introduced to the work of Kurt Schwitters. First impromptu poetry readings on the dining tables of the canteen at Medway College of Design. Reads at the Lamb and Flag public house in Maidstone, Kent, with the Out Crowd poetry group (aka Rob Earl and Bill Lewis). Forms the Pop Rivets as singer, with Bruce Brand on guitar, Russ Wilkins on bass, and Russ Lax on drums. They play their first gig at the Detling Village Hall.

1978 Accepted into the painting course at St. Martin's School of Art (as a student who lacks the normal entry qualification but shows outstanding artistic potential). Attends for half a term before quitting. Riding his bicycle in London he attempts to run down Johnny Rotten outside the Roebuck public house, King's Road, Chelsea. Meets and falls in love with Sanchia Lewis. On the dole.

1979 Meets Poly-Styrene Detector (later known as Sexton Ming) at a poetry reading in the back hall of the York public house in Chatham. Records first album. Tours in Germany and Switzerland. On the dole. Forms the Medway Poets with Bill Lewis, Sexton Ming, Charles Thomson, Miriam Carnie, and Alan Denman. Founds Phyriod Press with Sexton Ming.

1980 Employed as a ward porter at Oakwood Hospital, Barming. Forced to quit due to giving advice on patient care to ungrateful doctors. Sanchia Lewis leaves him, and he consequently suffers severe depression lasting several years. Films *The Man with Wheels* (unreleased), based on a collection of his poems about the life of Kurt Schwitters, directed by Eugene Doyen. Forced off the dole by the election of Margaret Thatcher. Reapplies to St. Martin's School of Art where he is once again accepted (as a student who lacks the normal entry qualification but shows outstanding artistic potential). Meets Peter Doig. Reads Charles Bukowski and John Fante.

1981 Learns to play guitar and forms the Milkshakes with Mickey Hampshire, Banana Bertie, and Bruce Brand. Tours in Germany. Plays the (former) Star-Club in Hamburg. Has sex with Janet, a prostitute on the Reeperbahn, and imagines she is Sanchia

Lewis. Meets Jeannine Guidi in a Hamburg bar and falls in love. Founds Hangman Books. Father is arrested for drug smuggling. Expelled from St. Martin's School of Art for the publication of an "obscene" collection of poetry. Begins a period of fifteen years of "painting on the dole." Paints first large collection of work. Ernst Schwitters, son of Kurt, reads Childish's poetry collection *The Man with Wheels* and sends "Mister Childish his kind regards." Invited to read at the International Cambridge Poetry Festival. The opening party is held in Sir Clive Sinclair's mansion, where Childish and Sexton Ming are wrongly accused of vomiting into the host's grand piano. Childish counter-accuses Michael Horowitz of "having only one fucking shirt!" Charles Thomson informs Childish that he will hire bouncers to keep him out of any future Medway Poets readings. Filmed for television with the Medway Poets, his poems are branded "totally un-broadcastable." Application to Maidstone College of Art to study painting turned down.

1982 Stops painting in seasonal blocks and commences painting two pictures a week. His grandfather Charly Hamper dies in All Saints' Hospital, Chatham. John Rice, the literary officer for South East Arts, tells Childish that he will secure him no further poetry readings unless he stops writing obscene material. Childish tells him to go fuck himself. Adopts the alias William Loveday. Meets and falls in love with Tracey Emin, who is studying fashion at Medway College of Design.

1982–84 Fifty-seven LPs released.

1982–87 Has a studio in the family home in Walderslade, Chatham.

1983 Starts writing his first novel, *My Fault*. Contracts herpes and gonorrhea by sleeping with Bernadette, a prostitute in Wurtzburg, Germany. Tracey Emin acts as administrator for Hangman Books. Marries Shelia Clark at the Brixton registry office in a secret ceremony. Films *Quiet Lives*, directed by Eugene Doyen and featuring Childish with Tracey Emin. Reads *Journey to the End of the Night* by Louis-Ferdinand Céline. Meets and falls in love with Kyra De Coninck while playing with the Milkshakes in Brussels. Beats up his father on John's release from prison.

1984 Turns down the offer of having his paintings filmed for the BBC 2 show *Something Else*. The Milkshakes release four albums around the world on the same day in an attempt to commit commercial suicide.

1985 Kyra De Coninck arrives from Brussels to live with Childish in Rochester, Kent. They both feature in the short film *Cheated*, directed by Eugene Doyen. Legally changes his name to William Charly Hamper.

1985–89 Forms Thee Mighty Caesars with John Gawen and Graham Day.

1986 Teaches poetry with Bill Lewis at the "Lifers" summer school in Maidstone Prison. Has first show abroad, *40 Wood Cuts*, at De Media, Belgium. Adopts the alias Jack Ketch. Tracey Emin stops working for Hangman Books and Kyra De Coninck takes over the administration.

1986–93 Founds Hangman Records—a non-profit-making label specializing in releasing the unreleasable.

1987 Diagnosed as dyslexic. Edits and publishes *The Man Who Created Himself* by Sexton Ming, *Six Turkish Tales* by Tracey Emin, and *The English Scene* by Vic Templer for Hangman Books. Features in the short film *Birdman*, directed by Eugene Doyen.

1988 Moves his studio to his mother's front bedroom in

Whitstable, Kent. The Medway Poets reform to do a charity tour of Kent for Amnesty International. Has first one-man painting show at 5 Dryden Street, London. Edits and publishes *One Clever Kid* by Joe Corkwell. The first English edition of Louis-Ferdinand Céline's *Cannon Fodder* cotranslated with Kyra De Coninck and published by Hangman Books. Thee Mighty Caesars invited to play at the Bad Music Seminar in New York, organized by Tim Warren of Crypt Records.

1989 Application to enroll in an MA in painting at the Royal College of Art turned down. *Conversations with Dr X.*, a student documentary about Childish directed by Andy Crabb, is nominated for the BP Film Award. Selected poetry, *En Carne Viva*, published in Spanish by Stultifera Navis. *All Metal and Other Men's Wives*, the first of three titles by Neil Sparks, published by Hangman Books. Spends early spring writing in Crackington Haven, Cornwall. Adopts the alias Charles Hangman. Forms the blues and punk group WOAH (Thee Worshipful Order of Ancient Headcoats) with Bruce Brand.

1990 Spends another spring writing in Crackington Haven, Cornwall. In Hamburg for second one-man show, organized by Eckhard Karnauke. Paints thirty paintings over a two-week period. Meets Jeannine Guidi again in Zurich after nine years and falls desperately in love. Music and poetry in Oslo, Norway.

1991 Tours in the United States with Thee Headcoats. Editor and publisher of *May My Piss Be Gentle*, the first of two books by Mark Lowe to be released by Hangman Books. Editor and publisher of *Lonely Hearts and Casualties*, the first of two books by Chris Broderick to be released by Hangman Books. The Milkshakes reform to play three dates in Tokyo, Japan. Exhibits in Belgium, and spends the winter painting in Zurich.

1992 Makes the short film *Girl of Matches*, featuring Kyra De Coninck, for Sub Pop Records, Seattle. Sub Pop also releases the double CD *i am the billy childish* to celebrate over fifty releases of his LPs. Edits and publishes *Self Hate in a Phone Free Heaven* by Dan Belton for Hangman Books. Wolfram Aue and Tim Neuger curate the show *The Kelly Family*, with Mike Kelley, Jim Shaw, Billy Childish, and Raymond Pettibon, at the Esther Schipper Gallery, Cologne, Germany.

1993 Quits drinking alcohol. *Hunger at the Moon*, his first American poetry collection, published by Sympathetic Press in Long Beach, California. Invited by Louis Behre to read at the One World Poetry Festival in the Hague, the Netherlands. Learns meditation with the Friends of the Western Buddhist Order. Starts practicing Iyengar yoga. Begins seven years of intense psychotherapy.

1994 Peter Doig and Matthew Higgs curate his first major London show at the Cubitt Gallery, King's Cross. He is included in the *War Child* exhibition curated by Brian Eno at Flowers East Gallery in London. Ten-day retreat with Vipassana meditation.

1995 Selected poems, *Druhovia v Mrtvom Clne*, published in Slovakia by Timotej in Košice. Founds the Friends of the Enemies of the Western Buddhist Order.

1996 Application to enroll in an MA in painting at Goldsmiths turned down. Publication of his first novel, *My Fault*, by Codex Books. Publication of his selected poems, *In 5 Minits You'll Know Me 1985–95*, by Sympathetic Press in the US. Performs and gives readings in the US. Starts the Messerschmitt paintings.

1997 Publication of *Notebooks of a Naked Youth* by Codex. Performs and gives readings in the US. Meets Julie Winn. Reforms Group Hangman with Dan Melchior. Writes first Hangman manifestos.

1999 Asked by Charles Thomson to be cofounder of the Stuckist art movement. Cowrites Stuckist manifestos. By mutual agreement, parts with Kyra De Coninck. Chosen as Tracey Emin's "Artist of the Day" at Flowers Gallery, London. Birth of his son Huddie. Thrown out of Tate Gallery for distributing anti–Turner Prize manifesto. Tracey Emin severs their friendship after Childish refuses to heed her demand never to speak to the press about his influence on her work. Thee Headcoats disband. Forms a new group, the Friends of the Buff Medway Fanciers Association (named after an extinct breed of chicken), with Wolf Howard and Johnny Barker.

2000 Marries Julie Winn in Seattle.

2001 Leaves the Stuckists. His wife Julie moves to Chatham and takes over administration of Hangman Books. The filmmaker Larry Clark asks Childish to write a screenplay of his first novel, *My Fault*.

2002 Paul Tickell makes a Channel 4 profile of Childish and his work.

2003 One-man show at the aquarium (gallery), London. Starts his association with Steven Lowe.

2004 Over two months, he paints thirty paintings for the exhibition *Handing the Loaded Revolver to the Enemy: A Homage to Vincent van Gogh* for the aquarium (gallery). One-man show at the Simon Finch Gallery, London. Publication of his third novel, *Sex Crimes of the Futcher*. Forms the Chatham Super-8 Cinema with Wolf Howard, Simon Williams, and Julie Hamper.

2005 Turns down a "substantial offer" to appear on Channel 4's *Celebrity Big Brother*. Virgin Books republish his first two novels, *My Fault* and *Note Books of a Naked Youth*.

2006 The aquarium publishes *the man with the gallows eyes: selected poetry 1980–2005*, *gun in my fathers hand: selected lyrics 1977–2006*, a paperback edition of *Sex Crimes of the Futcher*, and *Thoughts of a Hangman: Woodcuts by Bill Hamper* to coincide with an exhibition of paintings, *Our Friend Billy Childish*. Billy and Steve Lowe organize an exhibition of June Hamper's pots at the aquarium.

2007 The aquarium moves to Farringdon Road into a building that was bombed by a zeppelin in 1915. Billy researches this, finds out it was Zeppelin L-13 that bombed London that night, and the aquarium becomes THE AQUARIUM L-13. The first exhibition there is *Billy Childish: Against England*. Billy publishes his fourth novel, *the idiocy of idears*. Five hundred free anonymous copies are distributed via volunteers, who place them in bookshops around the country.

2008 Neal Brown apologizes to Billy for having to omit him from the book he wrote about Tracey Emin for Tate Publishing. In compensation, he writes *Billy Childish: A Short Study*, the first comprehensive analysis of Billy's art to be published. This is shortly followed by an exhibition curated by Neal Brown at THE AQUARIUM L-13. Curator Matthew Higgs offers Billy an exhibition at the nonprofit White Columns Gallery in New York for 2009, but the show is postponed due to the financial crash, which decimates the gallery's funding.

2009 *ART HATE. National ART HATE Week 13–20 July*, in collaboration with Steve Lowe, under the pseudonyms Dr. Albirt Umber and Harold Rosenbloom. Matthew Higgs renews his offer of an exhibition at White Columns in New York. This time concurrent with a larger exhibition at the ICA in London. Contributes poems to *Dwang*, published by Michael Curran's Tangerine Press, who go on to be Billy's main poetry publisher, specializing in limited-edition, hand-bound books. His daughter Scout is born. Commences writing the novel *All the Poisons in the Mud*.

2010 *Unknowable but Certain* exhibition opens in February at the ICA. Gallerist and art dealer Tim Neuger comes to the private viewing, due in part to his flight back to Berlin being canceled. He offers Billy an exhibition at neugerriemschneider, Berlin. Exhibition at White Columns opens in March. Steve Lowe receives an email from Tim Neuger with the subject line "Billy Childish Art Basel Attack"—an invitation to present a solo Billy Childish group of paintings at the Art Basel International Art Fair in June. Fifty paintings are shipped and they cause a sensation at the fair. All the paintings are sold. This is followed by Billy's first solo exhibition at a major commercial gallery at neugerriemschneider, Berlin. *World ART HATE Day, Basildon* is held to coincide with Art Basel. Then, on September 21, *Art Hate* on Cork Street. The first and only commercial Art Hate exhibition is met with more confusion. Tracey Emin reestablishes contact.

2011 *Storm of Defence: What Is Art Hate and Other Cuntish Questions*—a largely ignored and unseen but brilliant installation of Art Hate propaganda at the L-13 Light Industrial Workshop. First solo exhibition of paintings with Lehmann Maupin, New York. Becomes artist in residence at the Historic Dockyard Chatham and is awarded his studio above the Victorian Ropery to make paintings for an exhibition the following year. Hangman Books via L-13 is resurrected to publish *the sudden wren or painting lessons for poets and other mediochur cunts*.

2012 June 1 to September 30, *Frozen Estuary* exhibition at the Historic Dockyard's art gallery.

2013 CTMF formed. First exhibition with Carl Freedman Gallery, *darkness was here yesterday*. Starts making collaborative paintings with Edgeworth Johnstone. First solo exhibition with the Carl Freedman Gallery, London.

2014 Awarded an honorary doctorate by University of Kent for achievement in his field. *Our Friend Larionov* exhibition at Pushkin House, London, with collaborative paintings by Billy Childish and Steve Lowe under the pseudonym Heckel's Horse. This goes on to become the name for the collaborative paintings by Billy and Edgeworth. White Columns in New York hosts a critically acclaimed exhibition of June Hamper's pots. Solo presentation at Art Masters, St. Moritz, and exhibitions in Aachen and Hong Kong.

2015 Billy edits and publishes a book about his mother June's pots with Steve Lowe through L-13. *The Ward Porter* by "Odysseus" published as a free "proof edition" by Tyburn Press via the L-13 Light Industrial Workshop. As with *the idiocy of idears* some years earlier, *The Ward Porter* is left by volunteers in bookshops, buses, trains, and on park benches, etc. This time, 3,000 copies are sent out worldwide. Solo painting exhibitions in New York and Milan. Forms the MIC (Medway Indian Clubs) under the name Xerxes, with Mahrek and Arras. Swinging Indian Clubs, Iranian Meels, and Shena.

2016 Work starts on the first Billy Childish Studio Editions book of Billy's paintings, which is to be a complete catalog of everything painted in the last couple of years. Solo museum show at Opelvillen Rüsselsheim in Germany.

2017 *unbegreiflich aber gewiss* (trans. "unknowable but certain"), the first Billy Childish Studio Editions book and complete catalog of paintings from August 2014 to January 2017, published through L-13. (Commercial galleries are unhappy as collectors should not know how prolific an artist is. It is agreed that only 113 copies be made available privately to L-13 subscribers to stem the crying.) Solo painting exhibitions, both commercial and museum-based, in Hong Kong, Berlin, and Dallas.

2018 Suffers a nervous breakdown but continues to paint every Monday. Billy takes restorative "field trips" to Paris, Auvers, and Arles with his son Huddie and Steve Lowe, as a pilgrimage to van Gogh. Scenes from these trips later become the subjects of paintings. Solo painting exhibition in Berlin.

2019 *Punk Rock Ist Nicht Tot! The Billy Childish Story 1977–2018*, a triple-LP album, is released by Damaged Goods Records. Solo exhibition in New York and the inaugural show at the new Carl Freedman Gallery in Margate.

2020 Continues to paint and record music prolifically during the global pandemic and lockdowns. Records thirteen LPs. Curates his own exhibition in Berlin called *skulls wolfs nudes rope pullers and a nervous breakdown* at neugerriemschneider between lockdown restrictions. Commences recording a series of LPs of Bob Dylan songs as the William Loveday Intention. Hangman Records is resurrected to release the first of these, *The New and Improved Bob Dylan, Volume 1*, swiftly followed by volumes 2 and 3 as part of his "career in a year" project to release thirteen LPs in a year. Vipers Tongue Press imprint founded to publish poetry pamphlets. *Billy Childish Photography 1974–2020* published by L-13 and photos shown at Lehmann Maupin's project space in London, with a two-day residency making paintings on-site during the exhibition.

2021 *the student—a novella in thirteen parts* published by Vipers Tongue Press for subscribers, who are sent a new installment each month and a custom-made box to keep them in.

2022 Billy's mother June passes over.

2023 Publishes *Vipers Tongue* quarterly of international poetry and prose with his wife, son, and L-13. Continues working on *All the Poisons in the Mud*. Commences further prayer and fasting.

Acknowledgments

This book could not have been produced without the selfless assistance, cooperation, and goodwill of many people, all of whom have renewed my faith in the kindness of strangers.

Top of that list is **Billy Childish**, who has provided his time, memory, guidance, and humor without limit, and whose honesty is some kind of superpower the likes of which I've never previously encountered. A unique, inspirational character and collaborator with whom I hope to remain entwined.

Thanks and praise also go to:

Steve Lowe for his patient, good-humored attention to detail and availability, in particular collating the final section of images, and for reading the book's 100,000-word first draft in a Word document over email.

Eugene Doyen for generously providing unbidden a memory stick of black-and-white treasures.

Julie Hamper for regularly allowing me into her house and telling me a lot of things that she probably considered none of my business.

Huddie and **Scout Hamper** for permitting my intrusion into their lives with such polite nonchalance.

Sanchia Lewis, Kyra De Coninck, and **Sarah Crouch** for kindly inviting me into their homes and entertaining my incredibly personal questioning.

Ian Ballard for all of his detailed help, memories, and time.

Graham Day for meeting me even though he had a headache (and for the Last Forefathers).

All of the following picked up a phone or clicked a Zoom link, donating much time and truthful insight:

Stewart Lee, Keith Gulvin, "Button Nose" Steve Simmons, Bruce Brand (twice), Russell Wilkins (twice), Miki Berenyi, Tracey Emin, Bill Lewis, Wolf Howard, Rachel Lehmann, Michael Curran, Rachael Hudson, Antonia Crichton-Brown, Holly Golightly.

Thanks again, too, to **Clare Gildersleve** and the Hughes family for letting me watch Sean Hughes's documentary.

Bureau of Internal Affairs

Thanks to:

Special agent **Becky Thomas** of Lewinsohn Literary for always asking the right questions and having my back at all times.

Lee Brackstone at White Rabbit for enthusiastically commissioning *To Ease My Troubled Mind*, as well as the general broadsweep of encouragement.

Sophie Nevrkla, Clarissa Sutherland, and everyone at White Rabbit and Orion involved in this project.

Liz Dexter for prompt and accurate transcription (as well as keeping me on my toes by wondering "how on earth you're going to put all this together!").

Niall Doherty and **Chris Catchpole** for holding down the *New Cue* during my deadline-chasing sabbatical.

Mostly, thank you **Jean, Jagger,** and **Joey** for putting up with my ever-changing moods in the midst of writing.

Thank you for reading.

Photo Credits

Section 1

Photos of Billy on the train and Billy, Gabriel, and Button Nose Steve at the Vortex on plate 2 courtesy of Steve Simmons. Photos on plate 7 by and courtesy of Rikard Österlund. All other photos courtesy of Billy Childish, with additional thanks to Sanchia Lewis.

The montage in section 1, plate 4, features the following, L-R:

Row 1 Billy Childish, 1978; Rachel Waller and Childish, 1978; Childish and Sanchia Lewis, 1979; Childish and Sexton Ming, 1980; Sanchia, Childish, and Sexton, 1980

Row 2 Childish and Bruce Brand; Childish before ward porter interview, 1980; Childish in jacket and tie; Childish and Sanchia Lewis, 1979; Sanchia and Childish, 1979

Row 3 Childish and Jeannine Guidi, 1981; Childish, 1980; Childish, alive and well and dying in Chatham, 1981; Childish and Scout Hamper, photo-booth strip, 2020; Childish and Julie Hamper, photo-booth strip, 2020

Row 4 Childish, early 2010s; Childish with neckerchief; Childish with mustache

Row 5 Childish and Julie Hamper; Childish and Julie Hamper; Childish with Huddie Hamper, 2004

Row 6 Childish and Huddie, 2020; Childish in bush hat; bird mask and hat

Section 2: Eugene Doyen Gallery

All pictures by and courtesy of Eugene Doyen.

Section 3

All artwork by Billy Childish, courtesy of Steve Lowe.